# The GREATER GENERATION

## Also by Leonard Steinhorn

*By the Color of Our Skin:*
*The Illusion of Integration and the Reality of Race*

# The GREATER GENERATION

## In Defense of the Baby Boom Legacy

## Leonard Steinhorn

THOMAS DUNNE BOOKS
 St. MARTIN'S PRESS
NEW YORK

THOMAS DUNNE BOOKS.
An imprint of St. Martin's Press.

www.stmartins.com

Library of Congress Cataloging-in-Publication Data Available upon Request

ISBN 0-312-32640-8
EAN 978-0-312-32640-1

First Edition: January 2006

10  9  8  7  6  5  4  3  2  1

For my children,
Ariella & Max,
the next great generation

*It's not just what you do when the lights are turned on,*
*it's what you do when no one is watching.*
—Muhammad Ali

# Contents

# Prologue

It was springtime a couple of years ago when I mentioned to one of my honors students that I was thinking of writing a book on the Baby Boom generation. She had just completed an excellent paper on the press, and she always had intelligent things to say in class about politics and media. This was clearly a bright and interesting student. But after hearing about my book idea, she paused for a moment, then mumbled a few words about Vietnam, then said something about Boomers doing drugs when they were young, and then quite innocently asked what else Boomers ever accomplished and why on earth I would write a book about them.

Momentarily taken aback, I decided against launching into a long explanation and instead asked her a few simple questions: What did she think of women's liberation? Was it better when women deferred to men? Should diversity be a priority on college campuses? Is there anything wrong with interracial dating? Should gay people hide their sexual orientation? Should kids be raised to think on their own or follow their elders? Would she prefer working in a hierarchy or in a flatter organization? Should environmental protection be a major concern? On every question she gave what would be considered a fairly liberal response, and when we talked further it was clear where she stood—yes on women's rights, yes on diversity, yes on equality, yes on accepting gays, yes on independent thinking, yes on more democratic workplaces, yes on the environment, yes on greater personal freedom. But then she asked what our conversation had to do with my book. The connection between these issues and the Baby Boom generation never occurred to her. It's as if she had taken for granted that the world has always been this way. And so the main idea of my book was born.

Today we live in an America that is more free and equal than at any other time in our nation's history. In the span of a few short decades we have tackled some of the most intractable wrongs and entrenched inequities that have haunted our country in the two hundred years since its founding. Racial and sexual inequality, officially sanctioned prejudice, denial of basic rights, disparaging those outside the cultural mainstream, indifference if not hostility to the environment, double standards that privilege some and frustrate others, individual freedoms suppressed through law, compulsion, guilt, or fear—with rare exceptions most previous generations have overlooked or ignored or accepted these blights, all the while professing their devotion to American ideals. But one generation refused to play along, and that generation is the subject of this book: the Baby Boom generation.

Yes, the Baby Boom generation, that giant cohort of Americans born between the mid 1940s and early 1960s, roughly 80 million strong. It's the generation that came of age amid the idealism and tumult of the period largely defined by the Sixties, with early Boomers old enough to see President Kennedy inaugurated and to march on Washington with Martin Luther King, Jr., and the youngest able to remember Watergate and the fall of Vietnam. Known at first for their youth, and celebrated because of it, Boomers have now occupied the center stage of American life for more than half a century—indeed just mention the words "Baby Boomers" and everyone seems to know who they are. But it's not their numbers or when they were born that makes Boomers so recognizable and distinctive. No, what gives this generation its identity, what makes it cohere, what makes it more than just another age cohort is a shared sensibility, a unique worldview, a series of historical memories, and from these common touchpoints a set of norms and ideals to which most of its members generally subscribe. How Boomers have gone about implementing these ideals—and in doing so, how they have changed and bettered America—will be the central storyline of this book.

From the very moment they entered public life, Baby Boomers began to shape and transform our society and culture. Beginning in the Sixties, when they pushed for change, and in later decades, when they began effecting it, the Boomer ethos has increasingly defined American life, so much so that we can safely label these last few decades the Baby Boom era of American history. Over a single lifetime Boomers have accomplished what few generations before them were able or willing to do—to undo many of the accumulated hypocrisies and knotty contradictions that have tangled this country's history since its earliest days. What Boomers have made clear is that ideals matter not just in the abstract but in the very way we lead our lives. In the old America it was acceptable and appropriate to assume an African-American isn't smart enough to do the job or a woman can't rise above secretarial work or a man can't change a diaper or a lesbian is perverted and sick or a Jew is greedy or a business that pollutes should be allowed to do so in the name of progress. No longer. Boomers have overturned these norms and created new and powerfully egalitarian ones to replace them. So different are we today that it's hard to imagine we once lived by the bigoted and demeaning rules of yesteryear. But the very fact that it's so hard to imagine demonstrates how thoroughly Boomers have remade society. Our new norms seem so natural, so right, so much a part of our lives, so consistent with our national ideals and personal aspirations, that we never pause to think about how we got here and the people who made it happen.

To be sure, Boomers have built on the hard work and sacrifice of every preceding generation, without whom our present freedoms may never have flourished. The Revolutionary War generation changed human history by building a country not on nationalism but on ideals, setting a standard of freedom and equality against which all other generations must be measured. The Civil War generation gave its blood and tears to keep a cancerous subversion of liberty from strangling our Constitution and redefining America. The Progressive generation addressed the dangers posed by unchecked industrial capitalism, restraining its excesses to keep our food safe and our children out of sweatshops and coal mines. The World War II generation, now known as the Greatest Generation, fought the great battle against the most fearsome enemy of freedom the world has ever known.

Boomers will never go down in history as a generation that fought a great war to protect liberty, nor should they. But Boomers should go down in history as a generation that fought a great cultural war to expand and advance liberty. Taking very seriously what our founders wrote in the Preamble to the Constitution—"to form a more perfect union"—

Boomers have renewed institutions, rewritten norms, and generated more freedoms for more Americans than at any time in our history. And they've done it based on the core American creed that all people are equally deserving of dignity and worth, that no aspiration or race or lifestyle is better or worse than another, that those once scorned or forgotten or suppressed or demeaned are entitled to the same opportunities, respect, and rights as those sitting comfortably in the ethnic or cultural or religious majority. How much more American can a single generation be?

It's certainly legitimate to argue that Boomers could afford to be idealists because they were, as a whole, more affluent, educated, and exposed to the world than any generation before them. But there have been educated and comfortable Americans throughout our history, so one must ask why they remained wedded to prejudice and privilege whereas Boomers didn't. And then one must ask why other generations ignored our nation's hypocrisies in the Fifties and Sixties—or in fact embraced them—while Boomers didn't. No one will ever be able to say conclusively why a generation does what it does; that's the stuff of seminar tables, speculation, and theory. What led Boomers to change America is simply less important than the fact that they did it.

Does all this mean that every Boomer shares the same values with the same intensity? Not at all. Does it mean there isn't a vocal minority of Boomers who remain wedded to the ways and traditions of their elders? Of course not. But to define a generation solely by year of birth would render the concept of a generation meaningless, because the actions of a few could always be used to pick apart the sensibility of the many. Rather, generational identity develops when a critical mass seize their moment in history and form a shared consciousness about it. To say otherwise would mean we could never call the World War II generation a generation because their age group included lynch mob leaders on one side and on the other a small but vocal crowd of dissenting Beats. Or it would mean we could never infer qualities about the Revolutionary generation because there were many British loyalists among them. So the demographic definition of Boomers includes anyone born between those bookend years. But the operative definition, what we will use here, is all about the predominant norms, values, and ideals that continue to guide Boomer culture.

It's been said that history is the politics of memory, and it's precisely the political battle over the Baby Boom legacy that may help explain why my student had so little understanding of how far we've come in this one generation. In the 1960s Boomers were feted and praised for their idealism and commitment to bettering America. But it's always easy to applaud idealists and dreamers. More difficult is accepting the change and disruption when those dreamers begin to implement their ideals, especially so for those whose privileges and moral precepts are so tightly bound to the prejudices of old. Think of Greatest Generation Americans who felt betrayed when their Boomer children rejected the old ways, or religious and social conservatives who have never fully accepted their diminishing moral authority and the pluralism inherent in a diverse society. For them, the gains of this last generation are a threat, not a promise, and with the verve and determination of an aggrieved minority they have steadfastly resisted the social and cultural changes that began in the Sixties. But perhaps even more important than their resistance is how successfully they've articulated it, by building up and promoting an idealized image of America before Boomers corrupted it, a *Father Knows Best* image of a picket-fence Fifties filled with upstanding white World War II veterans motivated only by the purest of motives—faith, duty, and country. And they've then constructed a parallel image of Boomers consumed solely by self-interest, a generation for whom idealism is little more than a conceit, solipsistic yuppies forever stuck in a revolving Me Decade and whose irresponsibility and licentiousness have poisoned the American well and driven us away from our golden age. These images may be wholly inaccurate—caricatures detached from truth—but they are the images that too often define our mass-mediated conversations today, and that may explain how my student could wonder what if anything Boomers have accomplished. They did a lot of drugs, didn't they?

Diversity, feminism, multiculturalism, privacy, equal rights, individualism, transparency, social responsibility, political correctness—in our media food fight culture they've become sound bites almost devoid of meaning, sneered at by some, affirmed by others, all caught up in the politics of memory. But if we step back for a moment, block out all the noise, and look at the society we've created, there's so much to celebrate, so much to praise, so much to admire, all because so much has changed. Let us now look at this America and the generation that made it possible.

# The GREATER GENERATION

# Chapter One
# The Greater Generation

The employers will love this generation.
They aren't going to press many grievances.
They are going to be easy to handle.
—*Clark Kerr, President, University of California, 1959*

There's a whole generation, with a new explanation.
—*Scott McKenzie, "San Francisco," 1967*

**N**o one should ever doubt the valor and sacrifice of the World War II generation—the much-celebrated Greatest Generation, as they've come to be known. This was a generation that sacrificed their blood, their lives, and their futures to defend our country against implacable enemies of freedom. They suffered through the Great Depression without ever losing faith in the promise of America, and they bravely answered the call to fight a horrid and heroic struggle against fascism, preserving democracy for generations to come. Many hopes and dreams and aspirations were left on the brutal battlefields of Normandy and Iwo Jima during World War II, and we all should be deeply grateful for their service, courage, and sacrifice. For defending American freedom, they deserve every accolade they've been given.

But history is not hagiography. As hard as this generation fought for pluralism and freedom overseas, the question is what they did with those values when they came home. So we must ask how well America was living up to its ideals in the era of Greatest Generation ascendancy. Only then, only after a candid assessment of the Greatest Generation years, can we understand how thoroughly the Baby Boom has transformed and bettered America.

So we begin with something seemingly small but symbolically big about America in the Fifties: African-American hair. To an African-American in the United States today, having straight rather than kinky hair is largely a matter of style. But for blacks in the 1950s, style was the least of their

worries. This was the era of the Greatest Generation, an era now mythologized for its values, neighborhoods, human warmth, and decency. Yet in
black communities, young men and women desperate to look less black
would mix together lye, potatoes, and eggs, pour it on their scalp, and
brace themselves as this homemade potion burned fiery sores into their
skin while it straightened their hair. Nor did blacks simply try to emulate
white hair. They also bought skin bleaching creams with names like "Im-
perial Whitener" and "Black-No-More," all of them made with painful,
corrosive chemicals that stung bitterly when applied to the skin, products
that promised better looks and a lighter complexion but in truth did little
more than prey on black Americans who were told day after day that
their blackness made them unappealing and inferior, that the only way to
feel good about themselves was to deny who they were and conform to a
white standard of beauty.

In the America of the Greatest Generation, before multiculturalism and
diversity affirmed the humanity and worth of non-white Americans, and
before the much-maligned politically correct movement impelled our culture to change the national norm on race, it was rather routine and indeed
quite acceptable for whites to place little value on the lives and aspirations
of their black fellow Americans. Black World War II veterans, who risked
their lives fighting the enemies of freedom, returned home and found a
white society so repulsed by proximity to their blackness that they were
unable to buy a house in Levittown or any other white suburb. Ten thousand blacks worked at the Ford auto plant in Dearborn, Michigan, *Life*
magazine reported in 1957, but "not one Negro can live in Dearborn itself." White suburban communities re-zoned tracts from residential to industrial use simply to create large buffer zones between their pristine
neighborhoods and black middle-class communities nearby. Believing
they deserved the right to discriminate against blacks in housing would
remain a majority opinion among Greatest Generation whites for at least
another two decades. Of course if a black family somehow integrated
and wanted to join one of the organizations at the center of white community life in the Fifties—Rotary, Moose, Kiwanis, and Elks clubs, to
name a few—they would be laughed at and obviously rejected. "We're
not racists, believe me," a national Elks leader said in 1971, "but we feel

we're a private organization and we have the right to admit who we want in our lodge." Most industrial unions were no better. After World War II, whites simply believed they deserved jobs over blacks.

Not even success, not even fulfillment of the American Dream, could shield black Americans from white society's loathing in the era of the Greatest Generation. When baseball great Willie Mays moved with his Giants team from New York to San Francisco, no one would sell him a house until the mayor got involved, and then Mays was told how grateful he should be to the people of San Francisco. "What do I have to thank you for—for letting me spend forty thousand dollars?" asked Mays. But at least he didn't move to Boston, where the Red Sox manager in 1959 said, "There'll be no niggers on this ball club as long as I have anything to do with it." Or at least he didn't play professional basketball, where there was an unwritten rule limiting the number of blacks who could play on the court at the same time. And most of these incidents took place in the North, which was supposed to be more enlightened. As for the raw and pervasive bigotry in the South, it can be summed up by the white southerner who cavalierly asked why there was so much fuss about a lynched black teen found in a river, noting matter-of-factly, "The river's full of dead niggers."

Greatest Generation whites so dehumanized their black fellow citizens that large majorities felt completely comfortable telling pollsters well into the 1960s that blacks smell bad, laugh a lot, and are less intelligent than whites. Most appalling to whites of this era was any form of physical contact with blacks. When white singer Petula Clark quite innocently put her hand on Harry Belafonte's arm during a televised music special, whites—particularly throughout the South—deluged local stations with complaints. But incidental touch was nothing compared to the visceral disgust that almost all whites felt toward intimate contact with blacks. In a 1958 Gallup poll, 94 percent of whites said they disapproved of marriages between "whites and non-whites," and as late as the 1980s large majorities of Greatest Generation whites would continue to express quite openly the feeling that a white would never want to marry a black. Even indirect intimate contact with blacks repulsed most Greatest Generation whites, which a 1971 Harris poll found when it asked whether "self-respecting men would want to marry a girl they knew had been fooling around with people of a different race." Those who dared to cross the color line were met with abhorrence and rejection, such as a white actress and her inter-racial daughter who were handed a petition demanding that they move from their Manhattan apartment building. As *Newsweek* put it in 1963, "the greater the suggestion of physical contact, the greater the white antipathy—and even revulsion." So demoralizing and oppressive was this Greatest Generation culture to blacks that the most common signs at civil rights marches referred not to legislation or politics but to an affirmation of human dignity, with the simple words I AM A MAN. Many light-skinned blacks, those with no need to burn their skin with bleaching cream, sim-ply tired of pleading for their humanity and gave up altogether by passing for white and cutting off all ties with their darker-skinned relatives, sadly internalizing white America's loathing.

This contemptible cultural norm was not limited to race. Mainstream disdain for anything that didn't conform to white, Christian, crew-cut standards defined America in the Greatest Generation era. Pluralism was honored in name only. On the eve of World War II, as Hitler was herding Jews into ghettoes, a Roper poll for *Fortune* magazine found a majority of Americans supporting restrictions to keep Jews from "mingling socially where they are not wanted," and during the war Franklin Roosevelt chose not to welcome large numbers of Jewish refugees from Europe or to bomb the rail lines to Auschwitz for fear that Americans would resent fighting a war to save the Jews. Such overt bigotry became politically in-correct after the Holocaust, but the attitudes and practices remained for much of the Greatest Generation era. Ivy League schools maintained Jewish quotas, and even after they relented, Harvard's application material sent a clear message to high-school students with names like Schwartz or Spielberg by asking if they were related to a long list of people with An-glo names like Whiting and Eliot, a practice that lasted into the Seventies. For many Jews, the goal was to remain inconspicuous, not to stand out or call attention to themselves, to acquiesce even when the state forced their kids to read Biblical verses in the public schools. Some tried fitting in by putting up Christmas trees. Others, in a Jewish version of blacks passing for white, tried to deny their heritage and conform by fixing their noses and anglicizing their names, changing from Alvin Schneir, say, to Alan Stone, or Betty Perske to Lauren Bacall, or Bernard Schwartz to Tony Curtis. But even then acceptance was conditional. Many homes came with restrictive covenants prohibiting sales to Jews and blacks, and even when the courts struck these down the practice remained. For Jewish newlyweds looking for a honeymoon perch, resorts politely but firmly requested a letter from the couple's "minister."

Nor was ethnicity the sole determinant of what constituted a real American. "There were communities," wrote historian Geoffrey Perrett in his book about America in the Fifties, "where simply to wear a beard was to excite suspicion; a bearded stranger would be asked by the local police for identification." Indeed suspicion and intolerance of anyone different pervaded America in the Greatest Generation era. Senator Joseph McCarthy was ranked among the top ten most admired Americans in the early Fifties, and the chill of McCarthyism transcended politics and reached into every corner of American life. On college campuses, professors who dared to question the status quo were hounded, harassed, and sometimes fired. A 1954 poll found that only 12 percent of Americans favored allowing an atheist to teach in a college or university, and 60 percent said they wouldn't allow someone to make a speech in their community against churches and religion. It's not that Americans were overly devout, as Will Herberg observed in his 1955 study of religion in America, *Protestant—Catholic—Jew*, pointing out that more than half of all Americans couldn't name a single one of the first four Gospels. It's just that being religious and joining a church, Herberg explained, was a way to conform, to fit in the peer group, "almost automatic as an obvious social requirement, like entertaining or culture." Those who chose not to join were ostracized and disdained.

Life at the office was no different. Men climbing the corporate ladder were expected to act and dress a certain way—the proverbial man in the gray flannel suit—and company culture revolved around slavish obedience to the boss's will. In the regimented office of the Greatest Generation, a bell rang for coffee break, and clerks were prohibited from using the bathroom without permission. To get ahead, men needed a docile, cheerful wife to adorn them at company events and to entertain higher-ups with highball parties at home. A man's entire identity and social standing revolved around his stature at work, and heaven forbid he socialized with anyone below his level. As William H. Whyte pointed out in his classic book on Fifties culture, *The Organization Man,* it was the yes-man—no women allowed, of course—who got ahead, and questioning authority was a fast track to unemployment. Employers used personality tests to root out nonconforming employees, and success, according to Whyte, meant giving "the most conventional, run-of-the-mill, pedestrian answer possible." When in doubt, Whyte advised, tell them that you loved your father and mother, but your father a little more, that you don't care much for books or music, and that you love your wife and children but don't let them get in the way of company work. "Check out the norms and you will find that the advice is not flippant," added Whyte, who had analyzed these tests. You need to observe these rules "to get a high score."

Few paid a steeper price for this culture of conformity than gay and lesbian Americans, the most reviled and vilified of all groups during the Greatest Generation era, perhaps even more so than Communists, and unfortunately there was no politically correct shield to protect them. Many simply led a double life, full of lies, self-loathing, and secret indulgences—not unlike the blacks who passed for whites. Americans were unabashed in their hatred of homosexuals, calling them perverts and deviants, even sociopaths and psychopaths. So shamed were Greatest Generation parents with homosexual children that some committed their kids involuntarily to psychiatric hospitals, where psychiatrists were known to recommend such therapies as electric shock, induced vomiting, hormone injections, and even, in rare cases, frontal lobotomies. Universities expelled gay students and faculty, employers fired gay workers, and Congress acted to eradicate gays from government service—"One homosexual can pollute a government office," a 1950 Senate committee concluded. Across the country cities passed laws to prohibit gays from congregating in public places, as Miami did by arresting any bar owner who would "knowingly allow two or more persons who are homosexuals, lesbians, or perverts to congregate or remain in his place of business." In 1955, police in Boise, Idaho, interrogated fourteen hundred suspected gays and coerced them into naming others, and in 1958, Florida officials began a five-year investigation into homosexual influence at the University of Florida, grilling more than three hundred faculty and staff who were accused of homosexuality. America's revulsion toward gays reached so deep that women could face arrest for wearing men's clothing or looking too "mannish." New York police were known to arrest women wearing trousers unless they were also wearing at least three other pieces of women's clothing. In 1953, the Miami Beach police chief announced proudly that his officers would "harass those men who affect female mannerisms in public places and let them know in no uncertain terms that they are unwelcome on Miami Beach." So toxic was homosexuality that *The New York Times* routinely used the word "perverts" to describe homosexuals, writing in 1963 about how the "condition can be prevented or cured," and as late as 1969 *Los Angeles Times* refused to allow the word "homosexual" in its advertising. For years Gallup even avoided asking questions about gays for fear of arousing controversy. It was an attitude that Greatest Generation Americans would cling to for many years, finding even indirect contact with homosexuality repulsive, with substantial majorities well into the 1980s supporting a ban on library books with gay themes and opposing homosexuals teaching in college.

Today, with our sepia-toned recollections of the Greatest Generation age, we remember happy families and cheerful wives gazing worshipfully at their husbands, a generation of June Cleavers content with their role as domestic providers and ego massagers for their hard-working men. But again, the reality belies the nostalgia. For large numbers of American women back then, domestic bliss was really a domestic prison. Confined to the home and the role of supporting spouse, women had little choice but to swallow their frustrations, keep smiling, and make the best of it. Yet frustrated they were. The culture made clear that women should not have independent lives and thoughts of their own—and did everything to enforce it. So the frustration lay buried, unspoken, what the author Betty Friedan called "the problem that has no name stirring in the minds of so many American women." These were the Greatest Generation years—the years before feminism.

In a 1957 study by the University of Michigan, an astonishing 80 percent of adults said that a woman must be sick, neurotic, or immoral to remain unmarried. Indeed any form of female independence was greeted with hostility, resentment, and fear. Most Greatest Generation Americans disapproved of wives working outside the home, and those wives who did were seen as defying their husbands' authority. Even then, women had few options beyond a small and circumscribed set of "female jobs." Want ads were segregated by sex, with separate sections for men and women, a practice *The Washington Post* didn't end until 1972. In the "Help Wanted—Female" classifieds of the September 1, 1950, *New York Times,* women's choices were limited to bookkeeper, cashier, clerk, lab technician, maid, model, nurse, receptionist, secretary, stenographer, switchboard operator, or typist, and many ads described the perfect "girl" as "young" or "attractive," with one clerk-model job listing "5' 5"–7" in heels" as a requirement. Even bastions of enlightenment treated female aspirations with disdain. Of the 513 Harvard Law graduates in 1964, only fifteen were women, and they had to survive professors who refused to call on them and endure a first-year inquisition from the dean, who made them justify "taking the place of a man." Of course a woman's job didn't count for much anyway, as a wife's earnings could not be included when applying for a mortgage, and until the Equal Opportunity Credit Act of 1975, women had a hard time obtaining charge cards and wives couldn't establish credit lines independent of their husbands.

But it wasn't just women's economic independence that America suppressed in the Greatest Generation years. It was psychological and personal. In 1956, *Life* magazine—ever attuned to the cultural zeitgeist—interviewed five male psychiatrists who blamed female assertiveness and ambition for troubled households, anxious husbands, and even homosexuality in boys. Marital problems, the psychiatrists said, stemmed from "wives who are not feminine enough and husbands who are not truly male." And wives who weren't feminine enough and didn't send the right social signals could lead to husbands losing jobs and promotions. These sermons were of course mild compared to the censure aimed at women who asserted their sexual independence. Men who sowed their wild oats were met with a cultural wink and nod, while like-minded women were condemned as degenerates. Nor were these mere academic judgments. As historian Stephanie Coontz writes in *The Way We Never Were: American Families and the Nostalgia Trap,* "institutionalization and sometimes electric shock treatments were used to force women to accept their domestic roles and their husbands' dictates." Women were considered too emotional for politics, science, business, and even jury duty, and women who spoke too forcefully were labeled "hysterical," a word derived from the psychiatric term for a disorder characterized by uncontrollable, even violent emotional outbursts.

So overwhelming was this cultural ethos that large numbers of women felt compelled to internalize and believe it. In a faint echo of the light-skinned blacks who passed as whites and cut off ties with their families, more than one in four women—26 percent—told pollsters in 1946 that they wished they had been born as men (only 3 percent of men wished they were born as women), and in 1962, two out of three women said decisions "should be made by the man." But just as civil rights marchers holding I AM A MAN placards asked America to affirm their humanity, so too did the early feminists: "Women Are People Too" was what the little-known Betty Friedan called her 1960 article in *Good Housekeeping,* which she would eventually turn into her groundbreaking 1963 book, *The Feminine Mystique.* A nation that fought for human dignity and worth in World War II seemed to be ignoring and suppressing it here at home.

Nostalgia is a funny phenomenon because it puts a sepia-toned lens over the past and makes us yearn for the imagined good old days. But in truth the old days weren't so good. And in truth we live in a far better America today. It is a more humane America, a more equal America, a freer America, an America that no longer blesses the exclusion and debasement of people simply because of their background and gender. We live in the Baby Boom era of American history, and despite our flaws and blemishes as a nation, we are a more benign and virtuous nation than at any time in our history. The media may headline all the finger-pointing jeremiads about moral decline and a loss of virtues, but the real story of America in the Baby Boom era is how we've become a more open nation, a more accepting nation, a nation that's adopted a norm of democratic pluralism and tolerance for people regardless of who they are and how they act, think, or look.

Today's gauzy memories may bathe the typical Fifties community in a glow of welcome and warmth, but in truth these were communities built on ostracism and exclusion, which means they denied community to some as they conferred it on others. The Baby Boom norm is different: We expect communities and institutions to include, to reach out, to respect difference and find ways to accommodate it. Indeed if we're intolerant at all today, we're intolerant of the old intolerance. Rather than shame a black person for not looking white or a wife for not acting wifely or a gay man for not acting manly or a Jew for being too conspicuous, we now shame those who resist and disrespect this new norm. We now prize rather than punish people for expressing themselves—unless, of course, they're doing it in ways that exclude or harm others. People are free to conform or not to conform; mothers are free to stay at home or pursue careers; blacks and whites are free to fall in love and not fear harassment or worse; two men living together are free to call themselves a family; employees are free and often encouraged to speak their minds; citizens are free to dissent without risking censure for disloyalty; people are free to live and let live, to pursue their own version of happiness.

To be sure, not all Americans wholeheartedly embrace these choices, and we're far from eliminating those old habits of heart that demeaned anyone who didn't conform or spoke out or stood even a bit outside the mainstream. We may never eliminate prejudice, narrow-mindedness, and fear. But at a minimum we've created a new and compelling norm that shuns prejudice, narrow-mindedness, and fear. In a very fundamental way America in the Baby Boom age is closer than ever to its founding ideals of freedom and equality—not economic equality, which Americans never espoused, but a democratic equality, an equality of worth between people, a sense that all segments of society are equally deserving of respect, a belief in cultural pluralism that regards no race or belief or way of life as superior or inferior to another.

So natural and comfortable is our new liberal norm that most Americans seem to take it for granted, as if it's always been this way. Because we live in a changed America, we tend to forget what it was like before we embraced the principles of diversity, feminism, and Baby Boom individualism—we tend to forget how much better it is today, much like the proverbial female basketball star who spurns feminism without ever asking who put the ball in her hands. Today our political culture is riven by the notion of gay marriage, and pundits breathlessly report that gays are on the defensive because only 40 or so percent of Americans support the idea, far less than the number that supports the less ambitious concepts of gay adoption and civil unions. But to think that gay marriage would even be an issue, or to imagine civil unions as a possible compromise, or to see two men raising children let alone holding hands in public, or to have a majority call homosexuality an acceptable lifestyle, or to have nearly four in ten adults approving the marriage of two men or two women and a comfortable majority saying they're fine with civil unions—these would be mind-boggling and thoroughly incomprehensible during the Greatest Generation years, when gays could be arrested simply for congregating at bars and parents would commit their gay children to psychiatric hospitals. Today we haggle about the limits of affirmative action and politically correct thinking, but it would be hard to find many Americans who would support an accounting firm like the one in the 1980s that denied a woman partnership for failing to "walk more femininely, talk more femininely, dress more femininely, wear makeup, have her hair styled, and wear jewelry," which is precisely what most employers expected from women during the Greatest Generation era, when men were men and women were girls.

Today we see women going to work and men staying home to raise the children, black and white characters kissing passionately on television, universities training female prosecutors and male nurses, and Mississippi police departments once accustomed to arresting blacks now hiring black police chiefs. Today we see bottom-line business considerations giving way to environmental concerns, religious denominations blessing gay or female rabbis and ministers, lay organizations challenging church doctrine, corporate brochures promoting diversity, and a deeply conservative vice president of the United States praising the gay rights work of his lesbian daughter. We even see an attorney general known for his right-wing views authorizing a gay pride celebration at the Justice Department that his black deputy was asked to address, hundreds of thousands in hundreds of cities flocking to see a play celebrating female sexuality named *The Vagina Monologues,* and a southern senator driven from power for expressing segregationist sentiments. Most Americans barely raise an eyebrow when hearing these things today. It doesn't seem unusual anymore to see a female boss at work or a black and white couple lovingly embrace. But all of these would have been inconceivable in the Greatest Generation era. America has undergone what the scholar Ronald Inglehart has called a "broad cultural shift, with one worldview replacing another," and except for religious conservatives railing against it, the rest of America seems perfectly comfortable and has barely paused to notice. In fact when pollsters dig beneath the generalized nostalgia for the good old days, they find that only a small number of Americans would ever want to return to them, a fact that public opinion researcher Daniel Yankelovich learned more than two decades ago when he asked people if they had "any hankering to go back either to traditional standards of sexual relations, to the 'spic and span' housekeeping norms of the past, or to the male monopoly on working outside the home."

To say that America today is far better and more humane than in the Greatest Generation years is not to suggest that Greatest Generation Americans were in any way bad or indifferent people. Far from it. But when they returned home after the war and it came time to advance the freedoms they defended overseas, the Greatest Generation turned out to be generally resistant or mute. Perhaps it was because they were tired of fighting, or perhaps it was because they had experienced so much uncertainty that they just didn't want to rock the boat, or perhaps the white men didn't want blacks or women competing for jobs, or perhaps they were simply old-fashioned and liked things as they were. But whatever the reason, they acquiesced and remained largely silent. It was what Martin Luther King, Jr., meant when he wrote in 1964 about the reign of police terror against blacks in Birmingham, Alabama, "The ultimate tragedy of Birmingham was not the brutality of the bad people, but the silence of the good people."

The Greatest Generation's progeny, the Baby Boom generation, is often accused of being over-indulged and soft. In a curious and usually implied cultural condemnation, Boomers stand indicted for never having fought the Great War and never suffering through the Great Depression. But it's really a moot exercise to argue over how Boomers would have fared during World War II. What we do know is this: Millions of Boomers fought nobly and bravely in a pointless and duplicitous war their Greatest Generation parents bequeathed them, and millions more risked arrest, imprisonment, and ostracism for protesting and opposing the pointlessness and duplicity of that war. We also have no evidence or reason to believe that Boomers wouldn't have fought the Nazis with the same commitment of blood, bravery, and selflessness their parents gave, and indeed Boomer anti-war protesters said so at the time, distinguishing between the very just and necessary war against Hitler and the misguided, deceptive, and morally ambiguous war in Vietnam.

More relevant when examining these two generations is to focus on what they did when faced with the exact same circumstances, when faced with a culture, society, and political system that denied basic rights, suppressed aspirations, scorned anyone different, and made people outside the mainstream doubt themselves, their value, and their worth. In the 1960s, both Baby Boomers and Greatest Generation Americans witnessed the same society and its many flaws. One made the choice to accept and defend the status quo. The other made the choice to advance the principles of democracy, equality, and freedom, the founding principles of our country—they made the choice to end the hypocrisy of proclaiming but not observing our national ideals, to address the gap between the promise of American life and the reality of that life for so many Americans. The Greatest Generation deserves every bit of credit for protecting democracy when it was threatened; but Baby Boomers deserve even more credit for enriching democracy and fulfilling its promise when neither war nor catastrophe nor crisis nor necessity compelled them to do it.

Greatness can be measured not only by the decisions we must make, but by the decisions we choose to make. Two generations stared at the same shortcomings, inequities, and hypocrisies of American life, but it was the Baby Boom generation that chose to tackle them, to hold this country to its grand ideals, to agitate for justice when it would have been easier to remain docile and silent, and we are a better nation because of that. It is why this generation's accomplishments eclipse what came before it, and why the Baby Boom must be recognized as the Greater Generation.

One of our prevailing cultural assumptions today, fueled by the media's insatiable need for narrative arcs, is that the only path to greatness is through sacrifice and suffering. We have a bias toward the epic, toward the dramatic, toward the visual show of courage and grit, toward the *Saving Private Ryan* version of history. But what gets left out of this narrative is the heroism of daily life, of changing institutions and compelling society to live up to its ideals. What gets left out is the idealistic legwork of democracy. There's no rule in history saying you have to endure hardship or deprivation to be great—that only soldiers or ascetics have a claim to moral worth. Baby Boomers never had a good and triumphant war to fight, or a grueling depression to endure. And so many observers simply assume that the Baby Boom generation has lived off its birthright and hasn't accomplished much since energizing the civil rights movement and grinding the Vietnam War to a halt. But ever since Boomers burst into the Sixties and began challenging the status quo, they have relentlessly held themselves and their country accountable—morally and personally accountable—for expanding freedom and embracing pluralism. There may be nothing Homeric or visually compelling about bringing democracy to the workplace or effecting equality at home or ending the shame minorities feel simply for sounding or looking different, but these and other changes spawned by the Baby Boom are so far-reaching and fundamental that they will transform how Americans live in ways no war or New Deal ever could accomplish. Baby Boomers will never receive medals or decorations to document what they've done, but it's evident every day in our more open, inclusive, tolerant, equal, diverse, and environmentally aware society. The great advances of the last four decades didn't just happen on their own—it was, by and large, the Baby Boom that made them happen.

What Baby Boomers have done, as one author put it, is transform society through "a silent revolution in social values." Once the clamor from the Sixties died down, Boomers very quietly took the core values from that decade and began to remake society attitude by attitude, family by family, courtroom by courtroom, office by office, institution by institution. Empowered by their vast numbers and network of like-minded peers, they became a generation unafraid to examine the precepts on which society and their identity stood. These were regular people leading regular lives but unwilling to accept the obsolete norms of these regular lives, ordinary citizens who imagined themselves as agents of change. So

Boomers began to challenge old assumptions, modify outmoded laws, modernize personal and institutional relationships, and change the social values that guide the way we live and act toward one another. Demeaning and bigoted habits of speech—discredited. The sexual double standard—confronted. Deference to white men—challenged. Genteel prejudice—exposed. Discrimination against anyone outside the mainstream—rooted out. Racial and sexual taboos—defied. Imposing religious values on people who believe differently—rejected. The command and control workplace—discarded. Sexual harassment—outlawed. Entrenched authority—held accountable. Smoke-filled politics, cronyism, secrecy in government—unmasked. Toxic run-off and belching smokestacks—no longer tolerated.

Over the last four decades, the Baby Boom has created, reinvented, invigorated, or sustained most of the great citizen movements that have advanced American values and freedoms—the environmental movement, the consumer movement, the women's movement, the civil rights movement, the diversity movement, the gay and lesbian movement, the human rights movement, the openness in government movement. In its wake the Baby Boom has left not a single institution unchanged for the better, from the workplace to the university to the press to the military to the basic relationship between men and women. This is not to deny credit to those Greatest Generation legislators who sensed the cultural groundswell and voted for all the landmark civil rights laws in the Sixties. And many did it against the wishes of their white Greatest Generation constituents, who cheered Richard Nixon's cynical southern strategy in 1968, which exploited racial prejudice and fear, and who supported the segregationist George Wallace in the 1964 Democratic primaries, giving him as much as 43 percent of the vote in some northern states. But as Martin Luther King, Jr., pointed out repeatedly throughout the 1960s, a law can go only so far—it's the heart, the soul, the mind, and the deed that ultimately validate human dignity, that determine whether a black woman feels a need to bleach her skin, or whether a Jew feels a need to change his name, and until the Baby Boom tackled these matters of heart, the old norms remained unbowed and unchanged.

It was this evolving worldview that Boomers bestowed on society, a worldview that embraced change, pluralism, inclusion, and individual worth, that cast aside blind faith in tradition and fear of the other. Throughout human history new generations have always struck a bargain with their elders: Adhere to our traditions and conform to our values, the elders say, and we will let you assume power. Generation after generation acquiesced in the deal. But the Baby Boom said no, the Baby Boom refused to compromise its ideals, and in the span of a single generation the Baby Boom has overturned decades if not centuries of outmoded norms, attitudes, and discriminatory practices, replacing them with a more fundamentally democratic culture that reaches every nerve and synapse of American life.

Of course if most Greatest Generation Americans had their way, Baby Boomers would have transformed precious little in American life. As pollster Daniel Yankelovich has pointed out, America in the Greatest Generation era was governed by "universally held prescriptions" about how we should lead our lives, prescriptions that circumscribed personal freedom and upheld the prerogatives of white men at the expense of non-whites, women, and anyone who lived or loved outside the cultural mainstream. So stubborn and monolithic were these norms that the Greatest Generation resisted change even when the rest of society was metamorphosing around them, relenting only somewhat in their very twilight years. Well into the 1990s, polls showed Greatest Generation majorities opposing racial intermarriage, objecting to working mothers, supporting discrimination against gays, clinging to the notion that husbands belong at work and wives belong at home, and insisting on the old rule that young people should be taught to follow their elders, not think for themselves. When asked if people should obey the law without exception or observe their conscience when faced with an unjust law, large majorities of Greatest Generation Americans continued to espouse obeying the law without exception—no different from what they lectured young Baby Boomers on during the civil rights and Vietnam days. On issues involving the very nature of inclusion and pluralism, the Greatest Generation has repeatedly balked at the new Baby Boom norm. Through the end of the Eighties a majority of Greatest Generation Americans said they would vote for a law allowing a homeowner to refuse to sell his home to a black buyer. When asked in 1977 if they would try to end racial discrimination in a social club they and their friends belonged to, nearly 70 percent said "no"—and "no" remained the majority sentiment for this cohort till the end of the 1980s.

On all of these issues the Baby Boom has held diametrically opposed views ever since pollsters began recording their attitudes in the mid 1960s—when half, for example, expressed shame over our nation's racial problems. Indeed for Boomers, the generation gap is not merely a rhetorical relic from the Sixties—the persistence of Greatest Generation norms, manifested today in the conservative movement, has been a real and decisive barrier to the inclusive, equal, and democratic America that the Baby Boom has been shaping since the Sixties. To Boomer critics, if our nation had only stuck with Greatest Generation values—duty, faith, and deference—we would have become a stronger, stable, more united, and less divided nation. It was Boomers, they claim, who roiled society and stirred things up. But to Boomers, duty does not mean blind loyalty. It does not mean following authorities simply because they're authorities. It does not mean accepting unjust norms and resisting efforts to change them. During the climactic years of the civil rights movement, Martin Luther King, Jr., worried that too many Greatest Generation Americans preferred order to justice, "a negative peace which is the absence of tension to a positive peace which is the presence of justice." Boomers answered King's call, and as a generation they have never been afraid to challenge a status quo that needs challenging—they have always insisted on rights before deference and justice before order. And we're a better nation because of it.

Given the Baby Boom's staunch values, their devotion to egalitarian and inclusive principles, how curious that some critics accuse Boomers of lacking a moral compass and imposing a reckless relativism on the rest of society. Conservative critics such as William Bennett, George Will, Sean Hannity, and Robert Bork condemn Boomer liberalism for "unilateral moral disarmament," to quote Bennett, for an unwillingness "to make judgments on a whole range of behaviors and attitudes." But this analysis is flawed and misguided—it simply misreads Baby Boom culture. At bottom, what perturbs these critics is that their version of morality has been superseded by Baby Boom morality, and in a sly effort to undermine

Boomer liberalism, they attempt to trivialize it. But in the Baby Boom book of virtues, there's nothing equivocal about the Boomer view of right and wrong. Boomers condemn bigotry, intolerance, and discrimination. They reject moralistic constraints on personal freedom and don't like it when women are patronized and not treated as equals. They find pollution objectionable and see nothing moral in imposing religious beliefs on others. They believe a moral upbringing is teaching kids to think for themselves, not to follow arbitrary rules or blindly accept the status quo. And they have a hard time seeing the morality of ostracizing those whose sexual orientation and private behavior do no one any harm. What Boomer culture embraces are the very American values of pluralism, privacy, freedom of choice, tolerance, and respect for others no matter how different they are from you. To Boomers, authority should be earned, government should be open, conscience should trump rules, the environment should be protected, people should feel free to express themselves, and we should have as much democracy as any organization or institution will allow. These are core Boomer values, and they're as moral as the values of any previous era. To the oft-repeated accusation that Boomer culture has eroded the traditional family and all restraints on personal behavior, not at all. Boomers simply accept that people are different and have a right to make their own choices and lead their own lives, and that the moral imperative is not to condemn those who are different but to include and support them. Diversity is not just a slogan—it's a moral value in Baby Boom America.

Historians looking back will probably say that Baby Boomers turned Greatest Generation morality on its head. Whereas the Greatest Generation imposed its morality on private behavior and personal relationships, the Baby Boom projected its morality onto our social behavior and public relationships. Whereas the Greatest Generation viewed sexual and other personal behavior as a moral or religious issue, the Baby Boom sees it as an individual choice and a private personal issue. Whereas the Greatest Generation accepted racial bigotry, sex discrimination, cultural conformity, and environmental degradation as unchanging realities, the Baby Boom deems them unconscionable realities that need to be changed.

What's clear is that the norms of the Fifties are no longer the norms today, and the norms today were never the norms in the Fifties. To suggest that Fifties morality is the only type of morality is to misunderstand the very nature of morality. The William Bennetts of the world deride Boomer morality as parvenu morality, a politically correct indulgence of educated elites. They just don't recognize that today's morality is as exacting as any morality—it asks for self-restraint, it demands consequences, it involves making judgments. Or perhaps they just don't like the results of this new morality. Boomers are making a moral statement when they confront a politician who disparages gays or a sportscaster who demeans blacks or a businessman who condescends toward women. But when Bill Clinton "did not have sexual relations with that woman," even Boomers offended by his lying simply shrugged at his wrongheaded personal behavior and instead shuddered at the invasion of his privacy, to the great bewilderment of Greatest Generation pedants who wailed about an American society morally adrift.

To Boomers, of course, it was the old America of the Fifties that was morally adrift. As the first generation weaned on television, Boomers grew up seeing the flickering images of racial injustice and political McCarthyism, and they began to ask how there could be such public listlessness and conformity in a society that clearly wasn't living up to its founding ideals. Nor were they alone in this assessment. In 1960, President Eisenhower warned that an America "worshiping material success" could "become emptied of idealism," and to combat national aimlessness he created a Commission on National Goals charged with restoring a sense of purpose and direction in the country. His concerns were confirmed by sociologists who found Americans uninterested in civic life, unwilling to get involved, and unmotivated to learn about politics. One 1959 study of New Haven, Connecticut, found Greatest Generation Americans barely engaged in their communities or participating in any public concerns—"citizens are not interested, concerned, and active," the study concluded. In 1960 *Life* magazine worried about a growing gap between American ideals and the reality of excessive materialism. The social critic Paul Goodman diagnosed the Greatest Generation with a condition he called "the nothing can be done disease."

One lesson the Greatest Generation taught Boomers was to respect

American history, to honor our wars for democracy, and to revere the ideals encoded in the Constitution and Declaration of Independence. So Boomers took the founding American values to heart: freedom of speech, equality before the law, respect for privacy, distrust of power, individual liberty, open democracy, the pursuit of happiness, and constant vigilance against the tyranny of the majority. But as they looked closely at Greatest Generation society, they began to question how much America was living up to these ideals, the ones they were so earnestly taught in school. Drilling deeper, they wondered how a president could send young people to fight a war without telling the truth about the war or showing how it would protect democracy. Or they wondered how white Christian Americans could claim the mantle of American tradition when in fact this nation was built by a multicultural cast of whites and blacks, Christians and Jews, Europeans and Indians, deists and religionists. Or they wondered how our leaders could pontificate about our freedoms when so many Americans were unable or afraid to exercise them. To Boomers, a truly moral America would end this hypocrisy, which is precisely what this generation set out to do.

Recently, in a widely celebrated book called *Bowling Alone,* the prominent sociologist Robert Putnam labeled Greatest Generation Americans the "long civic generation" largely because so many built bonds of trust by belonging to social organizations like the Elks, Kiwanis, and Lions clubs. Sadly, Putnam argued, civic life in America has fallen apart in the Baby Boom years. But to Boomers there was nothing civic about belonging to private clubs that excluded blacks, Jews, and women—and nothing civic about blindly accepting that status quo. A social trust built on distrust of others seemed contradictory at best, poisonous at worst. Rather, Boomers understood "civic" the way Eisenhower articulated it, as a moral cause to advance American ideals. Much like other idealistic generations—the Revolutionary generation or the Progressive reformers of a century ago—Boomers were warned not to defy received tradition, not to question the established way of life, not to distrust their elders. But as they emerged onto the American scene in the Sixties, Boomers saw an America riddled with hypocrisy—they saw an astonishing gap between our founding ideals and the reality of American life—and as a generation they

refused to accept it. And ever since the Sixties, Boomers have s[
lives quietly agitating to bridge that gap.

In their neighborhoods and offices, in universities and the courts, through nonprofits and loosely organized grass-roots groups, in the home and in personal relationships, Boomers have sought to create a public morality that would square American ideals with the way we lead our lives. And in doing so Boomers have forged new bonds of trust—what Putnam calls "social capital"—between people who never would have met through an Elks or Moose club, or who never would have been allowed to join one of these clubs. This Boomer determination to transform our social values and create new forms of social capital first became evident on the increasingly diverse campuses of the Sixties, and today it is evident in every corner of Boomer culture and life. A Simmons Market Research Bureau study in the early Nineties found Boomers considerably more likely than other adults to participate in public meetings, work on local civic issues, volunteer in politics, give time and money to charities, and write letters to officials, newspapers, magazines, and product manufacturers. And to many Boomers it's more than just a civic duty—many have dedicated their lives to improving America. The number of nonreligious nonprofit and advocacy groups has mushroomed from fewer than thirty thousand in the late 1940s to nearly nine hundred thousand today, with nonprofit employment nearly doubling since the late 1970s, and in Baby Boom America there are advocates for any and all Americans locked outside the corridors of power, from consumers to minorities to working parents to small investors to plain old citizens seeking a more open and accountable government not beholden to special interests. Nor does that even count all the grass-roots groups and impromptu networks dedicated to social action, legal services, environmental protection, zoning laws, community festivals, and countless other local activities.

Boomers also put a great deal of their civic energy into transforming a new center of community life in America, the workplace, where they have successfully challenged corporate structures, flattened organizational hierarchies, and pushed for more flexible, inclusive, non-discriminatory work environments. Boomers may not flock to Kiwanis clubs, but most do work, and the office has become a new town square for people of all different backgrounds to build bridges, socialize, and band together for a common cause, so it's natural that Boomers would insist on making it better. It's the same spirit behind Boomer involvement in the environmental movement. In the 1950s and 1960s, few Americans considered the environment a national problem, placing it near the bottom in a Gallup poll of public concerns, and anyone criticizing industrial practices was accused of obstructing progress. But that was before Boomers took on the cause. By 1970, more than twenty million Americans would participate in Earth Day celebrations; by the early Seventies, under pressure from Boomer students, universities across the country were establishing environmental studies programs; by the Eighties, membership in environmental groups would multiply ten-fold if not more; by the Nineties, local chapters energized by grass-roots members would challenge zoning laws and sue for stricter environmental enforcement; and by 2000, curbside recycling would take hold in more than nine thousand communities, up from six hundred in 1988. A similar time line could be written about the rise of racial inclusiveness, or the growing equality for women, or the emerging acceptance of gays and lesbians, or the increasing tolerance for all forms of diversity. If membership in a Kiwanis club can merit a civic label, it would be difficult to call the Baby Boom anything but a great civic generation. Or as one writer put it, Americans have been experiencing "not the extinction of civic life but its reinvention."

It also would be difficult to call Boomers anything but patriotic. No, it's not patriotism in the flag-waving and chest-thumping sense, but in many ways it's as meaningful a patriotism because it recognizes that American nationalism is built not on pride or hubris but on ideals and how we uphold them. And it's a patriotism that doesn't feel a need to demonize others to prove how good we are. In fact the Baby Boom culture may best be judged by something Boomers haven't done. After World War I, the war to save democracy, an America seized by Red Scare fears arrested thousands of immigrants, charged many with sedition, and passed such restrictive immigration laws that they limited entry primarily to Anglo-Saxons and were later used to keep Jewish refugees fleeing Nazism from finding safe haven in this country. In the Thirties, millions of Americans cheered the anti-Semitic rants of Father Charles Coughlin, the "radio priest," who needed ninety-six clerks to answer the eighty thousand grateful letters he received weekly. In the Forties, as the Greatest Generation fought Hitler, we rounded up 120,000 Japanese-Americans and locked them away in internment camps. Then in the Fifties, the shroud of Mc-Carthyism cast a shadow of persecution, suspicion, and fear over anyone different from the ideological or cultural mainstream. This was all a part of the patriotism of old.

Now fast-forward to today, to America under the Baby Boom. Except for some law enforcement excesses and random but rare acts of violence, there was no Red Scare equivalent after September 11, no credible calls to persecute or imprison or deport Muslims and Arabs, no public imagery depicting Arabs with exaggerated or stereotyped features, but rather a sincere if at times awkward attempt to reach out and bridge any differences and reinforce our new ideology of inclusion. Observed the *New York Times* essayist Edward Rothstein, "at a time in which a war on Islamist terror is working itself out in so many incarnations and with so many controversies, what seems noteworthy is that there are now so *few* examples of graphic American propaganda and none using ethnic or racial caricatures." It's the same with the American response to the millions of Latinos and Asians who have emigrated during the last four decades: Unlike the malevolent nativism, bigotry, and 100-percent Americanism that greeted Russian, Polish, Italian, and Jewish immigrants a century ago, a norm of diversity shields today's immigrants. As a culture we've marginalized nativism and rejected stereotyping, and the worst it gets is the occasional initiative to limit government benefits for illegal immigrants, which is then dissected for xenophobic motivation and denounced if it's found. This is Baby Boom public morality, Baby Boom patriotism at work.

As we peer through the media looking glass today, most images of Baby Boomers seem stuck in the Sixties, when youthful Boomers quite brazenly confronted status quo values and norms, setting off a Newtonian process of action and reaction that pitted Boomers against their Greatest Generation elders. Many Boomers themselves harken back wistfully to these "glory years," a time when their generational adrenaline flowed, when they challenged a misguided war, two lying presidents, and a society that devalued minorities and women. To them, Baby Boom history stopped right about then. Now there's no question that the Sixties experience is a central helix of the Baby Boom DNA. But to focus only on the Sixties is to miss the more significant story of how this generation, ever since the Sixties, has transformed our institutions and changed our norms. In the simplistic narrative of mass media, the fact that Boomers were no longer marching or protesting or in-your-face demonstrating meant that Boomers had eschewed their ideals. But that narrative says more about the media's need for a good storyline than it does about Boomers. For the Baby Boom reverberation didn't end with the Sixties— it began with the Sixties and in the process suburbanized and institutionalized the Sixties. That is how this generation's story unfolds.

There will no doubt be critics who argue that the Baby Boom's generally liberal attitudes are not widespread and merely reflect the values of cultural elites, particularly activists from the Sixties who have moved into media and the universities. But research on public attitudes belies that argument. On social issue after social issue—from race to family to religion to personal behavior and choice—a large majority of Boomers fall squarely in the column of greater inclusion, freedom, equality, and acceptance, and an equally large majority of Boomers hold attitudes diametrically opposed to those of their elders in the Greatest Generation.

Where these critics stumble upon a kernel of truth is in describing the role of well-educated Boomers in setting the tone for this generation back in the Sixties. And there's a reason it happened this way. In the early Sixties, as America began to emerge from the smokestack industrial age, the technological demands of our changing economy required an increasingly educated workforce. That happened to coincide with the first group of Boomers entering early adulthood. For other generations a job and marriage were the sole options, but for better-educated Boomers the preferred choice was college, and many went. As employers clamored for smarter workers, campuses once reserved for WASP elites began opening their doors to an increasingly diverse student body. The result is that colleges that had previously reflected social privilege began to reflect another phenomenon: generational identity. And as is wont to happen at college, students don't simply get trained for a job. They begin to ask big questions, think critically, and question the status quo—which is precisely what Boomer college students began to do in the Sixties, and needless to say they had plenty to question. The result, as Daniel Yankelovich describes it, was a "cultural revolution" that was incubating on the college campuses in the Sixties. "Initially," Yankelovich notes, "its true nature was disguised by the Vietnam War protests, but when the war ended the unrest on campus turned out not to be essentially about antiwar protests and radical politics but rather about cultural values." These new Baby Boom values represented a sharp break from traditional values, and as Yankelovich puts it, we've moved from the old "lockstep social conformity" and "puritanical, repressive attitudes" to a new worldview characterized by greater diversity, less hierarchy, and a more pluralistic approach to knowledge and society.

But perhaps most interesting is how these values spread from campuses to the rest of the generation. And it happened through another quirk of history—the fact that Baby Boomers were really the first mass media generation. Transistor radios freed Boomer media from parental control and enabled Boomers to create a common youth culture on the airwaves. Through rock music Boomers heard the beat and the words that spoke to their desires, hopes, ideals, and frustrations. Television enabled Boomers to see what no generation had seen before: streaming images of Americans brutalizing other Americans who simply wanted to exercise their civil rights. As the Sixties progressed, FM radio and alternative weekly newspapers further sharpened the Baby Boom critique of Greatest Generation America and disseminated it beyond the campus gates. Nor was there the type of media clutter we have today with our many hundreds of choices—Boomers heard the same rock music and saw the same news programs and struggled with the same compelling issues about war, equality, bigotry, and official hypocrisy.

So what emerged was a youth culture of shared imagery, issues, and expectations that began to transcend the class, race, and ethnic barriers that had divided all previous generations. Boomer youth culture became a conveyer belt that spread campus concerns to the rest of the generation, even to younger brothers and sisters too young to remember the Sixties but old enough to be troubled by the fallout from Vietnam and Watergate. In the early Seventies, Yankelovich was the first to notice how broadly this generational identity was taking shape, as he found "the gap between college and noncollege youth" closing through "an astonishingly swift transmission of values formerly confined to a minority of college youth and now spread throughout this generation." And it wasn't long before these values permeated the rest of America, to the point that by 1980 Yankelovich could find no more than 20 percent of Americans who did not subscribe "to at least part of the new value orientation," a finding confirmed by scholars who wrote in *The American Journal of Sociology* that between the 1970s and 1990s, the social attitudes of college graduates and the less schooled "became more similar," to the point of "significant" convergence.

So yes, the Boomer silent revolution may have started on the campuses, and it may be anchored in the protests of the Sixties, but there's really nothing elite about it. More accurate is to see it for what it is: a generation-wide movement to repudiate stifling norms and fulfill American ideals, one of the great mass cultural transformations in our nation's history. That we remain a far from perfect society today should not obscure the fact that we are a much better society today. And to say that the Baby Boom has made it so has nothing to do with generational vanity, as some critics might charge, but rather with giving credit where credit is due. Indeed it's safe to say that World War II–era Americans, for all their virtues, wouldn't be so honored today were it not for the fact that their children, Baby Boomers, have spent their lives righting the wrongs that the Greatest Generation condoned, accommodated, or never addressed.

# Chapter Two
# The New Silent Majority

*We Are the People Our Parents Warned Us Against*
*—Nicholas von Hoffman, 1968*

**Immediately** after the 2004 presidential election and all the news reports that "moral values" motivated more voters than any other issue, my e-mail in-box began to fill up with messages of despair. Friends, former college classmates, and disbelieving Baby Boomers all were asking the same plaintive question, "Are we out of synch with the country, are we outside the mainstream?" The e-mails were from a dry cleaner in upstate New York and a suburban mom who works part-time and a stay-at-home mom who volunteers and an emergency room doctor in New Jersey and a high-tech wizard in the Pacific Northwest and from countless other Boomers chilled by the media spin du jour, that evangelicals represent the heart of our country and that real Americans can be found only in socially conservative pews. "Ordinary people, the people in the red states," is how the conservative media critic Bernard Goldberg framed it, and a chastened press seemed to be saying amen.

But as so often happens with the media, a good storyline simply got in the way of in-depth analysis, so even as the 2004 election caricature hardens into conventional wisdom, it's time to put it in proper perspective. Despite all the post-election claims about a socially conservative mandate, the very fact that one-fifth of voters cited moral values as their top concern means that four-fifths didn't, and while voters in eleven states approved amendments banning same-sex marriage, exit polls found that three in five voters nationwide supported marriage or civil unions for gays. If anything, the research suggests that America is moving in a more socially liberal direction, and the reason it's not immediately apparent is that the most traditional and socially conservative voters, pre–Baby Boomers, are living much longer and voting in very large numbers—voters sixty and over accounted for a quarter of the electorate in 2004, and their views on social issues are the most decidedly conservative among all age groups. Once younger voters begin to replace them, the socially conservative vote will dwindle. So I reassured my e-mail correspondents. Social conservatives no more represent the mainstream today than Prohibitionists did in the Twenties, and in fact it's the Baby Boom sensibility spawned in the 1960s—a sensibility characterized by social tolerance and personal freedom—that has become our new cultural center today. We must be careful not to confuse ballot box results with cultural trends.

What, then, explains the 2004 vote if it doesn't signify a retreat from Boomer values and a nod for the morality of old? One answer is that voters age sixty and over provided about 80 percent of President Bush's victory margin. Another answer is that he ran up such a large margin among white southerners, who represent only about a quarter of all voters, that it completely overshadowed the fact that he lost the popular and Electoral College vote in the rest of the country by a substantial amount. But an even more basic answer is that elections in general are a poor indicator of social and cultural trends. Quite typically, the primary influence on voting and party affiliation is family, and if not family then immediate economic concerns or global uncertainty or even candidate trust and likability. We should take the 2004 election focus at face value—that it was all about who had the leadership qualities in a time of terrorism and global uncertainty. Because of September 11, millions of voters repulsed by the religious right agenda still voted for the sitting president. Nor should we forget that people often vote their small-bore frustrations, which are important personally but hold little or no ideological value: a small business owner tired of paperwork, a doctor sick of nuisance malpractice suits, a veteran trying to make sense of the government bureaucracy. And the simple truth is that most Americans—rightly or wrongly—see politics as an abstraction set in Washington, largely disconnected from their daily routine, and thus they don't see their vote making much of a difference in how they lead their lives and exercise their freedoms. "Politics just isn't as important for most of us as other facets of civic engagement," wrote the late public opinion scholar Everett Carll Ladd.

We heard much the same talk about the rise of conservative social values in the Reagan Eighties, yet scholars who have studied attitudes in that period say there's little evidence to suggest there was any reversal of the social liberalism that began in the 1960s, particularly on issues involving family, women, morality, sexuality, and overall tolerance. According to Tom Smith, director of the highly regarded General Social Survey at the National Opinion Research Center (NORC), the rise of a socially conservative mainstream was more a political myth than a social reality. Americans had no interest in returning to the old ways, Smith wrote in 1985, and on most cultural and social issues "support for liberal positions [has] grown substantially over the last twenty years and now a solid majority of Americans favor liberal positions." And in the two decades since the Eighties, according to the research, even Greatest Generation Americans—those most resistant to Boomer culture—have been inching ever so slowly away from their old insular social values and toward the Baby Boom norm. To some extent, and with obvious exceptions, we are all becoming Baby Boomers now.

That the Baby Boom consensus marches on regardless of who inhabits the halls of power is perhaps the best evidence of the breadth and resilience of Boomer values in America. "From women's issues to environmentalism," wrote *American Demographics* magazine, which follows trends and attitudes in culture and society, "the emblematic values of the 1960s are being embraced by more and more Americans." In the institutions that define us, and in the very basic ways we lead our lives, Boomer norms now prevail. Call it the suburbanization of the Sixties, or the Baby Boom nation, or what some scholars have termed the new "liberal consensus." But from the home to the office to the bedroom to the classroom to the press and even to the pulpit, America has undergone a fundamental paradigm shift in attitudes and perspectives over the last generation, and even the most desperate efforts of social conservatives will not succeed in reversing it, no more than the Catholic Church's threatened excommunication of Galileo four centuries ago succeeded in making people believe that the sun revolved around the earth. As the British historian Arthur Marwick observed, the Sixties movements "did not *confront* . . . society but *permeated* and *transformed* it."

Nor is this mere assertion. To the academics and experts who study cultural values and norms, there's plenty of convincing evidence to support this view—that those born after the early 1940s have pushed American culture in a more liberal direction over the years, creating what some have called a "plateau" of liberalism or egalitarianism that characterizes our social norms today. And there appears to be no turning back. On core social issues involving race, gender, and overall questions of tolerance, opinion research shows few countertrends against Baby Boom social liberalism. Even the most traditional of religious institutions haven't escaped Baby Boom scrutiny: On the bellwether question of ordaining women as priests, most Catholics born before the Forties oppose it, whereas a large and growing majority of those born during and after welcome the change.

The evidence that America has been trending toward Baby Boom liberalism is compelling enough, but when pre-Boomer opinions are factored out of the findings, the consensus is far more liberal than the overall research suggests—and what emerges is an even more powerful case for the preeminence of Baby Boom values. It's certainly true that the elderly are gradually adopting the more socially liberal norms of the Baby Boom era, but they're still significantly more conservative than everyone born after them, and so their views skew the numbers away from the Boomer mainstream. Most scholars agree that as the more socially liberal cohort of younger Americans takes the place of their aging elders, the Baby Boom paradigm should be solidified for generations to come.

Consider some findings on race. On interracial marriage, according to NORC's General Social Survey, which is considered the most comprehensive ongoing study of American attitudes, large majorities of Greatest Generation whites would reject a close relative marrying a black, but barely one in five white Americans born from 1943 onwards have such concerns, a finding confirmed by a recent *Washington Post* poll showing a significant increase in "tolerance and even acceptance" of biracial couples. On what they would do with racially restrictive social clubs, most Greatest Generation adults over the years said they would stay in an all-white social club and do nothing to change it, while a large majority of Americans born from 1943 onwards say they would never accept such a policy and would try to confront it. How widespread Boomer values on race have become can be seen in the fact that sixty-five leading corporations—the very heart of the old conservative establishment—wrote a Supreme Court brief calling affirmative action essential and saying that a "racially and ethnically diverse" student body is crucial "in preparing students to be the leaders this country needs," a sentiment echoed by a poll showing that 80 percent of Americans believe it is important "for a college to have a racially diverse student body." Today there's nothing unusual about reporting for jury duty and seeing the training video feature an African-American judge and prosecuting attorney, or about turning on the television and seeing black news anchors and reporters or even a black and white couple kissing. Even the civil rights leader Jesse Jackson, no friend of the status quo, acknowledged in a 2003 *New York Times* interview that America today is far different from when he ran for president in the Eighties. "You look at the number of mayors, you look at the number of legislators, you look at the number of congresspeople, the number of blacks and browns on boards, the number of blacks and browns in college, the number of blacks and browns with MBAs. There is a steady growth curve." The norm on race clearly has changed.

And so has the norm on gender. It was a big deal back in 1970 when Mary Tyler Moore played the role of a single career woman on her signature show, but nowadays the independent and strong woman is the norm in our media and culture. Indeed we barely notice it anymore. According to the NORC surveys, large majorities of Americans born from 1943 onwards strongly reject the old view that families and children suffer if mom works full-time or if mom works and dad takes care of the kids. Among these younger Americans, few agree with the Greatest Generation notion that mothers should stay at home, that husbands should earn the money and women should keep the house, that women's needs are secondary to men's, or that all women want are a home and kids. In surveys throughout the Nineties, most Americans born before 1943 say it's better for a man to work and a woman to tend the home, while nearly three-fourths of all the younger cohorts disagree. In fact only 6 percent of those born from 1943 onward say that moms should stay at home once the youngest starts school, with almost half saying they should work full-time if they so wish—and a majority now say moms should work even when they have a child under school age. Americans have completely accepted the female as professional, as a doctor or lawyer or banker or professor—a far cry from the old condescending practice of hiring women only as stenographers or for how they looked in heels. Market research also shows that Americans are tuning out ads that stereotype women as homemakers concerned only about cake mix and detergent, and in fact the new trend is to portray men increasingly involved in the home and women with a say over which new car to buy. Even one of the great taboos of America past—the notion of women as sexual beings—is now being accepted and celebrated, with a healthy majority of Americans born from 1943 onwards saying they have no problem with sex before marriage. As three scholars writing in *The Public Opinion Quarterly* concluded about the changing role of women, America has undergone a "fundamental and profound shift in public expectations."

Even the most reviled of all during the Greatest Generation years—gays and lesbians—are moving toward mainstream inclusion. In 1977, the singer Anita Bryant led a nationwide "Save Our Children" crusade to repeal a Miami law that protected homosexuals from discrimination, winning nearly 70 percent of the vote. Empowered by her success and all the media attention, Bryant vowed a full-scale national effort against legitimizing this "perverse and dangerous" lifestyle. But rather than being on the leading edge of something new, Bryant's victory was really a last gasp of a Greatest Generation culture asserting itself. Twenty-five years later, an effort to revive Bryant's crusade and repeal Miami's new anti-discrimination law failed miserably, and across the state in conservative Sarasota, 73 percent supported an anti-discrimination law similar to Miami's, adding to the more than two hundred cities and counties nationwide with such laws.

Indeed the public opinion research on this issue is clear: All age groups but one—pre-Boomers—overwhelmingly say that society should recognize homosexuality as an acceptable way of life. It sounds almost trite these days when pollsters ask whether gay teachers should be fired, a Greatest Generation norm that most Americans now reject, so much so that corporations, charities, and local governments are withdrawing support from the Boy Scouts because it brazenly excludes gay scoutmasters. Nor are Americans simply outlawing discrimination—companies such as IBM and Proctor & Gamble now affirm gay relationships, providing health and other benefits to partners of gay employees. So pervasive is this new norm of acceptance that in 2002, a North Carolina newspaper right in the heart of the Bible Belt, *The Fayetteville Observer,* published a same-sex civil union announcement almost a month before *The New York Times* and *The Boston Globe* agreed to do the same, and while a few local ministers railed and more than fifty readers canceled subscriptions, the furor soon died down and the next civil union notice barely raised an eyebrow. Today more than five hundred newspapers run these announcements. Gay themes and characters are also fairly routine on television—on prime-time shows such as *ER, Will & Grace,* and *Queer Eye for the Straight Guy,* none of which suffer in the ratings—and supporters of gay marriage now include Homer Simpson, who became an ordained minister over the Internet in one episode so he could preside over gay weddings. Perhaps most deliciously ironic was when Chicago mayor Richard Daley announced he would have "no problem" if Cook County began granting same-sex marriage licenses—the same Cook County ruled with an iron fist by his father, the legendary Richard J. Daley, hero to the Greatest Generation for his avowed hatred of Baby Boom reforms and culture.

These are, of course, only the most obvious changes in American life, but in countless other ways America has embraced Baby Boom norms. We see it in a healthy distrust of what William Whyte called the organizational mentality of the Fifties, the old corporate culture that commanded absolute deference and conformity from workers and impugned critics for interfering with the American way of life. So now consumers have rights, workers flatten hierarchies, environmentalists offer an alternative vision of progress, and individuals no longer feel shunned for registering their concerns. Those who worry that social relations have become less ordered and more messy forget one thing: They're now more fair and democratic.

We also see the new norm in the wholesale insistence that personal behavior is private behavior, that people who do no harm to others have a right to conduct their lives as they wish, that religious or moral judgments are not absolutes but matters of perspective, that all people have an equal right to call themselves mainstream. We now value choice over tradition. Cohabitation before marriage remains shunned behavior for most older Americans, acceptable to less than 20 percent of them, but to Boomers

and everyone younger, it barely registers as an issue. Americans now reject the Greatest Generation norm that you prepare children for life by
teaching them to obey rules and follow elders, instead saying that kids
must be taught to make their own choices and think for themselves. Irreverence is no longer hidden and scorned but prized and accepted,
showing up throughout popular culture—on Comedy Central or *Saturday Night Live*—so much so that these shows are a must-do even for presidential candidates. Nor has religion escaped this culture of choice, with
Americans perhaps as religious as ever but neither bound to any denomination nor obligated to any family tradition nor shy about questioning
religious authorities. We worship the choice to worship and accept the
worship of choice. As a pregnant Gloria told her enraged father Archie
Bunker on *All in the Family,* "We decided to let our own child make up
its own mind about its religion." It's not that all is relative and there are
no moral judgments today. Americans are making judgments and choices
all the time, but they are judgments and choices based on individual ethics
and personal preferences rather than rigid rules and hidebound traditions.
When Boomer culture wields its moral authority, it's when individual
choices have serious social consequences, as in bigoted behavior that undermines equality or pollution that damages the environment. Let people
be themselves as long as they don't harm someone else.

The magnet of Baby Boom norms is so strong that demographic
groups stereotyped as socially conservative are actually more liberal than
commonly assumed. An article in *The American Journal of Sociology* describes how Catholics from the mid 1970s onwards "became more similar to religious liberals in their views on abortion, family gender roles, and
sexuality," and another researcher, after studying reproductive attitudes
and behaviors such as premarital sex, contraception, and approval of sex
education, found significant liberalization among Catholics since the 1960s
and few differences between Catholics and Protestants by the mid 1980s,
with Catholics generally "more liberal rather than more conservative
than Protestants" on these issues. Hispanics too seem to be breaking with
tradition and church teachings, with increasing numbers adopting more
liberal attitudes toward birth control and family planning. A 2003 study
by the Pew Hispanic Center found that Hispanics born or reared in the

United States hold social values that are much more liberal than their immigrant parents, with successive generations moving even closer to the Baby Boom norm.

Even conservative activists acknowledge the new norm, albeit in a backhanded way, by appropriating Boomer language and messages to achieve their ideological goals. Abortion opponents, for example, defend proposals to require twenty-four-hour waiting periods before women can get an abortion by saying their goal isn't to restrict abortion but to give women a choice. Outspoken opponents of gay marriage similarly protest that they are not bigoted or intolerant, that they respect the dignity of gay couples but only want to protect tradition. "We're not even allowed to discuss it without being called bigoted and hateful," one said bitterly. And when they're not co-opting Boomer language, they try co-opting Boomer style, posing as hip and irreverent even when their ideas aren't, as when they claim the Sixties mantle by labeling themselves rebels against the liberal establishment, or when a conservative talk show host such as Joe Scarborough plays the Beatles' "With a Little Help from My Friends" to promote his show bashing contemporary ideas and culture.

Conservatives had hoped that Boomers were an aberration, that the generations to follow would return to Greatest Generation values, and they were cheered when younger cohorts scoffed at Boomers and seemed so focused on their careers, as if these were signs of nascent conservatism. But a look at the attitudes of these younger Americans shows that they too have fully embraced Boomer culture and are in essence Boomers without the Sixties—that in terms of values, norms, lifestyle, and sensibility, there really is no generational divide between Boomers and younger Americans. They may be different generations demographically, but not in worldview.

On race, homosexuality, premarital sex, gender roles, the environment, and issues involving personal choice and freedom, their views are almost identical, and if anything, younger Americans are pushing the country in an even more tolerant and liberal direction—they may in fact be the most socially liberal generation in our nation's history. This is a generation that grew up watching shows like *Party of Five, Ally McBeal, Dawson's Creek, Buffy the Vampire Slayer, ER,* and *Friends,* all with storylines that unapologetically reflect the new cultural freedoms and norms. And so it comes quite naturally to them, and they have little patience for closed-mindedness and intolerance. In the NORC surveys, Boomer and Generation X attitudes are uncannily similar. Barely 18 percent of Boomers and 16 percent of Generation X say that gender role reversals hurt the family; only 23 percent of Boomers and 22 percent of Generation X would object to living in a half-black neighborhood. On a close relative marrying an African-American, 28 percent of Boomers and only 17 percent of Generation X have concerns, compared to 55 percent of pre-Boomers; on whether the government should ask about sexual orientation even for secret and top-secret jobs, 59 percent of Boomers and 63 percent of Generation X say no, compared to 34 percent of those born before 1943. What Boomers ushered into American society, everyone afterwards has internalized. "They will be the first generation to accept mixed races, 'nontraditional' families, and gender-bending sex roles as mainstream," *American Demographics* wrote about children of Boomers in 1995.

It may be a good media storyline to write about Boomers versus Generations X and Y, but except for surface differences it's a storyline without substance. Various studies, including one by NORC and another by the senior citizens advocacy group AARP, have shown virtually no generation gap between Boomers and their kids, and nothing close to the generational chasm that separated Boomers and the Greatest Generation. "Unlike the original baby boomers, most will think their parents are cool," *American Demographics* wrote. One survey of Boomer kids—also known as Millennials, Generation Y, and Echo Boomers—found that 94 percent share their parents' values, or as an army recruiting document put it, they "identify" with their parents. Pepsi may have caught it best with its recent commercial showing a teenager at a rock concert who turns around and finds his dad nearby in a mosh pit. What we have in America today, in short, is a more socially conservative pre-Boomer cohort and the vast majority of everyone younger leaning the opposite way.

The very fact that Boomers have transformed America should make it a story of great historical significance, but unfortunately it's a story the press has largely missed. Partly it's because news media feast on conflict and therefore highlight all the culture war clamoring from social conservatives, suggesting that there are two Americas in pitched battle with each other. But it's also because the media are like the proverbial generals who fight the last war and miss all the signs of something different and new—in this case they're reporters covering the last culture war.

What the press continues to do is make amends for missing the rise of Greatest Generation anger during the Sixties—the old silent majority, as Nixon called them. Historian Godfrey Hodgson writes how networks and newspapers that covered the police riot at the 1968 Democratic Convention in Chicago were completely blindsided by the thousands of abusive letters from viewers and readers denouncing their coverage and defending the police, some suggesting that the networks must have hired cops to beat up the youthful protesters. Journalists were astonished, Hodgson notes, that polls showed a "large majority in the country were shocked by the demonstrators, and sympathetic to the police." But rather than redouble their efforts "to convince the public that their reporting had been right all along," a contrite media compensated by shifting its coverage away from the emerging values of Baby Boom America and instead began to feature silent majority stories that turned the barbershop and the bar and the American Legion hall into the archetypal America and made the campus and the educated and the prototypical Boomer into elites out of touch with average Americans. What the press did, in effect, was ignore the process of change underway and instead report a snapshot of the silent majority of that time. The problem is the silent majority has changed, but the snapshot hasn't. So while Boomers and their cultural offspring represent today's silent majority of mainstream Americans, and the culture is becoming more in tune with Boomer liberalism, the press continues to feature yesterday's silent majority as if they really represent the current American mainstream.

What we have in America today is a new silent majority—not the socially conservative silent majority of old, but a new silent majority that embraces Baby Boom norms but doesn't shout about it in the press, a silent majority led by Boomers and upheld by Boomer kids that subscribes to the egalitarian and expressive values of Boomer culture. It's a silent majority found in cities and suburbs, in offices and PTAs, on co-ed softball teams and high-school newspapers, in churches and unions, and yes, in coffee shops. It's certainly stronger among the majority of Americans who have attended college, but the values have spread to Americans of all socioeconomic and educational backgrounds. This Boomer majority has become the new mainstream.

Of course, the press reports conflict, and the ones making noise today are those wishing to turn the clock back to Greatest Generation norms. So the obvious question is why this new Boomer majority is so silent when it was so aggressive three and four decades ago. And the main reason is they're largely content with American society and the new norms that guide it. There was a reason why Boomers expressed so much outrage in the Sixties—because there was so much to elicit outrage. To Boomers, the Vietnam War was a symbol of all that had gone wrong in America—the hypocrisy, the conformity, the bigotry. But America today is a far better country, a country that's seen breathtaking changes in race relations, women's rights, and individual freedom. There is no culture of conformity to tell people they can't gain fulfillment by doing their own thing. Americans today are accepted for who they are, not for who they ought to be. To the press, a report that Boomer children trust the military or the government is a nice news hook to show how Boomers' kids are rejecting Boomer values. But a more accurate interpretation is that these institutions are better and more accountable than they were in the Sixties, so there is more of a reason to trust them. The military has in fact become one of our most egalitarian institutions, ironically so, providing advancement opportunities for minorities and training officers to detect unconscious bias against women and blacks. Because Boomers were anti-military in the Sixties does not mean they or their kids should be anti-military today. That's nothing more than another simplistic media caricature. The truth is that most institutions today have been molded by Boomer norms and values, so there's no compelling reason for Boomers or their kids to reject them.

This very contentment may breed the complacency that keeps the Boomer majority silent. It's simply hard for Boomers and their progeny to imagine America regressing to Fifties values and undoing the hard-won gains of the last generation. Writing about Boomers in 1988, the historian Paul Light observed this trend toward Boomer silence. "In the absence of some strong catalyst, like Vietnam or civil rights, they may take their post-material world for granted, settling into a pleasant complacency, even disengagement." But Boomers and their kids will not remain silent if their freedoms and values are truly threatened. At James Madison University, a campus at the edge of the Blue Ridge Mountains in Virginia not known as a hotbed of student activism, the conservative board of trustees voted in 2003 to prohibit the student health center from dispensing an emergency contraceptive known as the morning-after pill, which it had been doing since 1995. The trustees, concerned that the pill was a form of abortion, simply assumed the students would go along with the policy. But they didn't. With only thirty-six hours before the last student senate meeting of the academic year, the students needed to gather 1,500 signatures on a petition to force a vote on the issue. Led by a nineteen-year-old who never saw herself as a feminist, the students not only met their goal but vastly exceeded it, gathering 2,714 signatures. These students rose up because they saw their rights violated and their choices restricted, and they resented the imposition of conservative values on their everyday lives. Very quietly a few months later, the trustees reversed their ban. Even at a supposedly conservative college campus, the Baby Boom culture prevailed, and it's a microcosm of what could happen nationwide if the social conservatives overreach. Threaten Boomer norms and this new silent majority will no longer be so silent.

What the media may have missed has not escaped the notice of those seeking political gain. Perhaps the greatest testament to Baby Boom preeminence is how socially conservative Republicans run campaigns to make Americans think they accept the new norms when in fact their platforms and policies do just the opposite. Indeed this manipulation of voters is a dirty little secret in Republican circles, but occasionally it leaks out, such as the Orwellian "Straight Talk" memo from the Republican strategist Frank Luntz urging the party to use "environmental communications" as a cover for their environmentally unfriendly policies ("the three words" Americans want to hear are "safer," "cleaner," and "healthier," Luntz says), or in other memos telling Republicans to appear more inclusive and adopt the language of empathy and fairness. On women,

Luntz writes, "I do not subscribe to the notion that we must change our substance or create a separate women's agenda. Listening to women and adapting a new language and a more friendly style will itself be rewarded if executed effectively and with discipline."

What the Republicans learned in the Nineties, and what they see in their focus groups today, is that blatant appeals to culture wars and harsh conservative rhetoric turn off mainstream voters, so the only way to promote their agenda is to cloak it in the language and values of Baby Boom culture. A conservative *New York Post* editorial writer, fearful that "the *Boomerization* of America" could portend "the end of the conservative movement," observed that George W. Bush's "compassionate conservative" label was an effective "marketing phrase" because "conservatism as an ideology must be blunted to be presentable to the boomer-heavy electorate at large." So in 2000 and 2004, Bush covered his opposition to affirmative action by calling for "affirmative access," and he diverted attention from his anti-abortion views by saying that he supports a "culture of life." At Republican conventions, religious right leaders are hidden from prime time, moderates are made the face of the party, and women and minorities are given prominent speaking roles, so much so that one conservative columnist called the 2000 convention "a parody of inclusiveness" with black performers on stage and whites in the stands as if "watching a basketball game with the Utah Jazz." Nor was it any different in 2004: Among the six delegate profiles featured on its convention Web site, there were three African-Americans, two Hispanics, one white woman, and not a single white man. And just to make sure the viewing public gets the message, operatives work in network control rooms pointing out black delegates, so during Colin Powell's speech at the 2000 convention, 42 percent of reaction shots featured blacks even though fewer than 4 percent of the delegates were black. Then there are the countless photo opportunities that show Republicans embracing tolerance and diversity, as when conservative legislators somberly linked arms before a memorial to Martin Luther King, Jr.,—even though most have few dealings with blacks and generally oppose policies to promote diversity, integration, and minority political representation. "Histrionic displays of diversity at GOP events" is how one conservative cynic described it.

In nearly four decades, Baby Boom norms have worked their way into every corner of American life—into our language, our homes, our politics, our relationships, our offices, our schools, our choices, our values. But as positive as these changes have been, haven't Boomers misfired at times, haven't Boomers overstepped in their zeal to remake America? And the honest answer is yes, of course they have. Any sweeping transformation of society is bound to include bad judgments and mistakes. Critics pounce on any alleged Boomer misdeed, but they are right to point out that too many Boomers made excuses for criminal behavior, believing society and not the criminal was at fault, or that Boomers in the Sixties and Seventies made all drug proscriptions seem illegitimate just because some were, or that Boomers for too long projected Vietnam onto all foreign policy decisions, reflexively distrusting political authority. But what the critics never mention is that as a generation Boomers err on the side of egalitarianism, that the Boomer impulse is to be fair, that Boomers sometimes bend over backwards to accommodate those who lack power and voice—which is to say that even when Boomers stray their motives have virtue. And the truth is that every generation has its vices and makes its mistakes. The difference with Boomers is that the media glare magnifies every one of its excesses. But strip away the hagiography and imagine how the Revolutionary generation's support for slavery would fare under the media spotlight today.

So yes, it's easy to decry Boomers as a therapeutic generation, a bunch of self-referential gabbers in the Bill Clinton mold. But who would prefer it the old way—the silent dads, obedient wives, and spouses that never talked with one another? We could certainly denounce Boomers for placing rights over responsibilities, for writing laws and filing lawsuits without regard to how much they all cost. But who wants a return to the old days when white men and large corporations had all the rights and everyone else had all the responsibilities? And we could no doubt blame Boomers for subverting authority wherever they see it, for disrespecting the proper order of things. But who would prefer the days of a supine press, a secretive government, a lying White House, unquestioned wars, and a culture that gives complete deference to political, corporate, and religious leaders?

The American idea of a nation was built not on class, ethnicity, race, or the rights of property owners. No, it was built on universal ideals, on self-evident truths, on the pursuit of happiness, freedom, equality, and justice, all for the common good. The true measure of a generation is whether it has advanced these ideals and made them possible and real for the greatest number of people, regardless of who they are and how they were born. And it would be hard not to acknowledge that Boomers have done precisely that. Boomer culture has embraced diversity, liberated women, demolished discriminatory barriers, democratized institutions, freed up individual expression, fought for a healthier environment, and annulled the shame of being different. To accomplish these goals Boomers have fought a silent war not in the trenches but in the office, the neighborhood, the courtroom, the nonprofit, and the home—which is perhaps why so few in the press have noticed. But with each quiet battle, Boomers have changed the social norms of this nation and brought them closer to our founding ideals. Yes, Boomers are a determined generation, and they've made their share of bull-headed mistakes, but it's a determination unremittingly targeted at roadblocks to opportunity and bigotry in any form. Only the most closed-minded ever would want a return to the way things were.

# Chapter Three
# The Revenge of the Luddites

He's as blind as he can be,
Just sees what he wants to see,
Nowhere Man can you see me at all?
   —*The Beatles, "Nowhere Man," 1965*

And don't criticize
What you can't understand.
   —*Bob Dylan, "The Times They Are A-Changin'," 1963*

In 1966 *Time* magazine broke with its usual custom of naming a prominent world or national leader its Man of the Year and instead chose the Baby Boom, what it then called the under-twenty-five generation. Writing before the more turbulent years of the late Sixties, and therefore free to depict Boomer traits without passing them through the prism of culture wars and political passions, *Time* drew an uncannily accurate portrait that in retrospect stands the test of time. It was the dawn of the Baby Boom era, when the Greatest Generation felt secure in its authority, but *Time* understood how Boomers were about to shake up the sediments of American life. *Time* saw how Boomers had little patience for their elders' pretenses and fears—how they repudiated the "dishonesty and double standards" that excused bigotry and inequality, stereotyping and mass conformity. These were young people filled with idealism but focused on change, determined to redeem "social imperfections" and deeply committed to making America "a kindlier, more equitable society." To *Time*, "This was not just a new generation, but a new kind of generation." As *Time* confidently predicted, Boomers would "shape the course and character of nations" and "infuse the future with a new sense of morality, a transcendent and contemporary ethic that could infinitely enrich the 'empty society.'"

What *Time* understood then is what many future historians will conclude about now, that ever since the Sixties Boomers have been quietly but doggedly insisting that American life truly reflect American ideals—that America, as *Time* put it, redeem its social imperfections. In every area of American life—race, gender, work, religion, politics, education, the environment, individual freedom—Boomers are accomplishing what they set out to do when *Time* crystallized their generational worldview nearly four decades ago. It's sometimes halting, by no means perfect, too often messy, sometimes excessive, occasionally mistaken, and certainly not friction free. But in the everyday lives of people—minorities, women, gays, youth, anyone who works in an office, anyone who practices a different religion, anyone who marches to a different drummer, anyone who wants to breathe cleaner air, and anyone who ever faced discrimination or shame or exclusion simply for being different—the impact is palpable and real.

Yet when it comes to discussing Boomers, to assessing their role in American life, to appreciating the breathtaking changes of these last few decades, these social and moral gains seem to matter little. Instead of recognizing the Baby Boom contribution, instead of lauding the idealism, instead of applauding the more inclusive cultural norm, instead of acknowledging how much better our nation has become in the Baby Boom era, the opposite has happened: It's been open season on Baby Boomers, who are regularly derided, condemned, and criticized in the media, and blamed for a litany of execrable culture war crimes, everything from selfishness to permissiveness to children's obesity to moral relativism to political correctness.

## Boomers Under Fire

*Time* predicted that Boomers would enrich the empty society, but it's the Baby Boom generation that is routinely called empty. "Those insufferable baby boomers," one critic wrote. "The nation's noisiest generation," wrote another. "Unbelievably annoying," wrote yet another. "The crummiest generation" and the "most spoiled generation in history." A newspaper database search linking the Baby Boom to the words "spoiled," "selfish," and "self-absorbed" turns up hundreds of hits. Boomers are self-centered, childish, and self-indulgent—or they're elitist, narcissistic, judgmental, self-righteous, and grandiose. "As the world now knows, what's on the Boomers' minds is themselves and their riveting encounters with the routine phases of life." They're hypocrites, never practicing what they preach, and their hip image simply masks their materialism and greed. They're also consumed by an "adolescent" fixation on their youth—"a true Boomer reached his or her emotional peak at fourteen." Throw the slightest hardship their way and they whine endlessly—their "wailing has never stopped." Even worse, they'll continue to remind us how important they are. "Long acknowledged and often reviled as the most self-absorbed generation in memory, the aging cohort of Americans known as baby boomers is greeting the coming twilight with an outpouring of—you guessed it—more navel-gazing." As one critic put it, "Probably no generation has inflated each moment of its social, political, and cultural life to such historic dimensions as the boomers have." Or in the words of conservative writer George Will, no friend of the Boomers, they "believe that their existence, in all its perfection, is the great and final goal toward which the universe has been striving since the Big Bang."

Just look at two unsavory characters that in the last few years have become poster children for Baby Boom excess—John Walker Lindh, the callow American Taliban captured in Afghanistan, and Sarah Jane Olson, the 1970s Symbionese Liberation Army terrorist who avoided arrest for nearly three decades and in the process transformed herself into the proverbial Midwestern soccer mom, complete with minivan and kids. Lindh, the child of Boomer parents, is a veritable feast for Boomer critics intent on showing the reckless self-indulgence of Baby Boom culture. In almost every account of Lindh's life, he's described as the offspring of misguided Sixties liberalism, the evolutionary result of alternative lifestyles and Marin County hot tubs, a granola child whose parents raised him amid such self-absorption and nonconformity that he couldn't tell right from wrong. "His hyper-liberal parents wanted nothing more than that their rebel son should seek his own way, find his own path," sneered conservative columnist Andrew Sullivan. "He grew up in a veritable ideological Disneyland of moral relativism, political correctness, and not-too-subtle anti-American multiculturalism," chafed another conservative pundit, talk show host Sean Hannity. A narrative that held Lindh, and Lindh alone, responsible for his actions wasn't sufficient enough to feed the media beast—the Baby Boom context was just too good a story. And it's been no different with Olson, a fringe character in the early Seventies whose arrest in 1999 and trial in 2001 unleashed a cascade of critical stories that turned her bombing and bank-robbing escapades into a parable about a generation that threw a tantrum in the Sixties and continues to flatter itself that the days of rage really meant something important. These are not serious people, the storyline goes, and by implication this is not a serious generation.

In the span of a few short decades American culture has come full circle: It's Baby Boomers, not their parents, that are now subject to mockery, contempt, and scorn. "That most maligned of demographic groups" is how a *Washington Post* book critic recently described the Baby Boom. How unlike the early 1970s, when millions of Americans bought Charles Reich's book, *The Greening of America,* turning his windy prose into a nationwide bestseller because it somehow articulated how Baby Boomers would triumphantly rescue America from the barren society their parents created. In its 1966 Man of the Year piece, *Time* magazine also lauded a Boomer culture that refused to replicate the "spineless and gray-flannel-souled" Greatest Generation. These were widespread, not isolated, judgments at the time as Boomers wrestled to free America from the Greatest Generation straitjacket of overt racial bigotry, disparaging stereotypes about women, environmental degradation, and a mass conformity that led us to the Vietnam War and demeaned anyone different. It was the Greatest Generation on its heels back then, defending a society that in significant ways was indefensible. And Boomers were heralded as the tribunes of change.

But today, Baby Boom defenders are rare, and those who valiantly argue their cause do so defensively. Resisting Vietnam was no doubt controversial in the Sixties, but there was a principle involved, the notion that it was just to oppose an unjust war, which even some war supporters respected because it spoke to our national ideals. Nowadays, with memory clouded by media narratives of wartime heroism, the principle is forgotten and Boomers who resisted Vietnam are routinely accused of selfishness, of ducking the war, leading many to feel that they need to make excuses for what they did in the Sixties, as if opposing and trying to end a pointless war needs an excuse. In fact our media culture is so driven by caricature that the entire Baby Boom experience has been compressed into a triptych of narcissism, self-indulgence, and excess, and then juxtaposed with a Norman Rockwell image of a lost America with cheerful families, dutiful fathers, and picket-fence neighborhoods, with the expectation that Boomers must repent for challenging the old virtues and unleashing the personal freedoms that wrecked it all. So absurd is this assault on Boomers that they are regularly mocked for drinking a latte or a glass of wine, as if going to a bar and downing a Bud are somehow more authentically American. The best Boomers get is gentle ridicule for selling out their principles, as in the classic Pepsi commercial that spoofs the bad LSD warning made famous at Woodstock, "Stay away from the green pesto sauce. It's a real bummer."

So why are Baby Boomers almost universally disparaged these days? How did the cartoon image of Boomers come to predominate? Why are Baby Boom accomplishments so easily diminished and overlooked? The first and most indirect source comes from Boomers themselves: the need to come to terms with their parents—the Greatest Generation—as they begin to pass on. Boomers may have fought their parents and found their society wanting, but Boomers still love their parents, and as the fever-pitched generation gap from the Sixties fades into memory, Boomers long for their parents more and more.

So in retrospect, Boomers—often at their own expense—glorify the neighborhoods, virtues, and moral clarity of their parents, and overlook all the bigotry and hypocrisy and double standards and blind obedience that came with it. Indeed it's partly because Boomers freed America of most Greatest Generation demons that America can so comfortably celebrate Greatest Generation accomplishments. In the sentimental mist of history and hagiography, the Greatest Generation's flaws are forgotten or brushed aside, buried by universal praise for their sacrifice and suffering, mentioned only as a throwaway line that simply shows how human they were. As a generation they stand above all others in our cultural narrative today. Only the Greatest Generation endured a depression, fought the noble war, and like the Horatio Alger story pulled themselves from hardship to build America. Only the Greatest Generation postponed gratification and lived for duty, honor, faith, and country. Only the Greatest Generation gave selflessly to its kids, its neighborhoods, its democracy—the "long civic generation," as sociologist Robert Putnam put it. When NBC news anchor Tom Brokaw crystallized this sentiment in his 1998 paean to his dad's generation, calling his book *The Greatest Generation,* the label resonated and the book became an immediate bestseller.

This glorification of the Greatest Generation may not have been created to rebuke the Baby Boom, but it effectively serves that purpose. "Put bluntly," one Baby Boom critic wrote, "boomers have never proved their mettle, at least in ways that gained the respect of the 'greatest generation' before them—a generation whose accomplishments can't be replicated." In many ways Baby Boomers are seen as the profligate children of honorable parents. Boomers are portrayed as the anti–Greatest Generation, a generation that takes but doesn't give, a generation that demands but doesn't sacrifice. If the Greatest Generation is admired for its "towering achievement and modest demeanor," to use Tom Brokaw's words, the Baby Boom is disparaged for its frivolous achievement and arrogant demeanor. "In the World War II generation, ordinary people found common cause, made extraordinary sacrifices and never whined or whimpered," Brokaw wrote. "Their offspring, the baby boomers, seem to have forgotten the example of their parents." Senator and presidential candidate Bob Dole, now lionized as a World War II icon, compared the virtue and heroism of his generation to Baby Boomers who "never grew up, never did anything real, never sacrificed, never suffered, and never learned." Listen to some critics and all Boomers have to show for themselves is Bill Clinton, or at least a caricature of Bill Clinton, the embodiment of what one Baby Boom writer called "his generation's alleged sins: the moral relativism, the tendency to pay more attention to marketing than to substance, the solipsistic callowness," all wrapped in "almost hilarious self-involvement" and "childishness." America has become one terrible country in the Baby Boom era, hasn't it?

Deifying the Greatest Generation is not the only way Boomers have inflicted such bad press on themselves. It was only a matter of time before the irreverent, anti-authority impulse so central to Boomer culture would be turned against Boomers themselves. A generation so attuned to hypocrisy in others has found its own glass house scoured for imperfections. Indeed it was Boomers in the 1970s who first coined the phrase "politically correct" as a way to needle peers who seemed a bit too sanctimonious for their liking. Contrarian Boomers have always been among their generation's fiercest critics, particularly snarky Boomer journalists who relish the opportunity to flay Boomers for their failings and unmask any Boomer pretense of moral superiority—and in the process prove their own moral superiority over all other Boomers.

This type of criticism first crystallized when the author Tom Wolfe chronicled the Boomer Seventies as the Me Decade, and then gathered momentum in the Eighties with the media's discovery of yuppies, a phenomenon blown all out of proportion to their actual numbers but which satisfied the media's need to revel in Baby Boom hypocrisy. The new media storyline indicted Boomers for egotism, self-importance, arrogance, and elitism, for accusing others of selling out but doing precisely that themselves, for boasting about their social concerns but pursuing careers on Wall Street, for caring little about civic life and only about themselves. As *Newsweek* wrote in its famous 1984 yuppie cover story, this was a generation that moved from hippie social consciousness to a "state of Transcendental Acquisition," a generation consumed by its "self-absorbed journey." Never mind that a number of these yuppies were women, who were trying to elbow their way into Greatest Generation male power structures but who were pilloried for wanting to "have it all," which to some women sounded like a veiled and underhanded criticism of their aspirations that was never applied to men. The bottom line is the yuppie label stuck. And then the media pile-on began, as if there wasn't a single Boomer not enamored with Brie cheese, Volvos, and balsamic vinegar.

Typical is the well-known journalist Christopher Hitchens, renowned for his mordant pen, who pounced on the alleged Boomer sins of hypocrisy and vanity in a 1996 *Vanity Fair* article, "The Baby Boomer Wasteland"—citing Boomers for deploring "waste and ostentation while getting a new model of car every three or four years," for preening their social consciousness yet "stepping around panhandlers," for resenting their parents for spending the inheritance, for bragging about the Sixties even if they had nothing to do with it, for feeling guilty but not responsible. Or there's the cultural critic Daniel Okrent, who similarly seized on

Boomer selfishness and selling-out in an essay for *Time* magazine. "Where once my generation was celebrated for its commitment to peace and justice, what we've grown to be—what we always were, probably—is a generation committed to nothing more (or less) substantial than what we appear to be leaving as our signal legacy to American culture: casual Fridays." To be sure, criticism like this can be healthy, a necessary check on the rationalizations every generation uses to justify its double standards and shortcomings. But it also must be taken for what it is, a media caricature, quite often puerile, and like much in the media, it ignores depth and perspective in favor of a clever phrase and good storyline, and in the process misses the real and abiding legacy of the Baby Boom generation. At least Boomers are taking it in stride and laughing at themselves, which wasn't the case when Boomers criticized the Greatest Generation, who dug in, grew resentful, and remained stubbornly resistant to change, to the point that well into the Nineties they were the only age cohort questioned in polls unwilling even to acknowledge the Baby Boom's "special contribution to society."

Further fueling the criticism of Baby Boom culture, unwittingly so, are Boomers most closely associated with their roots in the Sixties, those who work in the trenches of nonprofit advocacy. As it was in the Sixties, the Boomer impulse is to point out problems, to target hypocrisy and shortcomings, to demand change immediately. Seeing the glass half empty is a generational trait, and as the authors J. Walker Smith and Ann Clurman write in their book *Rocking the Ages,* flaws stick out to Boomers and every fight is "a clash of moral principles." So when liberal activists condemn the continuing blight of racism, or the discrimination that has yet to be flushed from society, or the ongoing difficulty many women face in balancing family and work, or global warming and toxic waste, it leaves the impression that we've accomplished little of worth over the past few decades, which then leads an otherwise thoughtful writer like Daniel Okrent to conclude that Boomers have contributed nothing more to America than causal Fridays. Boomers aren't the only generation in history to communicate a "woe is me" message—it can be traced back to our Puritan ancestors with their austere jeremiads warning that we're a nation of miserable sinners, that even good things are bad. But to indict

America for keeping blacks or women or gays as "second-class citizens" is to suggest that we've barely made any progress, when in fact the opposite is true. Boomers should take a page from Franklin Roosevelt during the Depression, who kept the focus on progress made rather than obstacles to overcome. To say that things are really bad, that not much has changed, that we have a lot of work to do is to send a message of pessimism and failure; to say that we've transformed America, that things have gotten better, that we're a more equal society but still have further to go sends a message of optimism, resolve, and accomplishment. Boomers too often dwell on the former, to their great disadvantage, when in fact the latter is much closer to the truth.

One might think that Boomer ubiquity in the media would enhance the Boomer image, but instead it has stirred even more resentment against Boomers, especially among younger generations. Largely because the rise of Boomers coincided with the rise of mass media in America, Boomer lives, events, issues, images, and interests have overwhelmed the media in the last few decades, the more so because the nostalgia industry and our fascination with early television have led to an endless loop of Boomer shows, music, and memories, particularly on cable TV. The problem is that those born after the Baby Boom feel smothered by Boomer culture, so smothered that they feel a need to distinguish themselves from Boomers, and since they share similar attitudes with Boomers and have no historical watershed to mark themselves as a separate generation, the only way to do it is to define themselves in opposition to Boomers, as better than Boomers, even though there aren't many real or substantial differences between them. So another source of anger at Boomers comes from the age cohort behind them, popularly known as Generation X, the perfect name for a group of Americans who feel the media pressure to proclaim a generational identity but don't know what it is. They look at TV "and they don't see themselves," *Age Wave* author Ken Dychtwald wrote. "They see the generation older than them."

The result is a generational Bronx cheer constantly directed at Boomers. To Generation X, the Baby Boom is a self-absorbed generation that still won't hand the youth mantle to anyone else and continues to choke all other generations with glorified images of its own. "They're so big and self-centered that every social and political issue orbits around their needs," wrote one Generation X author, adding that to Boomers, "no other generation matters." In his 1991 novel *Generation X,* which gave this age cohort its name, Douglas Coupland rarely mentioned Boomers as anything but sell-outs, as in "this horrible know-everything yuppie lawyer," or "Martin, like most embittered ex-hippies, is a yuppie." Others are less diplomatic. "Boomers are one of the most greedy, materialistic, and self-ish groups of people this country has ever seen," goes a typical comment, "and my generation has to cope with their irresponsibility." There's even a Generation X Web site called "Kill All Baby-Boomers." To be sure, Boomers aren't innocent victims here, having stoked this generational fire for years by constantly lording the Sixties over Xers, telling Xers that their defining moments and cultural touchstones just don't measure up. But strip away this generational chauvinism and the truth is that the Sixties did indeed contain more public drama than any decade since, and Boomers can't help it if theirs was the first generation ever captured so completely on television, with their youthful images and rhythms setting the standard for every successive generation. So the facts fuel the resentment, and no matter how similar Xers are to Boomers, they will always project selfishness onto all that Boomers do and cherish every opportunity to deride Boomers as sell-outs.

## Conservative Luddites

All of this generational jousting would probably amount to little more than harmless media entertainment were it not for one thing: It's been hijacked by conservative ideologues as a tactical weapon in their culture war against Baby Boom America. What angers these conservatives most is that their political victories of late have done little to reverse the triumph of Baby Boom values and norms, and their sense of grievance escalates the more they realize that politics, as fellow conservative George Will observed, "seems peripheral to, and largely impotent against, cultural forces and institutions permeated with what conservatives consider the sixties sensibility."

To social conservatives, almost everything about the Baby Boom era is anathema—the egalitarianism, the cultural diversity, the individuality, the insistence on rights over order, the willingness to question rather than obey received authority. They see the worm of the Sixties eating into an Edenic America, an America where people knew their place, an America where women, minorities, and anyone outside Norman Rockwell's white picket fence stayed docile and quiet, satisfied with the status quo, unwilling to question gradual gains, and deeply grateful for any gifts of equality and freedom thrown their way in the spirit of noblesse oblige. "Many conservatives regard the 1950s as a near-perfect past," writes Dinesh D'Souza, a prominent conservative author. Theirs is a patriotism frozen in time, a patriotism of Main Street parades and sturdy white men saluting the flag, a patriotism of dutiful women and thankful if not invisible minorities, a patriotism built almost exclusively on a defense of their "golden age," a world they fear has been lost. It's also a patriotism that ascribes unpatriotic motives to those who dissent from this view. Only grudgingly and after years of resistance did they even come to respect the memory of Martin Luther King, Jr., but only as a dreamer, not an activist. "Ordinarily this Kumbayah mentality amuses me for its naive idiocy," D'Souza writes. "But behind it there is an anti-American prejudice that I find less risible."

So the conservative culture warriors have found a backdoor way to undermine what they can't forthrightly change: They've taken the popular caricature of Boomers and turned it to political advantage, arguing that we can't take Boomers seriously so we shouldn't take their ideas seriously. As the conservatives lay out their case, the Sixties was just a frivolous tantrum by spoiled elites, so there really wasn't a problem with the way things were before, which means we should roll back all the recklessly adolescent ideas of the last forty years and return to the mythic golden age epitomized by the dutiful World War II generation. It's quite a clever approach, for as we've seen in politics, personal attacks quite effectively discredit political ideas, and that's precisely what conservatives have set out to do, launching the functional equivalent of a negative political campaign against Baby Boomers, pounding them day after day, week after week on talk radio, cable TV, and in newspaper columns, books, and speeches, all without rebuttal or reply. The goal, as D'Souza wrote, is to take "liberal culture" and "to undermine it, to thwart it, to destroy it at the root level." Or as conservative talk show host Sean Hannity declared, "It is therefore our job to stop them. Not just debate them, but defeat them."

This conservative strategy of trivializing Boomers in order to undermine Boomer ideas dates back to the Sixties, when conservative intellectuals, fighting to maintain their cultural authority, tried to discredit the challenge young people posed to Greatest Generation society by portraying it not for what it was, an assault on hypocrisy and injustice, but rather as a temper tantrum, an adolescent rebellion of Boomer youth against their fathers. Convinced of their own virtue, suspicious of dissent, fearful of passion, and defensive about the rigid Cold War culture they had helped to create, these conservative intellectuals discerned few serious flaws in American life and instead saw only betrayal by the young. Racial problems, the Vietnam War, cultural conformity—to conservative intellectuals, these had little to do with the emerging Boomer worldview. Rather, the Sixties arose from a generational Oedipal complex, a fit of impudence by spoiled, pampered, privileged youth. And that exasperated these conservatives even more, because they despaired over all the cultural damage this unserious generation would wreak.

Foremost in articulating this critique was the sociologist Lewis Feuer, whose widely read 1969 book, *The Conflict of Generations,* painted the Sixties as an outburst of elite, educated youth acting out a "rebellion against the father" and the father figures who ran our political, educational, military, and business institutions. Boomer social concerns had little to do with injustices in America but derived instead from a need to resolve their feelings toward dad—the need to "reject all that the fathers stood for," to sever "the psychological umbilical cord itself that united one to one's father, the elder generation." Thus it wasn't racial inequality Boomers were fighting but rather feelings of atonement and guilt. Or it wasn't an unjust war Boomers were protesting but rather their anger toward fathers who could no longer provide for them. Or it wasn't individual freedom Boomers sought but rather rejection of "the sexuality of the fathers." Boomer activism in the Sixties wasn't about issues but was really "a channel for aggression" and "a substitute for psychotherapy."

This analysis would become an article of faith among conservative intellectuals, who immediately understood its potential to discredit Boomer liberalism and over the next two decades began churning out scholarship to support it, all with variations on the theme. Boomers became activists because they viewed "their parents as cold and punitive and as weak or ineffectual." Behind the Sixties was "freedom from guilt over one's privilege." Rather than citizens protesting against injustice, "The sixties' revolution was more a rebellion of children against parents. . . . Its assertiveness was more in style than in substance." The Sixties "were above all a revolt of the privileged and overprivileged," or "the rhetoric of women's liberation was akin to a rhetorical tantrum by its privileged practitioners." In other words, society wasn't the problem—Boomers were the problem.

Status quo defenders reeling from the Boomer challenge in the Sixties and Seventies found this approach empowering, and it wasn't long before conservative pundits and politicians—desperate to reverse the tide of Boomer liberalism—began attacking Boomers as a "pampered generation" reared by the permissive Dr. Spock and spoiled by the immediate gratification of a television culture symbolized by the young child wailing in the classic Fifties cereal ad, "I want my Maypo, and I want it now." President Nixon and his vice president, Spiro Agnew, used this strategy to great political effect, finding that their support grew among an increasingly resentful Greatest Generation whenever they attacked youthful protesters as spoiled and ungrateful kids, "an effete corps of impudent snobs," in Agnew's words. The Me Decade caricature of the Seventies and the Yuppie stereotype of the Eighties fit perfectly into this storyline, as conservatives could claim they were right after all, that Boomers were in it only for their own gratification, that Sixties liberalism and its egalitarian spirit were thoroughly illegitimate because they sprang from the same privileged, selfish motives involved in ordering a "tall skim double-mocha latte, please."

Today's conservative assault on Boomers is built on the brilliant rhetorical foundation Feuer and his cohorts laid nearly four decades ago. Among the more relentless critics is the columnist George Will, a child of the Fifties who sees that era through "a roseate glow in my memory." To Will, the good and virtuous America of old has been upended and undermined by "the infantilism—impatience, hedonism, inability to defer gratification—that produced the cultural dissolution of the '60s." The only thing serious about Boomers from the Sixties is their "own self-flattering estimate of their seriousness," according to Will. This is a generation of spoiled, over-grown adolescents whose political attitudes stem not from social concerns but from the "moral vanity" and "narcissism" characteristic of teenagers, and as a result, Will writes, "their cause was always a style—an alternative consumption pattern—tarted up as politics."

Will has been touting this Boomer-as-adolescent line for years, but he's only the most prominent conservative spokesman for it. Author Ann Coulter calls Boomers "the Worst Generation" and sees them as egotists whose culture consists of little more than "hagiographic descriptions of youthful onanists smoking pot and listening to *The White Album* in their Berkeley dorm rooms." Dinesh D'Souza sees an ungrateful generation that's fed off the "frugal, self-disciplined, sacrificial generation of World War II," faulting the Greatest Generation only because it "produced the spoiled children of the 1960s." To talk show host Bill O'Reilly, the diversity impulse so central to Boomer culture derives not from conviction but from vanity. He writes, "This was the height of the 1960s: Many whites wanted to have black friends, just because that was considered cool at the time." In a book of essays by conservative authors, Boomers come off as "self-centered jerks," "endlessly pampered," "appallingly attached to material goods," "shallow about important things and deadly serious about frivolous things," and "an entire generation of spoiled middle-class brats" steered by "jejune and narcissistic" attitudes—all of which led one of the essayists to conclude that conservatives view Boomers as "the most depraved generation in memory, if not in history." Conservative politicians likewise see the value in this portrait of Boomers. Newt Gingrich flayed the Clintons as Boomer "elitists" and "counterculture McGovernicks," accusing Boomers of undermining the work ethic and values of the Fifties. *The Economist* called George W. Bush the "anti-1960s candidate" for the way he repeatedly chastised Boomers for their "childish behavior" and "if it feels good, do it" mentality.

These conservatives fervently hope that by undercutting Boomer seriousness they can undercut the seriousness of Boomer culture and ideas.

George Will therefore calls multiculturalism a "fetish," equating the effort to incorporate pluralism with an erotic fixation. Working mothers are self-indulgent, diversity is imposed by privileged elites, civil rights and gay rights are politically correct, environmentalism is fashionable, black and women's history are angry rants, self-expression is infantilism writ large, and liberalism is outside the mainstream. In one breath conservatives denounce Boomers for being "insufferable moralizers," presumably because Boomers don't tolerate prejudice and bigotry, and in another conservatives decry Boomer "moral laxity," for tolerating all sorts of private individual behavior—and conservatives don't see a contradiction here, only a reflection of Boomer adolescent behavior. If Boomers ever get praise from conservatives, it's of the backhanded sort—for becoming more materialistic and by implication more conservative. "They got wise to the ways of the world," said conservative writer David Brooks, author of *Bobos in Paradise,* a wry and savagely sarcastic critique of Boomer culture.

*Bobos in Paradise* may be the most clever and politically sophisticated of all the conservative tracts mocking the Baby Boom's alleged frivolity—so much so that Brooks parlayed it into a foxhole right in the heart of liberal America, a regular op-ed column in *The New York Times,* where he's become an influential pamphleteer for Republican conservatism. According to Brooks, "Bobo" is shorthand for "bourgeois bohemian," a deeply superficial and image-conscious Boomer who combines Sixties egalitarianism with Eighties materialism. Brooks will insist that he's talking only about the most privileged Boomers, but he does so with a wink because at other times he uses Bobo and Baby Boomer interchangeably (the alliteration is quite cunning), and it's not hard to see how his Bobo is really a pretext to stir up resentment against a Boomer culture and society that Brooks and his conservative confederates are determined to overturn.

As with other conservative critics, Brooks ridicules the usual Boomer suspects ad nauseam: the tall skim lattes, "gelato in such flavors as Zuppa Inglese," "Savannah dill" bread, "feminist lingerie," "all-terrain baby carriages," and every other ludicrous-sounding product or service available today—all to show that Boomer culture is at heart frivolous, elitist, and out of touch with real Americans. Brooks also flails at all signs of Boomer hypocrisy—the Boomers who had QUESTION AUTHORITY bumper stickers on their vans but now lead management seminars, or Boomers who denounced consumerism in college but now shop for $3,000 refrigerators. It's all fairly typical anti-Boomer boilerplate, but where Brooks takes it a step further, artfully so, is in tarring all Boomer interests, issues, and concerns as a pose, an air, an affectation—as a statement of image rather than a statement of values—and the result is a portrait not of a lapsed idealistic generation, which is how most critics describe Boomers, but of an artificial generation that has never been motivated by anything but vanity, a generation no one should take very seriously.

To Brooks, Boomers are all about status, about appearing hip, about buying organic because it looks good, about putting on "countercultural poses" that cover up their self-indulgence. "They have created an ethos of environmentalism, healthism, and egalitarianism that makes it bad form to live in the ostentatious style that characterized the old moneyed elite"—meaning that environmentalism and egalitarianism are self-conscious styles rather than real social concerns. They go to Fresh Fields supermarkets not to get healthier foods or support organic farmers, but to bask "in their reflected wholesomeness." Boomer intellectuals watch PBS and hike the rain forests on vacation not because these activities have any intrinsic value but because these intellectuals have "spent their lives building a reputation" and need to maintain it. In conversations Boomer women drop how they were "giving up Merlot during pregnancy," not because it was the right thing to do but because these women want to flaunt how sophisticated they are with wine and how righteous they'll be as parents. And just to show they haven't lost their roots in the Sixties, "health-conscious aerobicizers" work out in "Days of Rage" T-shirts. Everything's a pretense, it's all about image, these people never were serious and they aren't today.

Now in the long run of history, it matters not what type of bread someone buys or which type of coffee they drink or whether they buy a jogging stroller so they can run with their newborn. But that's the genius of Brooks and the conservative critics: They make it seem like it should matter, because in doing so they trivialize Baby Boomers and by implication, they hope, all that Boomers have accomplished. If a Boomer prefers French cheese to chicken-fried steak, then perhaps there's something un-American about all of these Boomer values and ideas. If a Boomer prefers traveling abroad rather than to Branson, Missouri, then perhaps there's something elitist about all of these Boomer values and ideas. Conservatives would never acknowledge that some of the organic foods they ridicule actually might taste good or help the planet, or that traveling and appreciating art from around the globe may reflect openness to other cultures and experiences, a value we supposedly cherish. Nor will they acknowledge that these Boomer tastes are spreading throughout middle America, with Starbucks in strip malls and Beef Merlot replacing Salisbury Steak in the frozen food bin—because to acknowledge that would deprive them of the Boomer-as-elitist stereotype they so desperately need to undercut Boomer culture. And they'll never disclose that other generations have also been indicted for materialism—it was conspicuous consumption in the Twenties and keeping up with the Joneses in the Fifties—because to do that would diminish their critique of Boomers as a singularly selfish generation. No, to conservative critics today their caricature of Boomers is the perfect propaganda tool in their effort to turn back the clock to the Greatest Generation days. What better way to make their case than to portray Boomers as elitist, hypocritical, vaguely anti-American, defined not by principle or ideal but by vanity and self-image? What better way to prove that the Sixties was an adolescent rebellion after all?

This Boomer bashing is serious business for conservatives because they see themselves in a prolonged culture war against Boomer liberalism and society. Some conservatives even see it as more vital than the old Cold War against the Soviet Union, which says a lot given how much they detested communism. "Now that the other 'Cold War' is over, the real cold war has begun," wrote Irving Kristol in 1993, one of the most influential conservatives over the last half century, commonly called the godfather of the neoconservative movement and a virulent critic of the Baby Boom throughout the Sixties and Seventies. "Sector after sector of American life has been ruthlessly corrupted by the liberal ethos," Kristol complained. "We are far less prepared for this cold war, far more vulnerable to our enemy, than was the case with our victorious war against a global communist threat." Kristol's battle cry is echoed throughout the conservative movement. Robert Bork, the Reagan Supreme Court nominee rejected by the Senate in 1987 because of his extreme conservatism, wrote that conservatives must unmask the Sixties because "the youth culture that became manifest then is the modern liberal culture of today." Said Bork, "Opposition to the counterculture, the culture that became today's liberalism, is precisely what our culture war is about."

To conservatives it's a desperate war, with fronts everywhere in our culture, from public schools, Hollywood, and higher education, to reproductive health, religion, privacy, and individual rights. When the Supreme Court in June 2003 ruled that gay Americans are "entitled to respect for their private lives," therefore tossing out laws that criminalized homosexual sex, the conservative justice Antonin Scalia eschewed any pretext of judicial impartiality and thundered in his dissent that "the Court has taken sides in the culture war," which revealed more about his perspective than the Court's, and he then justified it with a statement that parallels the Greatest Generation norm about Jews and blacks, "Many Americans do not want persons who openly engage in homosexual conduct as partners in their business, as scoutmasters for their children, as teachers in their children's schools, or as boarders in their homes." It's really the conservative agenda laid bare, a return to the norms of the Fifties.

Perhaps most revealing about Scalia's angry dissent was his dire warning that the ruling represented "a massive disruption of the current social order." For what Scalia and his socially conservative comrades refuse to accept is that "the current social order" no longer resembles the social order of the Fifties, that even the Supreme Court—an extremely traditional institution dominated by Republican appointees—has finally recognized in law the cultural norms and realities of the Baby Boom era, that it has in fact confirmed rather than disrupted the current social order. "Real change, when it comes, stems principally from attitudinal shifts in the population at large," wrote Justice Sandra Day O'Connor, a Ronald Reagan appointee. "Rare indeed is the legal victory—in court or legislature—that is not a careful by-product of an emerging social consensus." So what the Court majority recognized in this case is the very principle of Baby Boom egalitarianism, that the old norm "demeans the lives of homosexual persons," who deserve "dignity" and "respect for their privacy."

Nor was that the only pillar of Baby Boom culture the Court confirmed. In another high-profile case decided in 2003, one involving affirmative action in higher education, the Court majority called diversity "essential to the dream of one nation," not merely allowable under the law but good for the nation. And in yet another case, Chief Justice William Rehnquist, one of the most conservative members of the Court, stunned observers when he endorsed federal family leave laws and praised them for countering the "pervasive sex-role stereotype that caring for family members is women's work"—effectively acknowledging another Baby Boom norm, full and functional equality between men and women. Far from taking sides in the culture war, the Supreme Court has essentially conceded the opposite: that the culture war is over, and the Baby Boom has prevailed.

So why doesn't it seem that way? Why do social conservatives loom so large in our politics today? Why are they so dominant on cable news and talk radio? Why are publishers creating new imprints for conservative authors? How have Rush Limbaugh, William Bennett, and Bill O'Reilly become such loud and prominent voices in our public culture? Why are Boomers seemingly on the defensive?

To answer, let us draw on a parallel from history, the Luddites who terrorized Britain nearly two centuries ago. These were workers who traveled throughout the country smashing machines for fear that the Industrial Revolution would destroy their jobs and way of life. They were loud, and their tenacity gave the impression that they represented more Britons than they actually did, when in fact they were merely acting out their despair and outrage at a world that was passing them by.

Today's social conservatives are modern-day Luddites—cultural Luddites. They're certainly making plenty of noise, but what we hear is not a realistic alternative to modern life but the fury and rage over being left behind. Media personalities like Rush Limbaugh may think they're leading a movement, but all they're doing is banging loudly against the machines of Baby Boom America. And the reason we hear them so much today is because the media reward outrage—indeed as any news executive can document, television and radio generate high ratings not from rational discourse but from anger, controversy, and indignation. So the louder they bang, the bigger their platform, and the bigger their platform, the louder they bang, and as with the original Luddites, all the noise creates the illusion that they have more of a following than they actually do.

In the Sixties, Boomer voices predominated in the media because they were the ones outraged—against the intolerant and conformist norms of Greatest Generation America, against demeaning stereotypes and a war that lacked purpose and meaning. That led to the perception of liberal bias in the media, when in fact the media are biased not toward any ideology but toward the outrage and anger that brings in an audience. Boomer liberals today lack a loud media megaphone because they are much more restrained and quiescent than in the Sixties, and thus less appealing to the media, which makes perfect sense because there's less to incite Boomer outrage as the country marches haltingly and imperfectly but relentlessly toward Baby Boom norms. It's the angry cultural Luddites who command the media platform today.

In her influential 1970 book, *Culture and Commitment,* the anthropologist Margaret Mead anticipated the rise of conservative outrage, suggesting that "in most discussions of the generation gap, the alienation of the young is emphasized, while the alienation of their elders may be wholly overlooked." Her point was that the issue dividing America in the Sixties wasn't the Baby Boom's rejection of Greatest Generation social norms, but rather the Greatest Generation's resistance to the Baby Boom's new social norms. Defenders of the old orthodoxy, she wrote, would become increasingly "rigid and intractable" and "react with the greatest anger and bitterness," the more so as their hold on power began to slip and their belief in unquestioned authority began to clash with "a world in which conflicting points of view, rather than orthodoxies, are prevalent and accessible."

Social conservatives desperately want to believe that the majority of Americans support their moral vision, that Americans in their heart of hearts yearn to shed the skin of Boomer norms and return to a neo-Fifties golden era. To them, liberal Boomers have conspired to impose their norms on the rest of America. "Elitist liberals against ordinary Americans" is how Ann Coulter describes it. "It's the majority versus the elites in journalism and academia," explains former Reagan speechwriter and conservative author Peggy Noonan. As Mead anticipated more than three decades ago, these social conservatives simply live in fear that Boomer values have eclipsed their own. So they write, despite all evidence to the contrary, that working mothers "are a historical aberration; they represent a minority preference among women." Or they argue, again with no evidence, that most Americans reject Boomer individualism and egalitarianism—"the boomers did not expand the horizon of human experience but perverted it." Or they claim that middle America rejects diversity and multicultural-ism, ignoring that Americans increasingly embrace these values, that most people accept and appreciate diversity in culture, the workplace, and everyday life, and that most mainstream institutions—the military, busi-ness, and higher education—proudly promote diversity and support affir-mative action.

The strategy of these social conservatives is to feint moderation by using the Boomer rhetoric of tolerance and inclusion but to work stealthily behind the scenes rousing religious conservatives at the grass-roots level and filling the courts with ideologically conservative judges—all with the goal of restricting reproductive choices for women, eliminating evolution from public schools, limiting legal rights for gay couples, imposing their religious morality, and reducing government's role in the fight against race or sex discrimination. Conservatives have convinced themselves that Americans ultimately would wake up after these laws were enacted and say yes, this is the America we wanted after all, thank heaven the Sixties have been defeated, how nice that we've returned to Fifties morality, and how pleasing that all these noisy people, pushy minorities, and elitist women have been put in their place.

But even if they succeeded legislatively, over time it would prove to be an illusory victory, little different from the Prohibitionists who almost a century ago dreamed that by amending the Constitution to outlaw "de-mon alcohol," they could return to a golden age, to a time before loud and unruly immigrants invaded America. Society simply bypassed their constitutional amendment then, just as it would now, because the reality is that there's no turning back from progress, that America has been remade by the Baby Boom, and that most Americans now subscribe to the norms and values of Baby Boom culture. So however much political power these social conservatives may accumulate, theirs is a worldview that is becoming increasingly obsolete. As a leading conservative activist, Paul Weyrich, candidly acknowledged in a 1999 letter to his supporters, "I no longer believe that there is a moral majority. I do not believe that a majority of Americans actually share our values."

So what has all this sound and fury brought conservatives? Well, they've certainly succeeded in discrediting Boomers personally—surveys show majorities of Americans view Boomers as arrogant, ambitious, self-centered, selfish, materialistic, and less patriotic than others, and a respected newspaper like *The Washington Post* doesn't think twice about running a headline such as "A Generation Learns That the World Doesn't Revolve Around It After All." But that's a Pyrrhic victory at best because conservatives haven't succeeded in their larger goal of discrediting Boomer norms and values. Perhaps these conservatives target the Baby Boom so vociferously because they know deep down that most Americans—if they ever spent the time to think about it—might actually celebrate the fact that Baby Boom values have overturned Greatest Generation values. Notwithstanding all the critics, *Time* magazine got it right back in the Sixties: Boomers were on the leading edge of a new America. And the real Luddites, whatever happened to them? They eventually faded away, a footnote to history except as a symbol of angry, reactionary atavists unwilling to accept that the world had passed them by.

# Chapter Four
# The Baby Boom DNA

There's something happening here
What it is ain't exactly clear.
—*Buffalo Springfield, "For What It's Worth," 1966*

**T**his is a generation raised on Eddie Haskell, Bugs Bunny, and *Mad* magazine. It also was raised on World War II epics, stories of freedom against tyranny, civil rights stirrings, and comic book heroes defending "truth, justice, and the American way." One side is irreverent, one side liberal, and when blended together they make up a worldview Baby Boomers have assumed ever since the Sixties: liberally irreverent and irreverently liberal. Perhaps no two phrases better sum up the Baby Boom sensibility that originated in the Sixties and in the decades since has remade America.

Irreverence is central to Boomer culture. It's in their humor, their approach to authority, their take on tradition, their view of the status quo. No custom or institution remains inviolate in Boomer hands—not religion or the president or big business or the family. Boomers are equal opportunity critics, preferring to question rather than follow, never unwilling to confront sacred cows and pull the powerful down a notch if they betray the public trust. This is not a predictable or compliant generation. In a counterculture publication from the Sixties, the *Whole Earth Catalog,* a writer heaped praise on the magazine *Consumer Reports* for taking various corporations to task, no surprise there, but he then challenged the magazine's editors to print ads from the criticized companies, to "give the manufacturers a place to beef back, liven up the Liberal Hour." It's not that they didn't support the liberal side—they just didn't want it to get too smug and comfortable. And so it is in the Baby Boom culture today. This is a generation that accepts nothing at face value—it has no problem pulling the curtain away from the Wizard of Oz. Critics often accuse Boomers of having no sense of duty, but Boomers are actually quite dutiful as long as they get straight answers to justify it, and when they don't, Boomers never shy from speaking truth to power. They just don't suffer pretense or hypocrisy gladly. Boomers also insist that respect be earned, not given. The intense brand and political loyalty of old has given way to intense Boomer scrutiny of brand and political values. No one gets a free pass anymore. Knowing that the only constant in modern life is change, Boomers have little patience or sentimentality for old loyalties and out-moded ways. If it works, good; if it's beneficial, great; if not, either change it or move on to something better.

But as much as Boomers question authority and blind allegiance, they also have a very strong generational compass whose true north points to a set of liberal instincts and ideals—individual freedom, equal worth, respect for diversity, social responsibility, and the urge to include. Boomers are not afraid to shake up loyalties and institutions, but they do it with purpose, and what usually emerges is a more free-wheeling, inclusive, indepen-dent-minded, and egalitarian organization that rejects the formalities and hierarchies of old and affirms a commitment to Boomer ideals. But if Boomers are liberal-minded, they're also liberal with an irreverent twist, for while they generally adhere to socially liberal values, they spurn the old liberal reliance on big institutions and government programs to implement their values. It's more a personal than a programmatic liberalism. Govern-ment bureaucracies or labor unions, no matter how well intended, seem too impersonal, entrenched, and burdensome to Boomers, more likely to protect the old ways than embrace the new. Rather than set up a new agency, it's better to make change from within, through education or dia-logue or consensus-builiding at the grass roots, and if all else fails there are always the courts, which Boomers trust to impel us toward equality and justice. "The place to improve the world is first in one's own heart and head and hands, and then work outward from there," wrote Robert Pirsig in his 1974 bestseller, *Zen and the Art of Motorcycle Maintenance,* and that is precisely how Boomers have gone about changing their world.

So what are the roots of this Baby Boom worldview? Why are Boomers so different from their elders? How did irreverence and social liberalism—characteristics so contrary to the Greatest Generation—come to predom-inate? To understand how Boomers have shaped America requires an examination of how America shaped the Baby Boom. And that means we must detour into the Baby Boom's formative years to explore the four strands of cultural DNA that originated in the Sixties and remain the basic code for understanding Baby Boom culture today.

## Boomer Attitude 1: Questioning Authority

It's one of those gnawing little regrets common to so many Boomers today: how their parents cleared out the closet and threw away their old *Mad* magazines. To the many Boomers who sensed that something had gone awry in Greatest Generation America, *Mad* was a glimmer of truth, a benign but trenchant voice against hypocrisy and pretense, a way to laugh at parents who fretted over status symbols and authorities who talked one way but acted another. *Mad* was a symbol to Boomers that they weren't alone, that something really was amiss in society. "If you were growing up lonely and isolated in a small town, *Mad* was a revelation," recalled the comic artist R. Crumb. "Nothing I read anywhere else suggested there was any absurdity in the culture." According to some estimates, about half of all Boomers read *Mad* regularly as kids, and one survey in the early 1960s found *Mad* second only to *Life* as the most well-read magazine among high-school students.

Flip through old issues of *Mad* and you'll see why. In a playground that prepares kids for adulthood, there's a Showy Pyramid that teaches "the art of social climbing" and a Social Treadmill that "gets kids into condition for 'keeping up with the Joneses.'" A family swelters at home with all the windows shut "so our neighbors will think we've got central air conditioning." A *Mad* primer tells suburban parents what to teach their kids. "They must not lie. They must not cheat. They must not steal. Poor suburban children. They are so unprepared for the adult world!" Or there's the Super Patriot who hates liberals, intellectuals, moderates, pacifists, unions, minorities, teens, and people with foreign-sounding names. "Now you know what a Super Patriot is. He's someone who loves his country while hating 93 percent of the people who live in it." Or there's a Phony Liberal who hires blacks but never promotes them—an "Equal Opportunity Employer" who gives "Racial Minorities a chance to start at the bottom and stay there." And it mattered not which side of the cultural divide you were on—if you embodied authority, conformity, hypocrisy, or sanctimony, you were fair game for *Mad*. So *Mad* shows a self-righteous college student proclaiming his radicalism—until he has to graduate the next year. Or it shows hippies shutting down a hospital construction site so a drug addict doesn't get evicted—all "in the name of humanity." Then there's Alfred E. Newman sitting blissfully in maharishi clothing, levitated by the Beatles.

That there's a core of genius in *Mad's* satire is not in doubt, but it would amount to little more than a charming artifact of Boomer youth had it not articulated a very real bewilderment with what seemed like the many hypocrisies and contradictions of Greatest Generation life. And *Mad* wasn't the only cultural touchstone expressing this bewilderment. In Joseph Heller's *Catch-22,* a literary bible for Boomer youth, we identify with the anti-hero Yossarian whose commanders keep raising the quota of bombing missions required before anyone can take leave from the army, so whenever Yossarian and his fellow pilots reach one quota, they're told it's not enough. When Yossarian finally asks how to get grounded, he's told you have to be crazy, but when someone who's crazy asks to get grounded, he's no longer seen as crazy. "There was only one catch and that was Catch-22, which specified that a concern for one's own safety in the face of dangers that were real and immediate was the process of a rational mind," Heller writes. "All he had to do was ask; and as soon as he did, he would no longer be crazy and would have to fly more missions."

The movie *M\*A\*S\*H* also would use the backdrop of war to spotlight the deceptions of authority, but war wasn't the only venue where authority seemed so arbitrary and misguided. Social critics such as Paul Goodman, Ivan Illich, and Edgar Friedenberg wrote about schools that stifled creativity and individuality. Films ranging from the brooding *Rebel Without a Cause* to the seemingly innocent *Beach Party* to the more caustic *The Graduate* portrayed adults as phony and uninformed if not deceitful and hypocritical, and even family TV—*Leave It to Beaver* or *Father Knows Best*—showed parents plotting to deceive their kids. The rational seemed so irrational that it made the irrational seem benign, as in Ken Kesey's *One Flew over the Cuckoo's Nest* and the cult film *King of Hearts,* which made the mentally ill appear sane in response to the cruelty of their caretakers, a metaphor illustrating the invidiousness of authority and our need to defy it.

These cultural messages resonated with so many Boomers because they confirmed what Boomers were witnessing around them. Greatest Generation leaders proclaimed that they were bequeathing Boomers a society that had transcended the old ideologies, that merely needed fine-tuning, technology, and scientific management to solve its problems, that was a beacon of justice at home and freedom overseas. Boomers wanted to believe it—indeed through the mid Sixties Boomers expressed a great deal of faith in American institutions, according to surveys. The problem is that the reality of Greatest Generation America fell far short of the ideal—the America that Boomers beheld wasn't even close to the America they were promised. For Boomers it was hard not to conclude that their elders were saying one thing but doing another.

In the three American decades after World War II, Boomers raised to respect free speech saw disagreement attacked as disloyal. They heard politicians denounce communism for undermining freedom and democracy abroad, yet saw these same politicians suppress dissent, thwart integration, deny human rights, and condone police brutality at home. They saw Southern sheriffs jail and murder civil rights leaders—and saw what Southern justice meant when all-white juries acquitted the murderers. They heard endless lectures about the American Dream, but saw whites acquiesce in the bigotry and discrimination that denied it to blacks. They saw comedians prosecuted for using dirty language and publishers convicted for printing sensual photographs, and then saw politicians win votes and accumulate power for massively resisting racial integration. They were told to trust the American corporation and believe in progress, but then saw unsafe cars rolling off the assembly lines, toxic waste pouring out of chemical plants, and American industries falter because of arrogance, shortsightedness, and failure to innovate. They saw *Reefer Madness* and heard all about the evils of marijuana, but saw their parents down cocktails and sleeping pills, what the Rolling Stones called "Mother's Little Helper," and then wondered whether they were hearing the truth about drugs after trying pot and judging it harmless. It wasn't that Boomers saw all leaders as hypocrites—but it seemed as if those who stood for something good were gunned down, and all the rest seemed soaked in malfeasance and duplicity.

Yet it wasn't until the Vietnam War escalated that Boomer faith in Greatest Generation leadership completely unraveled. "Like a tumor on a small child, the Vietnam war has put all of American society in lopsided perspective," wrote the editors of *Ramparts,* a mid-Sixties protest magazine. What little credibility the authorities had left in the Sixties was completely undermined by the lies and deceptions that sent Boomers to fight in a war no one could justify. So it wasn't much of a leap for Boomers who were fined and imprisoned for burning their draft cards to equate their act of resistance with the jailing of Martin Luther King, Jr. Other Boomers found that the only way to beat the draft was to mock and dishonor the law—to report for their army physical high or drunk or with needle marks or acting weird or smelling bad or saying they're gay or jittery from high blood pressure after eating bag upon bag of potato chips. Boomers who risked their lives in the Vietnam jungles returned home feeling betrayed by their government, which seemed unable to articulate a purpose for the war yet like a conveyer belt kept sending fresh squads of Boomers to die for their country. "One, two, three, what are we fighting for?" was the question millions asked in a song made popular at Woodstock, but no one was giving them a straight answer.

For Boomers, Vietnam turned respect, reason, and trust in America upside down. As the *Ramparts* editors observed, "The war represents the consummate contradiction of all American values. We stand for freedom, yet we support dictators. We believe in truth, yet Vietnam has been a living lie through each dishonorable, escalating step. We say we play fair, yet we are selectively exterminating a people incapable of matching our technology of death. We build a better world in Vietnam, yet we must make a wasteland to do it." And if Boomers needed further proof that American authority was bankrupt, they found it in the police riots at the 1968 Chicago Democratic Convention, in the 1970 murder of four student protesters at Kent State ("four dead in Ohio," as Crosby, Stills, Nash & Young famously rendered it), and in the 1971 release of the Pentagon Papers detailing how the White House and military deceived Congress, manipulated us into Vietnam, and simply assumed they had the absolute and unchecked power to prosecute a war.

Watergate provided Boomers final confirmation that those in authority would stop at nothing to exert their will, that they would commit crimes, cover up the truth, and subvert the Constitution which they swore to uphold. To Boomers, Richard Nixon personified all that was wrong with authority in America—the vanity, the pettiness, the deceptions, the hypocrisies, the insecurities, the intolerance, the arrogance, the abuses of power. These were the same authorities who blamed student radicals and "outside agitators" for all the turmoil in the Sixties, but to Boomers, they were merely projecting their own responsibility onto others. For it wasn't the Baby Boom that undermined authority in America during the Sixties—it was authority that undermined itself, and Boomers quite sensibly have been questioning it ever since.

To Boomers, the lesson was clear: Beware the motives, reassurances, and excuses of those in power, because something perfidious or deceptive may be lurking behind them, and to acquiesce is to be complicit in the official rationalizations. Boomers then applied what they saw nationally to their own individual lives, seeing high-school principals as tyrannical, parents as arbitrary, and rules as inflexible, made to be challenged if not broken. Some even say that the political movements of the Sixties fizzled out because no one ever trusted anyone with enough authority to get things done. Popular culture articulated this distrust by romanticizing outlaws—*Bonnie and Clyde, Butch Cassidy and the Sundance Kid*—and ridiculing the protocols of the older generation and what Boomers disdainfully called "the establishment." To Boomers, those who accomplished anything did it by their own rules—the Humphrey Bogart characters that Boomers idolized, the secret agent men who operated outside the normal channels, the *Fantastic Four* and *Spiderman* comic book heroes who fought for justice but never fit in, and even the alienated Ben in *The Graduate* who disdained a future in plastics and used a crucifix to disrupt his girlfriend's wedding and escape with her to freedom. In art, Boomers drew inspiration from the objects of everyday life, not from the classics. In music, they embraced genres never accepted by the mainstream—blues, soul, folk, jazz, and of course rock. In journalism, they created alternative publications because the conventional ones seemed too cozy with power. What was the value of received wisdom, Boomers asked, if we weren't sure we could trust it. So Boomers simply charted their own cultural path, beholden to no tradition or authority but grounded in the values of freedom, equality, and inclusion that society taught them but failed to fulfill.

The result today is a generation that has little respect for the rules of old and a distrust detector for anyone too powerful and anything proclaimed from high above. We see it in Boomer humor—irreverent and always aimed at the hypocrisy of large institutions and national leaders, *Saturday Night Live* and *The Daily Show with Jon Stewart* being prime examples. We see it in the economy—from the flattening of business hierarchies to the ongoing shakeups, takeovers, and shareholder uprisings that show no regard for entrenched corporate culture. We see it in politics—from the rise of independent voters to the distrust of official Washington. We even see it in families, where Boomer parents don't pretend to have all the answers and let their kids have a say in family decisions.

From Vietnam to Watergate, Boomers saw our national leaders try to accumulate power and resist both in law and in spirit the checks and balances at the core of our democratic system. Boomers took to heart then and still do today the distrust of authority and concentrated power written into the Declaration of Independence and the Constitution and encoded into our national culture. To Boomers, the Sixties was a morality play about our democracy: Authority must be earned, not given; institutions must serve the people, not the other way around; and it's our civic duty to hold these institutions and the authorities who run them fully accountable. These are the basic American principles that Boomers have been using to shake up and recast society, and it's what places this nontraditional generation squarely in the American tradition of questioning authority.

## Boomer Attitude 2: A Nation of Ideals

Seared into the Boomer mind are the televised images of black Americans beaten by police and mauled by attack dogs simply for seeking the same rights as all Americans. We remember voting rights marchers beaten at the Edmund Pettus Bridge. Black children bombed at the Sixteenth Street Baptist Church. Freedom Riders trampled and shot. James Meredith barred from attending college. George Wallace. Bull Connor. Separate water fountains. A motel manager pouring muriatic acid into a swimming pool blacks tried to integrate. That our country was not living up to its ideals—that it was falling short of the American creed Boomers had been taught in school—became a motivating force behind Boomer activism in the Sixties. And holding America to its ideals has been the Boomer anthem ever since.

With Vietnam and civil rights and women's liberation as their real-life classroom in the Sixties, Boomers learned how power relationships shape the world, and their impulse since then has been to seek equal rights for all—for minorities, women, immigrants, gays and lesbians, for anyone abased by the dominant culture. It's what the historian Godfrey Hodgson calls the "Mississippi metaphor," as Boomers in the Sixties began to see the world through the prism of the most desperate of civil rights struggles, which meant identifying with anyone poor, powerless, or scorned for being outside the cultural mainstream. That America could deny rights to some showed Boomers that it could deny rights to anyone, and the more Boomers looked, the more they saw their own rights under siege. Indeed the black experience in America became an analogy for women and students and gays and anti-war protesters and anyone else trying to gain respect for their views and a seat at the table of power. "In Mississippi an autocratic and powerful minority rules, through organized violence, to suppress the vast, virtually powerless majority. In California, the privileged minority manipulates the university bureaucracy to suppress the students' political expression," said student organizer Mario Savio in 1964, who led the Free Speech Movement at Berkeley that year after spending a summer registering black voters in Mississippi. To be sure, as Hodgson points out, it was a bit much to equate white middle-class college students with Mississippi blacks, but as a metaphor it made sense, particularly as television magnified student protests and showed police storming college campuses in riot gear, wielding billy clubs and dragging students into paddy wagons. "It suddenly became possible for students on every campus in America to ask themselves whether there wasn't a little bit of Mississippi in all America," writes Hodgson.

To Boomers, it wasn't supposed to be this way. Scholars who studied Boomer children in the early 1960s found that they believed strongly in the laws and ideals of the country, seeing them as just and fair and admiring the authorities who enforced them. In schools, at home, and on the television set, Boomers were socialized to see the American system as a virtuous and benevolent democracy that empowered its citizens with rights and freedoms. The good guys always won, the law was moral, and Boomer heroes stood for "truth, justice, and the American way." But the flip side of Boomer idealism was a refusal to accept or accommodate any violation of that idealism. The same scholars who saw Boomers socialized by ideals also predicted that Boomers, no matter how disillusioned, would remain committed to those ideals and not walk away from them. It was a mindset reinforced by growing up in the shadow of Nazism and the Holocaust, which taught Boomers how raw power stripped of conscience can deny liberties and rights—and how important it was to defend them. So when Boomers saw America violate its ideals, they demanded change. When Boomers saw authorities enforce laws arbitrarily, they insisted on fairness. When Boomers saw injustice anywhere, they spoke out for justice everywhere. To Boomers, it was nonsensical to be told that we should go slow on ending racism or injustice or war—Boomers could see the problems in real time on television, and they couldn't understand the lack of urgency for real-time solutions. The Greatest Generation set out to raise moral kids who believed in America, who subscribed to the principles of freedom and justice for which the Greatest Generation fought in World War II, and in many ways they succeeded. But perhaps, from their standpoint, they succeeded too well. For in the decades after the war, as the Greatest Generation was defending America as it was, not for what it could be, Boomers were embracing America for what it could be, refusing to settle for the way it was.

As an idealistic generation growing up in the Greatest Generation era, Boomers found themselves inspired by America's promise, disappointed by America's shortcomings, and determined to do something about it— to reconcile America's reality with its ideals. For Boomers this dynamic played out in ways big and small, political and personal, with matters seemingly inconsequential even replete with meaning. At the national level Boomers witnessed the dramatic tension between hope and frustration in the civil rights movement, feeling exhilarated by the possibilities, indignant at the resistance, and shamed by the inaction. But it didn't take much more than a transistor radio or a high-school dance for Boomers to see a microcosm of it closer to home, when the Greatest Generation's self-appointed moral police attacked Boomer music—rock 'n' roll and soul—for promoting interracial contact and sexual intermingling, labeling it "race music" and "jungle music." What seemed natural and joyful to Boomers—a James Brown tune or a Motown single—shook their elders with anger and fear. So listening to music became a struggle, an act of defiance, a personal statement about racial equality and individual freedom.

Nor was it any different with Vietnam. Boomers imbibed the Kennedy idealism of the early Sixties, seeing America as a force for justice and human rights, flocking to the Peace Corps as an expression of American values. But when Boomers began to ask about Vietnam—how destroying a country in order to save it fit with American ideals, how Boomers in body bags advanced the cause of freedom, why a corrupt South Vietnamese government deserved our sacrifice—their concerns were dismissed as simplistic or un-American, and both their Greatest Generation parents and their schools told them that young people should be seen and not heard. And so Vietnam, like civil rights, permeated every part of Boomer life, and to Boomers all the criticism of their long hair, music, lifestyle, and clothing simply reflected the same intolerance that greeted their questions about Vietnam, making even the smallest personal decisions into idealistic struggles about individual freedom, rights, and ethics. The be-ins and long hair that shocked Greatest Generation America in the Sixties derived from a simple Baby Boom message: We have a right to express ourselves, so whether you like it or not you better get used to it.

For Boomers, it was never enough to change policies or enact laws. Boomer idealism demanded that assumptions, norms, and attitudes change as well—or as Pirsig wrote in *Zen and the Art of Motorcycle Maintenance*, it must come from within. Those who read their history knew that the Civil War and passage of the Fourteenth Amendment didn't materially change the lives of black Americans living in the South. They saw the Supreme Court outlaw school segregation but watched segregationists block the schoolhouse doors. They applauded suffrage for women, but saw even the most radical of anti-war groups relegate women to mimeographing and brewing coffee. Boomers who grew up decrying the hypocrisy of their elders would have felt hypocritical if they didn't put their own lives under the same microscope of scrutiny.

The result has been a generational crusade to make sure that the ideals we hold as a people are reflected at the most individual and intimate level, in our language, institutions, relationships, and actions. In the Sixties the personal became the political. What Boomers learned back then was that language and behavior carry powerful messages that often favor one type of person over another, and to achieve real equality we need to examine what we say and how we behave lest it impact an innocent individual. So Boomers adopted "Ms." so that women would not be judged by their marital status; they accepted homosexuality as an orientation rather than a preference, making it an issue of equality, not morality; they even began substituting "happy holidays" for "merry Christmas" as a way to show respect for religious diversity, which was a welcome relief to religious minorities like Jews, many of whom gritted their teeth and bought Christmas trees in the Fifties just to fit in. Demeaning labels, racist humor, acceptable prejudice, and disregard for minorities may have been fine with the Greatest Generation, but not with the Baby Boom. And what the Greatest Generation found most threatening in the Sixties—Black Power and Black Is Beautiful—Boomers embraced as an expression of equality, a needed corrective in a society that patronized minorities, stripped them of dignity, labeled them inferior, portrayed them as ugly, and denied their self-worth.

Boomers also began probing into the institutions and practices that frame our culture and perpetuate our norms, and what they found was a rampant bias against women and minorities that riddled our educational, financial, legal, and health care systems. A 1973 book about women's health, *Our Bodies, Ourselves,* would eventually sell millions of copies over the years because it gave voice to Boomer women seeking equality in health care and showed in a very fundamental way how Boomer ideals must be manifested in the most private parts of our lives. By the early 1970s, Boomer nonprofits, advocacy groups, research organizations, and legal aid lawyers were scouring society for inequities and institutional prejudice, beginning the process that continues today of moving daily life in America closer to its founding ideals.

Civil rights, women's liberation, the Vietnam War—they showed Boomers quite starkly how American realities fell short of American ideals, how complacency in the face of injustice furthered injustice, and how idealism meant not just lofty words but the practices, norms, attitudes, and actions required to implement them. We now live in a Baby Boom America that insists on diversity, inclusion, equal worth, and personal freedom—all core values consistent with what Boomers were taught as kids and shaped by the challenges Boomers faced in the Sixties. It's a long way from the Freedom Rides to "happy holidays," but it all derives from a commitment to ideals forged in this generation's formative years.

## Boomer Attitude 3: Do Not Fold, Spindle, or Mutilate

The popular image of Boomers—especially those who flirted with the Sixties counterculture—is that they rejected technology and, donning sandals, tie-dyes, and peasant shirts, set out for the land on a return to nature. Of course that was until they grew up, when Boomers came to embrace technology and progress and its attendant prosperity in the same way they condemned their parents for doing a generation ago. It all sounds so tidy and neat, another narrative of Boomer hypocrisy that Boomer critics love to regale and retell. But there's a problem with this image: It really isn't accurate or true. Like so many other storylines about Boomers, it rests on caricature and media stereotype. For the truth is that Boomers never really rejected technology and its benefits in the Sixties— rather, they rejected what technology came to represent. To Boomers, technology symbolized an increasingly mass-produced, bureaucratized, and depersonalized America, and it was that, not the actual technology, that Boomers disdained. "Technology, which could be a blessing to society," wrote the Students for a Democratic Society in their 1962 manifesto, *The Port Huron Statement,* "becomes more and more a sinister threat to humanistic and rational enterprise." Or as Robert Pirsig put it in *Zen and the Art of Motorcycle Maintenance,* "the real ugliness of modern technology" isn't in the technology itself, but in the relationship between

technology and people. Boomers envisioned instead a technology symbolized by the VW bus that they plastered with flowers and drove on
their many road trips back to the land: It should empower and free rather
than constrain and control.

To Boomers in the Sixties, everywhere they looked the America of
their ideals seemed to be turning into an America where the individual
no longer mattered. We live in a technocracy, Boomers were told, a society built on rationality and technology that would make us happy and
wealthy. But to Boomers, this idealization of the machine had its disqui-
eting underside. Boomers feared the machine's potential to control, its
impersonal quality, its tendency to reduce us to data and numbers and in-
terchangeable cogs that engage the gears and keep the machine going. To
them, politicians who were bad were "machine politicians." Inferior products were "machine made." Boomers increasingly began to associate technology and machines with all sorts of evil—Dr. Strangelove, Big Brother,
nuclear weapons, even the mechanized death machines of Nazi Germany.
The computer HAL, from the 1968 film *2001: A Space Odyssey,* became a
metaphor for a technology moving beyond the grasp of man. "I know you
and Frank were planning to disconnect me," HAL said, "and I'm afraid
that's something I cannot allow to happen."

It was this machine metaphor that Boomers applied to their own lives.
In school, they saw teachers and administrators not really educating them
but preparing them to join the rat race and to fit into what Norman
Mailer described as "the cold majesty of the Corporation." At college they
became computer punch cards—do not fold, spindle, or mutilate—and
Social Security numbers sitting in large lecture halls at what Berkeley's
chancellor Clark Kerr proudly called a "multiversity" or "knowledge factory." When they called an office they got bumped from one bureaucrat to
another and couldn't seem to get a straight answer from anyone. Peering
into the world of work, they saw a world of hierarchy, rules, organization
charts, junior executives, and status-seekers that valued yes-men, elevated
conformity over creativity, encouraged managers to cover their mistakes,
and treated workers as parts of a machine whose humanity was simply a
rational problem to be addressed through better personnel management
and improved gadgetry. From Ralph Nader they learned how corpora-

tions mass-produced cars and other products that executives knew were unsafe. It was a society, according to Theodore Roszak in his influential 1969 book *The Making of a Counter Culture,* built around "the relentless quest for efficiency, for order, for even more extensive rational control." And that which got in the way of progress was pushed aside, no matter what the cost to society, a fact driven home to Boomers when they opened the pages of Rachel Carson's 1962 environmental classic, *Silent Spring,* which documented quite chillingly how the chemicals used in everyday products and mass-produced food were poisoning us and ravaging the earth. "Lulled by the soft sell and the hidden persuader, the average citizen is seldom aware of the deadly materials with which he is surrounding himself; indeed, he may not realize he is using them at all," Carson wrote. "To find a diet free from DDT and related chemicals, it seems one must go to a remote and primitive land, still lacking the amenities of civilization." The factory smokestack, long the symbol of industrial progress and the pride of working Americans, had become anathema to this new generation of Americans.

But perhaps nothing more cogently illustrated Boomer unease with technology and the machine than the Vietnam War, which to Boomers represented the technocracy run amok, the mass production of war, the bureaucratization of murder. Boomers recoiled at the military's rationale of destroying a village in order to save it. From the military they heard the eerie bureaucratic euphemisms—pacification, collateral damage, surgical strikes, protective reaction strikes, incursions—all to cover up America's devastation of Vietnam. They then saw the same chemicals that promised us a better life at home burning the skin off peasants who ran from their torched and flattened hamlets shrieking in pain. "In another delta province there is a woman who has both arms burned off by napalm and her eyelids so badly burned that she cannot close them. When it is time for her to sleep her family puts a blanket over her head," reported *The New York Times* in 1965, typical of what Boomers witnessed throughout the war. And the dehumanization wasn't limited to the rice paddies of Vietnam—it also was reflected in the draft, which to Boomers denied them the individual, moral decision of whether to participate in what increasingly seemed like the senseless killing of this war.

To Boomers, the entire culture seemed pre-packaged, dehumanized, devoid of emotion and spirituality, built on big and small lies like planned obsolescence and better living through chemistry and winning the hearts and minds of the Vietnamese people. It was a culture of technocratic and bureaucratic euphemisms designed to cover up an irrational war and environmental degradation and social conformity and hierarchical thinking and cars that were unsafe at any speed. It was a culture that told Boomers the only way to protect themselves from a thermonuclear nightmare was to duck and cover. Increasingly it seemed that the same bureaucracies created to solve problems were becoming part of the problem. Dustin Hoffman in *The Graduate* spoke for many with his contempt for "plastics"— an emblem of technocratic America, an unresponsive and impersonal society that had forgotten the individual and stifled conscience and expression. Large and remote institutions, wrote the *Whole Earth Catalog,* no longer offer solutions; better to empower "the individual to conduct his own education, find his own inspiration, shape his own environment, and share his adventure with whoever is interested." So countless Boomers sought repose and meaning and personal connection in places diametrically opposed to technocracy and technology—in Eastern religions, holistic health, sensitivity sessions, self-help, and the mystical novels of Carlos Castaneda, J. R. R. Tolkien, and Hermann Hesse. Millions participated in the first Earth Day in 1970 and began to integrate environmentalism into their politics and way of life. "There is a time when the operation of the machine becomes so odious, makes you so sick at heart, that you can't take part," said Berkeley organizer Mario Savio as he spoke to students at one of the first major student protests of the Sixties, the 1964 Free Speech Movement. "You can't even passively take part, and you've got to put your bodies upon the gears and upon the wheels, upon the levers, upon all the apparatus, and you've got to make it stop. And you've got to indicate to the people who run it, to the people who own it, that unless you're free, the machine will be prevented from working at all."

So what really troubled Boomers about technology was not technology itself but technology as a symbol of the impersonal, mass society America had seemingly become. In fact some technology thoroughly captivated Boomers—the space program and moon landing, for example, because they furthered our horizons and examined the mysteries of the universe, because they expanded the human experience rather than mechanized it. The back-to-the-land *Whole Earth Catalog,* rather than portray life on a commune or organic farm, instead featured on its back and front covers photographic images of our universe and galaxy, one supplied by the astronomer Carl Sagan. In his 1970 book *Future Shock,* Alvin Toffler effusively described a breakthrough technology—"a personal computer"—that could empower the individual with vast amounts of knowledge and information. Even in the countercultural Sixties, Boomers gravitated toward technology that would enhance human potential and individual choice.

This Sixties approach to technology—an appreciation of its promise, a rejection of its by-products, and an aversion to its bureaucratic manifestations—has spawned a number of attitudes that shape American life today. In the Baby Boom era, progress is measured not merely by rational economic measures but also by its social costs and impact on the environment and society. We now praise risktakers and entrepreneurs and individual initiatives, while we disdain managers, junior executives, hierarchies, red tape, and any symbol of bureaucratic, non-responsive, intrusive, machine-like organizations. Technology must be user-friendly, no longer impersonal and detached from daily life, a means to liberate rather than burden. Government must be agile and responsive rather than bloated and bureaucratic. What the organization or corporation or government agency wants no longer determines what the consumer, employee, and citizen will choose. We simply refuse to see the individual as a cog in the machine. And so it makes sense that Boomers are demanding mass-produced organic foods, crafts that look custom-made, and even sport utility vehicles named Explorer and Tahoe that go off-road into nature—because they all seem to blend technology and environmentalism, mass production and personal freedom, gadgetry and empowerment, the various elements that define our culture and economy today. Yes, in many ways Boomers want it all—they want compassion and justice from government without the bureaucracy, they want four-wheel-drive vehicles that consume less gas, they want sophisticated technology that the individual can control, they want access to information but no invasion of

their privacy, they want more responsibility at work but not too many layers of management, and they want economic progress coupled with environmental awareness. These may seem like disparate phenomena, some
even contradictory, but they're all spun from the same Baby Boom thread
woven in the Sixties: discomfort with the impersonal technocracy and
bureaucracy of modern America. Do not fold, spindle, or mutilate.

## Boomer Attitude 4: Never Trust Anyone Over Thirty

In 2002, Honda unveiled a boxy, small SUV called the Element, which
was billed as a combined "base camp" and "dorm room on wheels." In a
full-scale ad campaign, Honda featured carefree and hip twenty-somethings
cruising to the beach with all their paraphernalia and gear. These were
fun ads, light with the promise of youth and evocative of college cama-
raderie and outdoor vigor. Honda's goal: to grab the youth market.
Honda's reality: Boomers began buying the car. In its first year of sales,
the average age of Element owners was forty-two. Honda's story is really
a parable about Boomers, and it begs the question: Why are Boomers so
fixated on youth?

"We have a saying in the movement," Berkeley protester Jack Weinberg told a reporter in 1964. "Never trust anyone over thirty." It actually
wasn't a Boomer saying at the time—Weinberg made it up in the interview. But it resonated with Boomers, and not because they took the
under-thirty thing literally. To Boomers, it was less a statement about age
than about youthfulness, about the youthful qualities of experimentation
and freedom and fun and open-mindedness that invigorated America in
the Sixties and remain central to our culture today. Boomers are often derided for not growing up, for not letting go of their youth, for fattening
the wallets of companies who sell them relaxed-fit jeans and progressive
eyeglasses that hide the bifocal line. But there's a reason why Boomers remain attached to youth, and it has nothing to do with wistfulness and
nostalgia and fear of old age. No, it has everything to do with keeping
current and not losing touch. They don't want to repeat the mistakes of
their elders.

Returning from World War II, the Greatest Generation simply assumed
that things would go back to the way they were, that the future would re-

main an extension of the past, that the elders would have all the wisdom, and youth would do as they were told. But what the Greatest Generation didn't comprehend is that America in the Sixties was entering a period of change, of constant, rapid, and profound change. As a nation we were becoming more diverse—and beginning to acknowledge the diversity we already had. Americans who once settled for fewer rights were now demanding equal rights. Television began to dissolve the old boundaries of distance and time, and in the comfort of our living rooms we could see images of war abroad and injustice at home. The birth control pill and antibiotics and other scientific advances brought us new choices and freedoms.

Writing about her own World War II generation in 1970, the anthropologist Margaret Mead observed, "Our thinking still binds us to the past—to the world as it existed in our childhood and youth. Born and bred before the electronic revolution, most of us do not realize what it means." It is in times like these, Mead concluded, in times of accelerating social and technological change, that the past no longer serves as a reliable guide for the future, and the answers of old often serve as obstacles to the new. And that is why youth must be heard, she argued, because only the young were born into change and have no preconceptions they want to impose on it. Much like the immigrant children who learn their new culture and try teaching it to resistant parents, it is youth that adapt to the new better than their elders, and as change quickens—as society transforms and technology mutates—we must rely on youth to shape it and translate it and incorporate it into our daily lives.

And so it was in the Sixties, when Boomers understood that America was somehow changing and began to chart out new norms and approaches to deal with it. As culture, politics, family life, and the economy began to churn and transform, it fell to Boomers to make sense of it, to manage and adapt, to embrace the new and eschew the outdated, to create new language and perspectives to interpret what was happening, to build a sense of urgency for change. And so they began talking about diversity and women's rights and personal freedoms and media choices and limits to power and a balance between progress and the environment.

It's not that Boomers in the Sixties had all the answers. But they were at least asking the right questions. As Mead put it, "They feel that there must be a better way and they must find it." And knowing that something was awry, Boomers weren't willing to wait. When their elders dug in and refused to budge from the old ways—telling Boomers they shouldn't listen to this music or they shouldn't protest a war or they shouldn't demand their civil rights or they shouldn't rush change or they shouldn't behave a certain way because it would violate their moral teachings— Boomers took it as an invitation to defy, seeing these admonitions as delay tactics, as desperate attempts by their elders to reassert control over a world that had passed them by. What emerged was a culture that increasingly looked not to elders but to youth for its cues to the future—in fact Baby Boom America may be the first society in history ever to transfer cultural authority from its elders to its youth. So in America today, not to be youthful is to be stuck in the past, to resist the new, to be captive and powerless in a modern world where change is the only constant and certainty. It is a lesson the Baby Boom learned quite well, and as a generation Boomers are determined never to be obsolete.

Youthfulness also meant freedom and adventure for Boomers growing up in the Fifties and Sixties, and they saw no reason not to have fun. Boomers saw their parents living under strict rules, stifling conformity, and lingering Victorian restraints—to have a living room wrapped in plastic furniture covers seemed to symbolize Greatest Generation culture. That Rob and Laura Petri in *The Dick Van Dyke Show* slept in separate beds seemed foolish and full of self-denial. That families routinely deferred vacations to please the boss seemed thoroughly self-defeating. That authorities could shut down beach parties and rock concerts seemed overly punitive. That a leading educator could call premarital sex "offensive and vulgar behavior" seemed so moralistic and rigid—as did rules at most colleges requiring male and female students visiting each other to keep the door open six inches and keep three feet on the floor at all times. Young men were sent off to war at eighteen, yet closing the dorm room door was prohibited? In the immortal words of the Beach Boys, it was "fun, fun, fun, till her daddy takes the T-bird away."

If that was what it meant to be grown up, if it was all about arbitrary rules and punitive morality, Boomers wanted to stay youthful, if not young. What Boomers wanted to avoid was what one author called "the split-level trap"—leading lives of self-denial, deferred gratification, no joy, and little fun. They wondered how a society dedicated to the pursuit of happiness could be so unhappy, how pleasure could induce such guilt. Growing up with the bomb further heightened Boomer urgency, because if it all could vanish in a blinding flash, it made no sense not to seize the moment. To Boomers, the American notion of freedom meant exploring frontiers, challenging traditions, testing boundaries, taking risks, reinventing oneself and society. It's the way generations of Americans had lived, whether as pioneers or immigrants or gold miners or patriots or entrepreneurs, all making this country what it was. But in the Greatest Generation era, Boomers were warned against expressing themselves. They were told that freedom meant conformity, that it meant order and logic and not rocking the boat, that it meant not questioning authorities when they told you what to do. And Boomers would have none of it.

So in the Sixties, the youth generation defined freedom the way they understood it—as experimenting with new ideas and not conforming to expectations or deferring to elders or going to church just because that's what you were supposed to do. It also meant smoking pot or dancing in the street or painting faces or backpacking in the Rockies or traveling to Mardi Gras in New Orleans. But the drugs and the music were less important than the experience and the kick, the breaking of boundaries, which Boomers now replicate with ecotourism, adventure vacations, and any number of avocations like parasailing and hang gliding. In the Seventies, the pollster Daniel Yankelovich found that Greatest Generation Americans and Baby Boomers both wanted to make money, but Boomers wanted it not as a symbol of status or success but rather as a means to excitement and adventure. To the Greatest Generation, doing your own thing meant that neighbors might whisper about you and ostracize you; to Boomers, expressing yourself is a given, and there's no reason to think that people won't accept or appreciate it. In Baby Boom America, as long as you're not hurting anyone, it's acceptable and even encouraged to be different—and it's no one's business to tell you to stop. Or as the marketers figured out in the Sixties, Boomers wanted to be the Uncola, they wanted to be a generation unbound. When Richie Havens sang "Freedom" at Woodstock, it was more than just a song—it was an anthem for this generation.

To cultural historians, Boomers may emerge as the one generation that finally pushed down the remaining walls of Victorian morality that governed the country from the mid 1800s onward. It was a stern morality characterized by sexual repression, behavioral rules, postponed pleasure, mass conformity, and social hierarchy. Young women and even engaged couples were chaperoned wherever they went. Prudery and deferred gratification were ways to improve onself, to fit in. To Victorians, this strict sense of virtue and duty was essential in maintaining the social order and keeping the gears of industrialism running smoothly. You were expected to know your place in society, and not to challenge it. Boomers certainly weren't the first and only Americans to find this culture stifling. Before World War I, a small but vocal group of young artists and intellectuals gathered in Greenwich Village and quite visibly revolted against Victorian lifestyle strictures. The Beats in the Fifties did much the same. Even the middle classes so associated with Victorian morality strayed at times, though never in public as they secretly hid their vices and transgressions. So Victorian restraints began to erode even before the Sixties, in both public and private life. But by the Sixties they seemed completely atavistic and out of touch in an America that was becoming increasingly open, diverse, free, and expressive. They were ready to be challenged en masse. To Boomers, it was their elders who held on to this moral system of old, desperately so. And it was young people who pushed for change and liberation. It all sent a strong message to Boomers that youth stood for change, that to be contemporary one must remain youthful, and it is a message Boomers will take to their grave and leave as a legacy for generations to come.

Now look at American society today. Baby Boom attitudes predominate in our culture, shaping who we are, what we do, why we do it, and how we look at the world. We see Boomer irreverence in our exuberant individualism, invigorating youthfulness, personal empowerment, distrust of entrenched authority, and suspicion of big institutions and the power they have. And we see Boomer liberalism in our embrace of diversity, insistence on rights, intolerance of intolerance, open-mindedness toward change, and emphasis on freedom of choice, environmental awareness, and the personal as political. America today is made in the image of the Baby Boom, and we are, thankfully, a better and healthier and more open nation because of it.

# Chapter Five
# Farewell, Donna Reed

All I'm askin'
Is for a little respect.
—*Aretha Franklin, "Respect," 1967*

**W**ithin a stone's throw of my house are four Boomer families like my own, all of us raising children, and I often ask how representative we are of the rest of America. It's an eclectic group, with incomes ranging from the modest to the comfortable and homes varying from a small two-bedroom to a more spacious house about ten years old. Among us are a public school teacher and a medical researcher and a furniture maker and a lawyer and a computer programmer and a nonprofit executive, and most of us settled in the area by chance and happenstance, hailing originally from other parts. Our kids range from newborns to late-teens and everywhere in between, and we don't seem much different from parents at the local school bus stop, or for that matter anywhere else in the country. Yet something does seem different about us: In every family the father is either the dominant childcare provider or a full and equal partner in raising the kids. There are two stay-at-home dads, another dad who worked only occasionally when his daughter was young, yet another who takes the after-school shift and shuttles his kids to their various activities. None of the dads feels inadequate or any less fulfilled in life—they're simply parents doing what's right for their wives and their children. To be sure, a block or so away it's a dash more like the olden days—a few more traditional families with stay-at-home moms, others in which it's the mom and not the dad who rushes home from work to greet the kids, and when the elementary school bus arrives in the afternoon there are still more moms than dads waiting with open arms. So I ask: Is my immediate neighborhood the exception? Or is it a sign of something new under way?

Perhaps we can find a clue in an unlikely source, the Food Network, certainly not the place where revolutions are made but maybe a harbinger of things to come. For what its audience numbers indicate is that something big may indeed be underway in American life: Men comprise 42 percent of its viewers, and it's closing in on 50 percent. According to a University of Minnesota study, more than a quarter of all men, 27 percent, act as primary food handlers for their families, which means they shop, cook, dice, chop, and do the main preparation for the dinner parties. Only a few decades ago the closest American men got to preparing a meal was at the barbecue grill, and a man wearing yellow dish gloves and an apron was a symbol of ridicule, contempt, and shame. But in the era of Baby Boom egalitarianism, even the most mulish of Greatest Generation norms are beginning to give way. My neighborhood may not be so unusual after all.

And change isn't taking place only in the kitchen. The office used to be the haunt of organization men unwilling to let any family issue get in the way of their work. But today, men are demanding more of a balance between their family and career commitments. "We hear almost as much about work-family issues from men as from women," said a researcher who has interviewed men and women about their satisfaction at work. One study of men in dual-earner couples found that one in six have reduced work hours and one in four have refused or limited their job-related travel, all to accommodate family needs. Other surveys show that an increasing number of men deem flexible schedules more important than high salaries or challenging work, and when changing jobs they look for companies with better hours, childcare benefits, and generous family leave. Of the twenty million American workers who used parental leave between 1993 and 1999, 40 percent were men.

In fact husbands no longer automatically assume their careers come first. There are surveys showing that a majority of working spouses see their careers as equal, there are studies showing that about a third of working wives now make more than their husbands, and there are statistics showing that men are doing more housework and spending more time with their kids than at any time in our history. Scholars describe "mounting evidence" of these shifts in family roles and worldviews—that married fathers "have significantly increased the time they spend with children," that women are doing less housework than they used to "and their spouses more than in the past," and that we're moving toward a culture that emphasizes "intensive parenting" rather than intensive mothering. According to a mid 1990s Census Bureau analysis of childcare practices in families with working mothers, about one in four fathers took care of their kids while mom was at work, and estimates since then suggest an even greater proportion today. *Business Week* notes that researchers are documenting "more and more" how "the roles are starting to change, evident in the increase in male executives working compressed weeks so they can have more time with children, in shift workers who are taking responsibility for daytime childcare, and in dads working from home so they can be closer to their kids."

Just think of the recent rise in children's sports activities—the proliferation of soccer, baseball, basketball, and hockey teams for boys and girls of all ages—which could not have taken place without many dads doing the coaching. Or look at public opinion surveys, where there's almost no gender gap in attitudes about family roles, particularly among Boomers and everyone born after—equally large majorities of men and women reject the traditional marriage of the Fifties and prefer to share work and home responsibilities. The contrast between then and now is perhaps best illustrated by the day their children are born: Only 15 percent of fathers in the mid 1960s expected to be in the delivery room, compared to almost 90 percent today. As *Newsweek* concluded in 2003, "They may not be perfect, but most husbands today do far more around the house than their fathers would have ever dreamed of doing. They're also more involved than ever in their children's lives."

For all the Homer Simpson and *Married with Children* caricatures, for all the popular culture portrayals of self-centered and boorish fathers, the truth is that the egalitarian norms of the Baby Boom have deeply changed men and will continue to do so for generations to come. Today's fathers are simply not the silent, psychologically distant dads of the Fifties, the ones whose emotional absence caused lifelong sadness in their sons and daughters. The "new man" image may be a cliche ripe for parody, but when asked by pollsters if they prefer to be viewed as "sensitive and caring" or "rugged and masculine," only 15 percent of American men choose the Marlboro Man norm and nearly three-fourths opt for sensitive and caring. When asked which was the best decade to be a man, only 12 percent of fathers say the Fifties. It's the stony guy, the strong and silent type, who seems out of place today. In advertising, which makes its money articulating the cultural Zeit-geist, the gruff and imperious male boss of yesteryear is typically portrayed as clueless, corrected by a more open-minded and sensitive generation of male and female employees. Increasingly men are shedding the conformist straitjacket of old and doing things the Greatest Generation considered un-manly and reserved for women—such as pursuing careers in the tradition-ally female fields of nursing and public school teaching, which more and more men are doing, or assuming primary responsibility for elderly relatives and parents, a third of whom are now cared for by men, or taking yoga classes, which are now a quarter men, or frequenting hair salons as much as barbershops. History has shown that it is much harder to give up privilege than to accept it, that it takes extraordinary effort to assume an image or role typically associated with a shamed or lower caste. But American men in the Baby Boom era have been doing just that—slowly but steadily em-bracing equality at home and at work, increasingly enjoying roles once rel-egated to women, and forsaking the *Father Knows Best* model of family decision making in favor of a more equal and democratic household.

Now this is not to say we've reached the promised land of full equal-ity, that men and women are putting in the same amount of time on housework and with the kids, that women are getting equal pay for equal work, that power is fully shared at work and at home, that some men aren't digging in and resisting change. Will women still need to litigate against discrimination and sue for pay equity? Of course. Must the glass walls and ceilings that keep women from job advancement come down? Yes, absolutely. Do women have reason to be frustrated and angry with the barriers they still face on the job and the disproportionate share of housework they still do at home? No question. But those who see the proverbial glass only half empty have unrealistic expectations for the pace of social change. Remember, the glass was almost completely empty only a generation ago. Centuries of family and gender relations—as with cen-turies of any other ingrained roles and behavior—cannot be completely unknotted in just a decade or two. But they are loosening and changing, rapidly so, moving toward greater equality, and what Boomers jump-started in the Sixties has been nothing less than a compelling transforma-tion of family and gender in American life.

So yes, fathers still spend fewer hours with the kids than mothers, but now it's double what it used to be; and yes, women still do about 60 percent of the housework, but that's far better than the 85 percent in the 1970s; and yes, women do most of the cleaning and chores in about a third of dual-earner families, but there are even more families in which the work is shared, which wasn't the case three decades ago. At mid-life, Greatest Generation Americans generally felt that women should take care of running their homes and leave running the country up to men; at mid-life, 90 percent of Boomers reject this formulation. In the course of a single generation, Baby Boomers have made equality the norm and equity the rule between men and women, and while the reality has not caught up with the ideal, it's moving inexorably in that direction. Indeed among couples that have most thoroughly imbibed Baby Boom egalitarianism, there's near parity in the amount of housework and childcare they do, with the men spending less time at work and more time with the kids than their less egalitarian peers, and according to the Census Bureau, dads in the more liberal Northeast are almost twice as likely as dads in the more conservative South to be taking care of their pre-school children while their wives are at work. And the more women enter the workforce and demand equality, the more their partners will adjust and listen, evidenced by the fact that men with working wives tend to be more supportive of equal rights and shared responsibilities than men whose wives stay at home. When a 2002 National Opinion Research Center survey asked whether men should do a larger share of household work and childcare, most Americans agreed; what that tells us is two things, that men should indeed do more of the family work, and that most Americans agree with the norm that men should do more of the family work. Except among the vocal conservative minority, there's no interest in turning back the clock to the old ways, and the more Boomer values take root, the more we'll move toward a truly equal society.

For women, the Baby Boom era has been one of breathtaking change— in a single generation, American women have effected one of the greatest social metamorphoses in recorded history. What women are able to do today would have been unimaginable four or five decades ago, at best the stuff of utopian fantasy or science fiction. For women to look back on life in the Greatest Generation days is to travel back in a time warp where everything is familiar but almost nothing is the same. Back then, women were to be seen, not heard, and economically dependent on men; to succeed in life meant not following one's dreams but marrying the right man; the norm was the dutiful, pleasant housewife, ready with dinner and the highball when hubby came home; women who chose a different path were stigmatized, and they typically had few choices beyond working as a teacher, nurse, librarian, stenographer, telephone operator, or domestic; girls who liked sports were demeaned as tomboys and amazons; higher education was a male thing, with some saying that college damaged women's health; dad supported the family economically but rarely spent much time with the kids and almost never cooked for them or, heaven forbid, changed their diapers; and much like Ricky Ricardo in *I Love Lucy,* he had little time or patience for his wife's silly aspirations and dreams.

Yet beneath the housewife's adoring gaze and smile, women of the Greatest Generation years had many aspirations and dreams, and they weren't silly at all. A 1946 Women's Bureau survey of women who worked for the war effort during World War II found that three-fourths wanted to keep their jobs after the war. In the two decades before the war women typically earned about two-fifths of all bachelor's degrees. Many women wanted an education and a career as well as a family. But the Greatest Generation norm of domesticity was so powerful that it not only shrank women's expectations but made those lowered expectations seem normal, the way things were and ought to be, so much so that both men and women internalized them and created patterns of behavior to accommodate them. So of the women who attended college in the Fifties, two-thirds failed to receive their bachelor's degrees, and of all the BA degrees granted in 1950, only 23.9 percent went to women. Even at elite women's schools, college was seen as a stepping-stone not to a career but to a good and respectable marriage, what many called the Mrs. degree. In a study of Radcliffe freshmen in the early 1960s, not a single one discussed how she planned to make money, simply assuming that was the man's role. When girls sought out their high-school counselors for career guidance, the counselors routinely put the list of men's jobs in the desk drawer and pulled out a short and narrow list of women's jobs, a message constantly reinforced in the classroom as girls found few role models in textbooks and almost no encouragement to excel in science or math.

Nor were these lower expectations evident only in schools: A government study of the high-school class of 1972 found that Greatest Generation parents had higher aspirations for their sons than their daughters. If women worked but didn't need the income, it was considered a pleasant interregnum in life, a nice experience not to be taken too seriously. Said one woman asked to be a guest editor of *Mademoiselle* magazine in 1953, "I wanted to do something really interesting and different before moving into the lock-step situation typical of women of my time." Women who dipped their toes in the career waters found nothing but a chilly reception. Applying for a job often meant getting rejected because the company's clients didn't want to have a woman on their account, and when hired, women were frequently relegated to back-room research positions because male colleagues found it distracting to have women at the table. Studies of the legal profession found male judges all too frequently according female witnesses and lawyers less credibility—calling women attorneys "honey," "babe," "lawyerette," "little lady," even "attorney generalette"—an attitude that lasted well into the 1980s until Greatest Generation judges began retiring from the bench. And much of the humiliation at work was hidden or, perhaps worse, accepted as commonplace—the sexual harassment and requests for sexual favors, the male managers who prohibited women from wearing pants and measured the length of their skirts, the presumption that women couldn't do certain jobs, the lower pay for the exact same job, the client work that went to the less-qualified man.

Everywhere women turned outside the home it was an uphill struggle, and every cultural marker pointed to staying at home. The laws made it difficult to obtain credit or buy a home without a husband; the culture called women unfulfilled without children; it was shameful for women to be economically or sexually independent; domesticity even drove women's health priorities, reflected in the scant amount of medical research devoted to women's issues, except, of course, when it involved giving birth. Women were simply valued for their relationship with men and their families. And woe to the housewife who expressed discontent—cheerfulness was the approved emotion, so there must be something wrong with her. Not surprisingly, some scholars have found that Boomer daughters growing up in this culture identified not with their mothers in their role as homemakers but with their fathers or their peers or others outside the family. Why identify with someone society deemed inadequate and unequal?

So total was this ideology that as late as 1970, a majority of pre-Boomer Americans opposed any effort to strengthen and change women's status in society. But Boomers weren't about to let inequality and degradation remain the norm—certainly not Boomer women, and as the last few decades have borne out, they had willing partners in many Boomer men. Our nation, our norms, our daily realities, and our personal expectations and relationships—all are profoundly different and more fundamentally equal because of it.

Today, record numbers of women are entering the professions, the pulpit, politics, the arts, and the law, their aspirations no longer seen as secondary to men's. Nearly invisible in the career track half a century ago, women now hold a significant proportion of jobs once reserved almost exclusively for men—a quarter of the doctors, half the pharmacists and economists and journalists, nearly a third of all lawyers and chemists and computer scientists, about three-fifths of accountants and auditors, a sixth of the clergy, and more than half the financial managers. Now compare that with 1950, when women were only 6 percent of the doctors and 3.5 percent of the lawyers and 8 percent of the pharmacists and 10 percent of the chemists and 4 percent of the clergy. Today there are women military officers and news anchors and corporate decision makers and sports executives, all rarely if ever seen only decades ago. Today we see female war correspondents and photojournalists when a generation ago women would have been judged unfit for such work. Today, women graduating from college receive more than half of all biology degrees and almost half of all chemistry and math degrees, and it's no longer unusual to have a female physics professor, which wasn't the case just twenty years ago when 55 percent of universities had no women on their physics faculty, compared to only about 10 percent of physics departments today. In 1962, women made up only 15 percent of executives, managers, and administrators, but nowadays they're about half, and according to 1999 numbers, a larger percentage of employed women are managers compared to employed men, 32.3 percent for women versus 28.6 percent for men. These gains seem even more impressive when compared to women overseas, who aren't close to the American benchmark of nearly 50 percent female managers—in Britain women make up only 30 percent of management, in Germany 27 percent, in Japan a meager 9 percent.

Only a generation ago the workforce was largely segregated according to male and female jobs, and while some of these patterns persist—nursing and elementary school teaching remain predominantly female while construction and architecture remain predominantly male—the employment wall separating men and women has been steadily eroding. And if higher education is any indication, this erosion will accelerate in the years ahead. Whereas men received about 65 percent of the BA and MA degrees in 1960, women receive about 60 percent today, and while women received only 3 percent of all professional degrees and 11 percent of PhD's back then, they now receive, respectively, 47 and 44 percent, with women making up about half of all medical and law school students. Insofar as education correlates with income, the wage gap between men and women will likely narrow as well. Women remain quite a distance from full pay equity, making just over eighty cents for every dollar men make, and while economists say that only about half of this gap is due to entrenched and outmoded attitudes, with the other half due to factors such as women choosing motherhood, it's still a substantial difference. But the gap has narrowed significantly in the Baby Boom years—it was fifty-nine cents for every male dollar in 1981. And many women—recent MBAs, younger women, and some in the professional fields—are just a whisker shy of full equity. Since 1992, the number of women in full-time jobs who earn more than the median income of full-time working men has grown almost 70 percent, to about ten million. Further evidence that women are gaining personal and economic power can be seen in an activity that was once the exclusive domain of men: Women now buy nearly half of all new cars, according to research by General Motors.

That the work world has grown more accommodating to women and their aspirations can be seen in the annual awards given to female-friendly corporations by the nonprofit group Catalyst, a research and advisory organization that works to advance women in business. When Catalyst gave out its first awards in 1987, it recognized the Equitable Financial Companies for forming a group of senior-level women to identify the career needs of female employees, and IBM for creating a childcare resource and referral service for its workers, the first major company in the U.S. to do that. But times and norms have changed: What IBM and Equitable broke ground doing then has become routine and quite ordinary today, according to Marcia Kropf, Catalyst's vice president of research and information services. In the Eighties, Kropf says, women had to rattle the corporate cage, to say "wake up, we have a problem," to point out the cultural and structural obstacles to equal opportunity, to show how the old "organization man" approach to work kept women from contributing most effectively to their companies. Today, "with a different generation in authority," to quote Kropf, most companies understand the problem and are seeking ways to deal with it, from instituting more flexible but equally efficient work schedules to rethinking how they evaluate talent to scouring their companies for evidence of subtle bias and discrimination against female employees. These are the types of corporate programs Catalyst now recognizes, and while the business world still has plenty of adjustments to make, and women continue to face a number of subtle obstacles men don't face and never had to face, it's hard to deny that in a mere two decades, a corporate America that is notoriously slow to change has made great strides in rooting out the old demeaning attitudes toward women. Or as Kropf puts it, we no longer have to concentrate on "raising consciousness" about the problem because people get it and are finding ways to "do something about it."

Of course many women today, empowered by Boomer egalitarianism, are unwilling to wait for all of these changes to work their way through the system. They ask: If my company doesn't yet see how subtle bias can influence work responsibilities and promotion opportunities, or appreciate the need for greater balance between family and work, why should I hold my livelihood, family, and job satisfaction hostage to the hope that they'll eventually get it? Surveys indicate that men at the office are increasingly accepting women as managers, but some still resist. More and more men accept the notion that sexual harassment is not just a politically correct rule but rather a serious form of discrimination, but some men still belittle the idea. Equal opportunity safeguards have counterbalanced the old boy network, but not completely. A majority of professional women are satisfied with their balance between work and home, but many still find their employers unforgiving. Women make up about half of all managers and have made impressive gains rising up the ranks, but there are still well-documented glass ceilings at the highest levels, and many women run into glass walls that keep them in human resource jobs and don't let them advance to the line positions that control profit and loss, the ones that lead to senior management slots.

So individual women, in true Boomer spirit, have taken the initiative and since the late Seventies have been opting out of the corporate world and starting up their own businesses. In the Eighties the number of female-owned companies nearly tripled, in the Nineties it nearly doubled, and by 2000 women were running nearly 40 percent of all small businesses in America. A 1995 Yankelovich survey of Boomer women in mid career, conducted for *Fortune* magazine, found that nearly 90 percent had made or were seriously considering major changes in their lives, and leading the list was starting their own business. "The message of the day is that change is possible," *Fortune* quoted one woman saying. "You don't have to get it right the first time." So while smaller companies are exempt from the 1993 Family and Medical Leave law requiring employers to offer twelve weeks of parental leave, a majority are offering it anyway, perhaps because so many women are at the helm. It's the Baby Boom ethos not to wait for change or accept the status quo but instead to do something about it, and that's exactly what these female entrepreneurs have done. And it's a spirit of initiative that spreads far beyond work and career. Home Depot reports that when it created Do-It-Herself workshops in 2003 to teach women how to tile, install fixtures, and fix the faucets, more than 100,000 women took the course in just the first year, and demand for the course has remained high. Imagine that in the Greatest Generation days.

If there was one sector of American life more sexually segregated than the workplace in the Greatest Generation years, it was the sporting world, the arena, where men were gladiators and women barely even spectators. Writes *Washington Post* columnist Sally Jenkins, "As late as 1973, women still played half-court basketball at many state high schools, for fear they would faint. The first athletic bra wasn't invented until 1977, and women weren't allowed to run the Olympic marathon until 1984." But again in the Boomer era, what was once all but closed to women has been pried open, and with the door now unlocked millions of women are proving through action that it wasn't their physical constitution that kept them from participating in sports, as previous generations assumed, but rather the outmoded attitudes of those previous generations. Since 1972, when Congress bowed to growing pressure and enacted Title IX guaranteeing gender equity in sports, high-school female sports participation increased 847 percent, from less than 300,000 girl athletes to 2.8 million today—meaning that only one out of thirty high-school girls participated back then compared to more than one in three today. It's been likewise at the college level, where the number of women participating in intercollegiate sports programs increased from about 15,000 in 1967 to 32,000 in 1972 to more than 150,000 today. In the past two decades, varsity women's soccer has been added at nearly 850 colleges and universities, and every game of the NCAA Division I women's basketball tournament is now televised. Women are even moving into sports few imagined them pursuing, such as ice hockey and wrestling, which claims nearly 4,000 high-school girl participants, some of whom compete on the mat against boys.

Nor is it only about female jocks. The moment Boomer culture validated athletics as an acceptable female pursuit, women flocked to the gyms and tracks and treadmills, comprising a significant part of the fitness craze in the Eighties that grew even more in the Nineties, when the number of women who participated annually in more than one hundred fitness activities increased by almost 25 percent, according to the Women's Sports Foundation. Nowadays it's socially acceptable and in fact desirable and even sexy for a woman to be strong and fit with good muscle tone, quite the reverse from the aspersions cast on such women a generation ago. This generational surge toward fitness and athleticism suggests that women always had as much pride and interest in their fitness as men but were simply never allowed to show it. And in the Baby Boom era it's also acceptable for women to be as much of an armchair athlete as men always were. In the classic Barry Levinson film *Diner*, set in 1959, one of the neighborhood guys would marry his girlfriend only if she could prove her devotion to football and his beloved Baltimore Colts, so in a memorable scene he grills her about the game and the team, the subtext being that following sports is something girls didn't do, so she really must love him to do it. That's certainly not the case today, with most professional sports leagues targeting the female fan as a major growth market. In 2003, almost thirty-three million women watched the Super Bowl, more than a third of the viewing audience, and even more telling, that was almost double the number of women who tuned in to the Academy Awards that year.

To be sure, the rise of women's sports at the collegiate level has come at the expense of some men's programs, such as wrestling, which a number of schools have eliminated, creating resentment among some men, understandably so. But as much as our culture cherishes sports and doesn't want anyone denied the chance to compete, the Boomer approach simply argues that men don't have any more of a divine right to athletics than women, and if resources are tight, Boomer culture errs on the side of equity, that women are entitled to pursue their athletic goals and aspirations and enjoyment as much as men. That men's sports used to dominate athletics budgets says more about the culture than it does about women or men, and because it used to be that way doesn't mean it always has to be that way. Just look at all the dads who cheer on their soccer or basketball or softball daughters—they're as demonstrative on the sidelines as the dads watching their sons, and they're just as adamant about making sure their girls have the same athletic opportunities as the boys have. From the field to the gym to the stadium stands, sports have become a real and tangible part of women's lives in the Baby Boom era, something almost inconceivable a generation before. It's Baby Boom egalitarianism, literally leveling the playing field.

To the socially conservative critics of Boomer culture, this egalitarianism has gone much too far. Unwilling to accept that history has passed them by, and unwilling to admit anything wrong with the Fifties, these conservatives have fought back by exploiting the popular caricature of Boomers and labeling Boomer feminism as nothing more than a tantrum of selfish elites and pushy career women intent upon imposing their lifestyle on the majority of Americans. "Today in America we have a 'she-ocracy' where a minority of feminist zealots rule the culture," declares the conservative talk show host Michael Savage. "Femi-nazis" is the way radio personality Rush Limbaugh describes them. To prove their point and discredit women's gains, conservatives rather relentlessly cultivate a stereotypical image of yuppie professional moms who rush back to work soon after giving birth with little regard for their children's needs. It's an image of self-absorbed career women who put their interests ahead of their families, relegating all the nurturing to nannies but narcissistically basking in the glory of their kids' accomplishments. Most women prefer the old gender roles, these conservatives declare, and moms would rather stay at home, but they've been steamrolled by this small minority of aggressive, angry, and self-absorbed feminist elites.

But there's a problem with this conservative image: It's wrong. Driven by ideology and not reality, it ignores the facts and doesn't reflect what people want and how they live—and thus amounts to just another propaganda tool in the conservative war against Baby Boom culture. Far from being the lifestyle whim of a few elites, Boomer feminism speaks for the vast majority of Americans and the choices they make. Indeed those who condemn career moms end up condemning a lot more than just a few Yuppies, for it's not just women in heels and suits who care about their jobs—it's most American women. When the National Opinion Research Center asked Americans in 2002 whether they agreed or disagreed with the statement that "both the husband and wife should contribute to the household income," fewer than 10 percent disagreed. And these opinion numbers track with what people are actually doing. In the Greatest Generation years, most women quit their jobs after giving birth, but only a quarter do today, and while only 17 percent of moms returned to work a year after giving birth in the early 1960s, 60 percent did in the early 1990s, with 52 percent returning after six months. Among all mothers with pre-school kids, about 70 percent are now in the workforce, according to the Census Bureau. From the socially conservative perspective, these numbers translate either to millions of yuppie mothers rushing to work every day, abandoning their children for their careers, or millions of hoodwinked moms misled by a small cadre of feminist elites. But the more realistic interpretation is that most women simply want to work

and see no personal or moral conflict between pursuing a career and raising kids, and that makes them neither yuppie nor elite, just normal people seeking economic independence and fulfilling lives. When women
are asked in various surveys whether they would continue working if
they didn't need the money, as many as two-thirds say yes. That—not the
Donna Reed stereotype of Fifties sitcoms—represents the mainstream
American sentiment today.

But it's not just the number of women who work and want to work
that matters. It's how they meet their many responsibilities that undercuts
the conservative critique. Far from the Eighties yuppie icon of the Boomer
career woman in a bow-tie and business suit who so badly wants to "have
it all" that she doesn't have time for kids, the working women in Baby
Boom America have begun to reconstruct their family lives along more
egalitarian lines and have found ways to have a career path and plenty of
mommy time too. Most women have no problem being nurturers and
providers at the same time, and in fact they like it that way, contrary to the
caricature that social conservatives put forth. When a 1995 Harris survey
of working mothers asked whether they wanted to give up some family or
work duties to help balance their lives, a significant majority said no, they
like doing both. All they ask is for more flexibility so they can do it all better with less pressure and stress. And the evidence suggests they're making
it work even with all the stress and all the obstacles in their way—they're
finding a way to navigate the patchwork of leave policies and flex-time
and childcare options available to them, and striking a balance with their
working husbands. And they're doing it with almost no government support for childcare arrangements, which conservative politicians continue
to obstruct. According to University of Michigan scholars John Sandberg
and Sandra Hofferth, working women in 1997 spent about the same
amount of time with their children as stay-at-home moms did in 1981, and
because fathers in these dual-income families have increased the time they
spend with their kids, parents in 1997 dual-income married families spent
more time with their children than parents in 1981 stay-at-home mom
families. Hofferth also has documented, based on 1997 numbers, that
stay-at-home moms spend only three more hours per week actually interacting with their kids than employed married mothers do. As Sandberg

and Hofferth conclude, claims that work undermines motherhood are simply "unfounded assertions."

The Baby Boom era has brought women closer to what they've long wanted but were always denied: choices, respect for their choices, and a degree of independence and control over their lives. Women used to quip that a wife has the most high-risk career of all—handing over her economic destiny to a man. But now women at least have options to lessen that risk. And it's not that women must work to be liberated. For moms, having a choice is what matters. Follow the news media and it's all about the regrets and difficulties of making this decision—one day there's a human interest story about a working mother's anguish, and the next day there's a story about a stay-at-home mom convincing herself she did the right thing. But what these stories miss is the larger point that women now have a choice and society will accept and respect them whichever way they go. Working is now as worthy as staying at home, and vice versa. The Greatest Generation contempt for the working mom may still be extant among some social conservatives, but it has largely vanished from mainstream society—in large part because mainstream society would be expressing contempt for itself. In Baby Boom America, young girls growing up—the future athletes, scholars, scientists, entrepreneurs, doctors, lawyers, bankers, teachers, and mothers—all have choices and aspirations their mothers and grandmothers never even imagined.

Nor are careers and aspirations the only ways women are exercising choice and seeking fulfillment in our culture today. Before the Baby Boom era, society judged women solely by their relationship to men, as part of Adam's rib, but that too has changed as well, and the old maid stigma that stalked so many unmarried women is now a relic of the Greatest Generation's musty old attic. Eight in ten adults in the Fifties called a woman sick, neurotic, or immoral if she never got married, whereas today, more than eight in ten say that women who never marry can be as happy throughout life as those who do. For women who thought it wise to live with a man before marriage, the shunning and shame that greeted them decades ago has largely dissipated, with cohabitation before marriage the recommended choice among Boomers and everyone younger, a complete shift from the generations before. One study found that among women born between 1951 and 1976, nearly half—45 percent—had been in at least one cohabiting relationship as of 1995. So accepted is living together that one financial planner quipped, "Twenty years ago, grandma might have looked down on the practice, but now she is doing it herself." And unlike the unluckiest of wives in the Greatest Generation era, the stigma and disgrace of divorce that once kept women trapped in bad, abusive, cheating, or passionless marriages are gone, as are the legal impediments that frustrated even those most in need of separation and divorce. Women are now comfortable enough in their choices that they're initiating divorces at more than twice the rate of men, according to the sociologist Andrew Hacker. No longer will they settle for an emotionally unsatisfying marriage that treats them as little more than procreators, mothers, housekeepers, and caregivers.

The Baby Boom era also bid farewell to a cultural straitjacket perhaps as confining as any in human history—the denial if not abhorrence of female sexuality. For centuries the sexual double standard told women it was shameful to have sex, and even more so to enjoy it. It was women, not men, who lost virtue if they had sex outside of marriage. It was women, not men, who were told they should feel stained or defiled after sex. It was women, not men, who were taught that their private parts were dirty. Boomers certainly didn't invent the sexual revolution—it was the birth control pill, approved in 1960, that freed women to have sex without fear of pregnancy, and by the end of the decade millions of women were taking it. But it was the Baby Boom, in the span of a single generation, that turned this medical advance into a cultural norm, overturning centuries of taboos and making it acceptable for women to be both sexual beings and respectable adults, just the way it's always been for men.

This new respect for female sexuality first gained widespread acceptance on the campuses of the late 1960s, and as the pollster Daniel Yankelovich has shown, it spread rapidly throughout the Boomer generation, to the shock and horror of a resistant Greatest Generation. But it wasn't just a simple matter of agreeing to have sex. Women in the Baby Boom era have had to unlearn the fear and shame that society had taught them to associate with sex and their private parts—and to learn how sexual relations can be pleasurable, enjoyable, and natural. And the more society has accepted female sexuality, the more the old taboos have fallen—taboos that kept "good" women from initiating sex or "good" girls from asking boys out on dates or older women from finding sexual partners and satisfaction, even with younger men, a phenomenon that AARP, the lobby for older Americans, attributes to a Boomer generation that "changed the perception of older unmarried women from being 'old maids' to emancipated feminists." In the old days even children were stained when their moms didn't follow the rules, labeled "bastards" and shunned by peers if their mothers were unwed or gave birth before the ninth month of marriage. Today, as millions watch *Desperate Housewives* and *Sex in the City* and follow the suggestive banter on shows like *The View,* our culture no longer punishes women for having sex. We simply accept it as an intrinsic part of life.

As for family life, is it better or worse for all these changes? A popular myth in our culture is that the families of old were much warmer and tighter and more loving than families today, and it was the Baby Boom that created a culture of selfishness that with centrifugal force has pulled Americans and particularly American women away from the hearth and the home. Life in America was *Ozzie and Harriet* and *Leave It to Beaver* and *The Donna Reed Show,* a nation of selfless mothers and eager kids and happy endings, or so we'd like to remember. But in truth the home was never the idyllic haven we now imagine it to be. As the demographer Cheryl Russell points out in her book *The Master Trend,* "family togetherness was more duty than choice" years ago, and according to a 1939 survey she cites, "spending time with the family ranked dead last among seven favorite activities," with even a night out playing cards the preferred choice over staying home with the kids. Today we live in quite an open and candid culture, so we tend to forget that the parents of old rarely talked with their kids about intimate or personal issues, that the culture sanctioned more formal and distant and dutiful relationships between parents and their children, with aloof fathers more the norm than the exception. Typical is what teens told pollsters in 1974, when nearly half reported they were having "serious problems" with their parents, and a majority said they didn't feel comfortable speaking with their parents about personal matters. When college students in 1971 were asked about whom they most closely identified with, their families came in a distant third behind their fellow students and peers.

So if family life of old wasn't all it's cracked up to be, the question is whether families today are as bad as all our modern jeremiads proclaim them to be. And the surprising answer is that family relations in the Baby Boom era are much better and healthier than the conventional wisdom would ever admit. There's no generation gap dividing parents and children these days, and as a Gallup poll found in the Nineties, the emotional distance that characterized Greatest Generation families has largely disappeared, with more than nine in ten teens saying they're close to their parents and trust their parents to be there when they need them. "The level of disagreement and discord so evident between young people and their parents' generation thirty years ago has long since dissipated," concluded *The State of Our Nation's Youth,* a report published in 1997 by the Horatio Alger Association of Distinguished Americans. Young people today say it's their parents and not their peers who inspire them and serve as their role models—with boys and girls now looking to their moms for a sense of accomplishment, which wasn't always the case in a Greatest Generation culture that demeaned and diminished women. Fathers are much more demonstrative and involved in their children's lives, and as discussed earlier, working moms have found ways to spend almost the same amount of time doing things with their kids as mothers who stay at home. Surveys that showed large numbers of teens alienated from their parents in the Seventies now show about 80 percent having little or no difficulty getting along with their parents. One author who has written about the different generations in American history said this about Boomer parents and their children, "In the history of polling, we've never seen tweens and teens get along with their parents this well."

What we're seeing, in effect, is the Baby Boom worldview working its way through family life in America. A generation unwilling to accept entrenched authority, blind loyalty, rigid hierarchy, and stiff formality in the rest of society has applied these principles in the home. Critics scoff that Boomers try too hard to be friends with their kids, abandoning all authority in the process, but these critics mistake the Boomer insistence on explaining their parenting for not parenting at all. Boomers have no problem setting limits but also think their kids deserve to know why they're setting limits. And Boomers see no reason why they must place artificial barriers of authority between themselves and their kids. The result is that candor and openness—not rigidity and distance—have become the norms in American families today. Boomer kids "express confidence that their parents are not only interested in their problems and concerns but are also accessible and understanding," said the *State of Our Nation's Youth* study. According to surveys, most teens look to their parents for frank advice on drinking, money, careers, sex, and AIDS. Teens even praise their parents for keeping "up to date" on the music they like, with so many parents attending concerts that some arenas now have "quiet rooms" for parents to get a break from the sound. Or as the newspaper columnist Ellen Goodman wrote in 2000, "Now the whole culture encourages far more openness in families. Adoption is discussed among parents, children, and even birth mothers. Divorce, which was once hidden out of shame, is now acknowledged. So, increasingly, is homosexuality. And a whole lot of adults who were born eight pounds and six months after their parents' marriage now know they weren't premature." Whereas a generation ago young people loved their parents but felt they just didn't get it, Boomer parents today get high marks for reaching across the age divide, understanding their kids' choices, and guiding them through their predicaments—doing precisely what their parents rarely did for them.

To the critics who say that Boomers so loosened moral restraints that our culture now condones single parenthood and out-of-wedlock births, all at the expense of children, especially minority children living in poverty, it's a legitimate concern but ultimately one that blames the Baby Boom for social forces already in place by the time the first Boomer reached adulthood. The rise in out-of-wedlock births actually gained momentum in the early Sixties, under the Greatest Generation's watch, as factories deserted cities, the underclass began to grow, racial separation hardened, and no one had the foresight to address our crumbling industrial economy, which is what really harmed the most vulnerable families. In the mid Sixties, inner-city unemployment hovered at the Depression level of 20 percent, even higher for black youth, and the semi-skilled and unskilled jobs that had once pulled white immigrants out of poverty were rapidly abandoning the cities, leaving urban blacks with fewer opportunities and even less hope. An NAACP official warned in 1964 that if these trends weren't reversed, "we're going to have a permanent black underclass—permanent unemployables." A year later, Daniel Patrick Moynihan, then a Johnson administration official, warned that black families were under enormous strain because of severe and chronic unemployment, noting a 40 percent out-of-wedlock birthrate among blacks in Harlem.

So when the social conservatives attack single professional moms for undermining family values and setting a bad example—the *Murphy Brown* argument that Vice President Dan Quayle made in 1992, when he accused "today's intelligent, highly paid professional women" of "mocking the importance of fathers by bearing a child alone and calling it just another lifestyle choice"—they're simply foisting blame onto Boomers for a cancer that began to metastasize not in the days of *Murphy Brown* but in the days of *Leave It to Beaver.*

If anything, Boomers have simply recognized the increasing diversity of family life in America and in the spirit of Baby Boom egalitarianism have broadened the definition of what it means to be a family, accepting people for who they are, not what any moral or religious authority wants them to be. No longer do we define families only as married couples with kids. Families today might include a gay or lesbian couple raising a biological or adopted child, or a cohabiting heterosexual couple who have kids but just don't want to marry, or a divorced parent who merges clans with his or her new partner, or a pair of previously married senior citizens who glide into old age together. In the Baby Boom era, the structure of a family matters less than the love and interaction within it. In fact the apparent disintegration of families reflected by the relatively high number of out-of-wedlock births is somewhat misleading because about 40 percent of children born to "single mothers" are actually born to cohabiting parents, according to *American Demographics* magazine, and the Census Bureau reports that among all cohabiting households, 41 percent include children under eighteen, almost the same percentage as for married families. These statistics may even underestimate the actual numbers, the Census Bureau says, because many couples—particularly gays and lesbians—are reluctant to report their personal status to the government and thus describe themselves merely as roommates or housemates. All of this is not to say there aren't challenges when unmarried couples have children or when parents join two sets of kids under one roof. But there's no evidence that parents in these non-traditional households are any less loving or devoted to making a good home for their children.

Nor is it the case that Americans are spurning marriage—about 85 to 90 percent of American adults will marry at some point in their lives, a statistic fairly constant over the last century. But in the Baby Boom era there are simply other ways besides marriage to form a family, raise kids, and express commitment and love. Most divorced parents, for example, find new mates and return to the altar, but many choose cohabitation instead because they experienced a bitter divorce and dread putting themselves and their children through another, and many women who were abused in their first marriages fear getting trapped again and want an easier way out if the need arises. Interracial couples tend to cohabit longer before they marry—and some have kids in the interim—not because they aren't committed to one another but because they harbor lingering fears about the way society will react to them. So there are plenty of valid reasons why different types of families form, and with these many permutations we simply can't hold up marriage as the sole bellwether of family health in America. Ours is a more fluid and free society than it's ever been, with women in particular gaining rights and choices they never had before, and the family has responded organically and grown to accommodate these changes. The difference today, at least for most Americans, is that we no longer impugn the diversity and label these lifestyle choices immoral. The new norm simply tells us to accept the diversity and make it work.

What began with Baby Boomers burning their bras more than thirty years ago has turned into a prairie fire of change that reaches into every home, school, institution, office, and bedroom in America—into the most personal corners of our lives. In the span of a single generation, the Baby Boom has taken on deeply entrenched attitudes toward gender, family, women, and men—and has created choices and opportunities unimaginable just a few decades ago. For women, it's about getting the chance to express themselves in all aspects of life—and to give men that opportunity as well. Social conservatives may rail against the decline of the mythologized 1950s family, but Boomers and their progeny are as dedicated to strong families as any generation—only for them it's equality in a family that makes it strong. Progress certainly hasn't come friction free: From the personal to the political to the professional, old attitudes continue to circumscribe women's choices and lives, and neither government nor business has addressed the work-family balance in any systematic or comprehensive manner, leaving women and their families to deal with the enormous strain. But only the most blindly nostalgic would pine for the old days when women had no career options, when there were few legal protections against marital abuse, when independent women were labeled abnormal if not immoral, and when young girls who wanted more from life than marriage and kids found little if any support.

Recently a mother from Michigan wrote a *Newsweek* column about her five-year-old daughter who dreamed of playing ice hockey. The mom described her own ambivalence, wondering whether hockey with the boys was the right sport for her three-foot-nine-inch daughter. But when she finally relented and suited her girl up in shoulder pads and hockey skates, she filled with great pride at what her daughter was about to accomplish. To the mom, her daughter was a symbol of American freedom, a symbol of defiance against fundamentalist ideologies that attacked our nation on September 11. But in many ways her daughter was more a symbol of how far America has traveled in these brisk few decades of the Baby Boom era. This little girl was skating in defiance of what America used to be but thankfully is no more.

# Chapter Six
# All-American Diversity

Now I could understand the tears and the shame
She called you boy instead of your name
When she wouldn't let you inside
When she turned and said, "But honey, he's not our kind."
    —Janis Ian, "Society's Child," 1966


A black mayor? That'll be the day.
    —Lou Carruthers, soda fountain owner in the film
    Back to the Future, set in 1955


**T**here's a timeless quality to the wedding and celebration pages of the Sunday *New York Times,* where proud and beaming couples give the rest of us a peek into their vows and lives, and it was no different on May 11, 2003. But on that day, as it is every Sunday in the Baby Boom era, there was nothing timeless about the couples on these pages. Of the thirty-two couples featured, more than half were in interracial, interfaith, interethnic, lesbian, or gay relationships. The couples were black and white, Indian and Korean, Jewish and Italian, and various other combinations. Two of the weddings had "an interfaith minister" presiding, and one couple was married by a Presbyterian minister who "combined Christian and Jewish traditions." Three of the couples probably wanted to marry, but they were lesbians so their announcements described commitment ceremonies instead. In every case the celebrations seemed joyous and the parents appeared delighted to bless their children's happiness. But such bliss would have been shunned if not forbidden before the Baby Boom era, when it was taboo to marry across ethnic or religious or racial lines, and no newspaper would even have considered letting two women or men proclaim their love on its pages.

Nor were these weddings and celebrations an aberration that spring. If any of the couples honeymooned near Orlando, they might have run into the Gay Days celebration at Disney World, which attracted thousands of gays and lesbians in early June to the family-friendly theme park. Or if their destination was Washington, D.C., they might have come across a Joy of Motion dance recital full of suburban white kids moving to Street Jam and African rhythms. If they went to the cineplex, they might have seen God played by a black man in *Bruce Almighty,* which grossed almost $100 million its opening weekend. If they followed the news, they would have read all about the election of an openly gay Episcopal bishop, or about the retired generals and admirals who petitioned the Supreme Court on behalf of diversity in college admissions. Or if they preferred the gossip pages, they couldn't have missed the daily feed about Hollywood's hot couple du jour, a white guy from Boston and a Puerto Rican from the Bronx.

Or let's say some of these couples snuggled up and watched some television. They would have seen the most ethnically diverse year of TV come to an end, a year with fifty-one multiethnic ensemble series—*ER, The Practice, Without a Trace, Law & Order, Boston Public,* among others—compared to only thirteen in 1995, a 292 percent increase, which doesn't include all the reality shows with their ethnically diverse casts. If they were fans of *Dawson's Creek* and *Buffy the Vampire Slayer,* they would have bid adieu to two popular, long-running shows that embraced gay characters and storylines involving same-sex intimacy. If they were soap opera devotees, they would have been buzzing about the first ever lesbian kiss on daytime TV, on *All My Children.* If they channel surfed on cable, they would have heard about a pair of shows that would become hits that summer, one a dating game mingling gays and straights, the other a makeover show in which five gay guys teach straight men how to cook, dress, and shop. And if they enjoyed theater and caught the Tony Awards on national TV, they would have seen two male songwriters lock lips after winning for the musical *Hairspray,* a kiss that would have shut down the CBS switchboard in the Greatest Generation era but barely raised a whisper today, with only seventy-eight complaints among the eight million viewers.

Look anywhere in American culture today and it's hard to avoid the cascade of images and events and personal statements that bespeak the very rich diversity of this country. An America characterized only decades ago by stifling conformity and rigid social hierarchies and impenetrable ethnic borders has become more flexible and tolerant and porous and inclusive than at any time in its history. Boundaries that kept people from interacting or expressing themselves are now routinely crossed if not erased altogether. Those once demeaned and disgraced for being different now feel free to affirm their rights and proclaim their pride. It's not that diversity is anything new—America has always been a diverse country. But only in the Baby Boom era have we stopped trying to deny it and sincerely tried to accept it; only in the Baby Boom era do people no longer feel the need to hide who they are. America may still not be the "beloved community" envisioned by Martin Luther King, Jr., and full equality remains more a goal than a reality for too many Americans, but in just a single generation we've created a powerful new norm—an equality of worth—that has eroded the barriers of ethnicity and religion and lifestyle that for centuries kept people from seeing the humanity of their neighbors.

Nowadays we celebrate Greatest Generation Americans for their many virtues, but we do so with a dash of willful self-deception, for when they came back from defending freedom and equality and individual rights and human dignity abroad, they readily accepted and even promoted assaults on those ideals here at home—segregation, discrimination, inequality, blanket conformity and uniformity, suppression of dissent, devaluing people because they were different. During World War II, the black soldiers that weren't cleaning latrines or cooking for whites were isolated in segregated units, and while asked to sacrifice their lives for the cause of freedom, they were given the indignity of being seated behind German prisoners of war at USO concerts. White veterans returning from war were often rewarded with pay raises and public displays honoring their service, but black veterans were frequently denied both. History textbooks in the Fifties depicted black children as carefree "pickaninnies" and slavery as "benevolent in intent and on the whole beneficial in effect," or as the jazz musician Wynton Marsalis recalls, the books always showed smiling "Negroes" on plantations with never a mention of abolitionists like Harriet Tubman and Frederick Douglass. So devalued were America's black citizens that neither condemnation nor ridicule nor shame greeted a prominent Georgia senator who in 1964 proposed an amendment that would result in the export of Southern blacks to the rest of the country.

But blacks were only the most egregious example in an America that degraded those who stood outside the white Protestant mainstream. In a 1948 survey, about half of Americans said they preferred not to work side by side with people of different ethnic groups, including Italians, blacks, Chinese, Jews, Mexicans, and Filipinos, among others. Houses came with restrictive covenants that kept entire neighborhoods not only free of blacks but free of Jews. So imposing was this denial of diversity that those with different attitudes or lifestyles or religious beliefs felt safest only when hiding them. Today we remember the 1967 film *Guess Who's Coming to Dinner* as a breakthrough social commentary about tolerance and intermarriage, but back then the director tried to conceal the interracial storyline for fear that the studio would spike the project—and even today two-thirds of Greatest Generation Americans would oppose a close relative marrying a black, and almost half would oppose it with a Hispanic, suggesting that if Greatest Generation whites still had their way, the attitudes back then would remain the norm today. In the Greatest Generation era, America may have been the home of the brave, but it was never fully the land of the free.

With the relative fluidity and egalitarianism of social relations today, we tend to forget what it was like back then, but it would be hard for historians to conclude that the change in America during the Baby Boom era has been anything but breathtaking. To create our culture of diversity, Boomers had to upend the rigid social structure of the Fifties and challenge centuries of entrenched norms and attitudes about race, ethnicity, religion, and sexuality. Boomers saw the Greatest Generation years as a cultural vise that forced a rigid conformity on people in seeming contradiction to our national ideals. So they asked how America could celebrate freedom and democracy when minorities and gay people didn't feel free to be themselves. And they asked how Americans could talk about equality when some among us were deemed lesser Americans simply because of who they were and how they looked. This denial of dignity was clear to Boomers, even if it wasn't to their elders. As Daniel Yankelovich found in a 1971 survey of college students, the vast majority were deeply troubled by America's treatment of homosexuals, blacks, Indians, and Mexican-Americans, with 84 percent citing widespread discrimination against homosexuals, and the others not far behind.

For Boomers, it's never been a matter of simply ending discrimination and leaving it at that. Just as peace is not the absence of war, equality is not the absence of discrimination. The civil rights movement and Holocaust made opposition to racism and anti-Semitism core parts of the American identity, but Boomers have taken it further. If hatred arises from denying the humanity of people, so evident in the Holocaust and Jim Crow, the only way to end hatred is to affirm that humanity, and thus Boomers have created a culture of diversity that seeks to validate the attributes of previously despised and outlier groups. In the Baby Boom era we have enlarged the melting pot to include all our differences, not just European ethnicity, with neither race nor nationality nor sexual orientation too bold or spicy or different to be added into the stew.

In the last decade or so, Boomers have made a cottage industry of studying their genealogy and family roots, with millions surfing the Net to learn their heritage, and they know that when immigrants arrived in America years ago, the Jews attended yeshiva, the Irish formed their political clubs, and the Italians, Poles, Germans, and almost all other immigrants built local ethnic societies that still endure today. Critics back then—much like critics today—accused these immigrants of isolating themselves, of un-American behavior, of failing to learn the language, wondering why they just didn't defer and fit in. But what these ethnic groups really were doing was enriching America, and it's because they held on to their differences that we're a more diverse and interesting society than we were a century ago. In many ways Baby Boomers celebrate diversity in the same spirit as their immigrant grandparents, but without the defensiveness of doing it in a culture that demanded 100-percent Americanism and scorned ethnics as unwashed masses. Boomers have simply restored the idea that diversity enhances society, that there should be no shame in being different, that America is poorer for uniformity, that all of us should appreciate the many ways to be an American.

Central to the Boomer culture of diversity is the idea that all people of all backgrounds and orientations have equal worth—that no one ethnicity or religion or lifestyle is better or worse, superior or inferior to another. This is democracy at its core, the notion that all of us, as long as we do no harm to others, deserve respect and equal rights in society, and that because of our differences—not in spite of them—each of us enriches the whole. Perhaps the most noble example of diversity in action is the disability rights movement, which is based on the idea that even those with the most crippling handicap can contribute equally to society if given the chance, and that because of their disability they have a unique perspective from which we all can learn. So as a country we've spent enormous sums of money to build ramps and hire sign-language interpreters and construct wheelchair-friendly buses, all to accommodate a small minority that was ignored and warehoused just a generation ago but now merits the same respect and worth as anyone else. It's an equality well worth the cost. In fact one reason affirmative action tears at our fabric is that it both embraces and violates the idea of equal worth—and thus when polls frame affirmative action as a tool to undo centuries of damage and give voice to a people long denied, majorities support it, saying it's worth the cost, but when polls frame it as simply giving preference to some over others, majorities oppose it, saying the cost is too high.

Getting to a culture of equal worth has not been easy, and it remains an ongoing challenge in Baby Boom America, one that Boomers have pursued with relentless determination and, thankfully, considerable success over the past few decades. For what it entails is peeling away layer upon layer of attitude and prejudice and even visceral disgust that the majority has felt for any number of minorities—a process that liberates and threatens all at once. A society that values equal worth must accept that minorities and all others outside the mainstream have the same talents, hopes, aspirations, emotions, and dreams as anyone in the presumed majority—and thus as a nation we must overcome longstanding assumptions that blacks and Hispanics and other minorities are lazy and unmotivated and lacking the same talents as anyone else. A society that values equal worth must accept that different people have different styles, that a West Indian who hums to herself at work is not slacking but instead is working just as efficiently as the buttoned-down white guy in the next cubicle. A society that values equal worth must re-imagine the term "all-American" so that it truly encompasses all Americans, meaning not just those with blond hair and blue eyes but people of every hue and background and ethnicity. A society that values equal worth must address the deep and oft-buried revulsion of the majority toward the minority, a revulsion that shows up in the offhanded but all-too-frequent comments among whites equating black people with monkeys, or the old polls in which whites say blacks smell different, or the occasional request for a different rental car because the last one smelled like a black person drove it, or the notion that a child is tainted if he or she has any black blood, or the physical disgust many heterosexuals feel toward effeminate men or masculine women or expressions of same-sex intimacy. A society that values equal worth must see the humanity of all its members. That is what diversity in Baby Boom America is all about.

For an entire generation, Boomers have been raising these issues and confronting these prejudices and drilling down into these deeply rooted and centuries-old preconceptions—and while critics accuse Boomers of creating a politically correct climate, the result has been a culture that values its different citizens in ways unimaginable just decades before. So today we see gay celebrities hosting daytime talk shows and hardened rap artists adding their voice to politics and movies like *Antwone Fisher, Monster's Ball, Philadelphia, The Birdcage,* and even a slapstick like *Meet the Fockers* portraying the human side of diversity—of young black men and gay couples and relationships that reach across racial and religious lines. Only those most resistant refuse to accept it. Indeed the evidence suggests that the more Americans are exposed to diversity, the more accepting and inclusive they become. Studies of diversity on college campuses show that students whose living and learning environments are most racially integrated at school tend to lead the most integrated lives after graduation. Other studies show that white students gain a broader perspective on issues when exposed to minority peers in the classroom. It works even at the most personal of levels: One study of college students found that the more they saw televised images of same-sex relationships, the more they grew accustomed to them and the less discomfort they felt.

Boomers have never been fans of artificial barriers, and as our culture continues to emphasize a diversity among equals, we're seeing more and more Americans do what was unthinkable a generation ago—crossing social boundaries once considered inviolable. These boundaries, besides separating people, also maintained the old social stratifications and in the process sustained the old prejudices and inequalities. So the very act of crossing these boundaries means that Americans in the Baby Boom era are shedding the ethnic hierarchies and social attitudes that for much of our history contradicted the democratic spirit of our nation—and what's unfolding is a modern America based on equal worth and constantly rejuvenated by an ever-fermenting social mobility. "Intergroup tolerance" has increased significantly in the last few decades, observed the director of the General Social Survey at the National Opinion Research Center (NORC) in 2001, and "antipathy among groups is declining as ethnic images become less negative and preference barriers to intergroup contact decline." We have become an America with a diversity of differences, permeable boundaries, and a growing appreciation for the many resulting permutations. Such is the context for the *New York Times* wedding and celebration pages of May 11, 2003.

So in America today, the most intimate and psychologically entrenched taboos are falling fast. Even as late as the 1970s, most white American adults opposed intermarriage, about half supported laws against it, and almost half went so far as to say that it would "violate God's law for people of different colors to marry and produce mixed-blood children." Nowadays, as many as half of all teens say they've dated across racial or ethnic lines, including more than a third of all white teens, and most of these are "serious" relationships. It's safe to say that most of these teens would not have been so forthcoming had their culture and their families not approved, and indeed among those who have dated interracially, 90 percent said their parents had no problem with it. In one survey that asked whites for their reaction if a family member was going to marry a black, only 9 percent said they wouldn't be able to accept it, and another survey found that only 15 percent of parents would try to dissuade their son or daughter from dating someone of a different race.

And teens aren't the only ones crossing racial and ethnic lines. Research on marriages during the 1990s shows that about three-fourths of Italian-Americans, four-fifths of Polish-Americans, nearly half of Jewish-Americans, two-thirds of Japanese-Americans, two-fifths of native-born Hispanic-Americans, and about half of native-born Asian-Americans were marrying someone from outside their ethnic group, all of which continues a trend that accelerated when Boomers began to take their vows in the

Sixties and Seventies. Nor is religion the impregnable barrier it used to be: According to the 2001 American Religious Identification Survey, nearly a quarter of all adults now live in households that cross denominational or religious lines, and with younger couples replacing their more homogeneous elders in the adult population, that number is likely to swell. "Almost no white American extended family exists today without at least one member who has married across what two generations ago would have been thought an unbridgeable gap," one demographer observed in 1993. Or as the author Gregory Rodriguez put it in an article for *The Atlantic Monthly*, "Americans cross racial lines more often than ever before in choosing whom to sleep with, marry, or raise children with."

As for the black-white boundary, the most impervious of all, the one hardened by centuries of intolerance and dehumanization, the one affirmed wholeheartedly by Greatest Generation Americans, there's evidence that it too is gradually becoming more porous in the Baby Boom era. Intermarriage rates for blacks still lag far behind those for other ethnic groups, no doubt a product of the old racial taboos, ongoing prejudice, and continuing residential segregation, but outside of the marital radar there's much more interracial commotion going on, with blacks and whites cohabiting at about twice the rate they're marrying. The latest figures show that about one in seven cohabiting black men lives with a white partner, that white women are about three times more likely to live with a black man than to marry him, and that black women are one-and-a-half times more likely to live with a white man than to marry him. As one scholar from the University of Michigan's Institute for Social Research observed after looking at cohabitation patterns, "Our findings suggest that there is much greater intimate contact between the races than marriage data imply. The social distance between racial groups is not as great as other studies suggest it is."

That these relationships are no longer forbidden fruit is also seen in how the children of black-white relationships are identified. It used to be that Americans simply accepted the "one drop of blood" rule, meaning that a child with one drop of black blood was black, a rule built not on any sense of black pride but on the dehumanizing idea that anyone with any black heritage is tainted and stained. But today in the Baby Boom era, interracial kids increasingly refuse to identify only with their minority parent; more and more they call themselves "multiracial," a category the Census added for its 2000 count, living proof that Americans are beginning to celebrate the crossing of boundaries that once kept us separated and apart. And that identity is bound to increase, one researcher estimates, for when all races are added to the mix, about one-fifth of adult Americans have a close family member of a different race, and according to a study by the Population Research Center in Portland, Oregon, 37 percent of African-Americans, 40 percent of Asian-Americans, and almost two-thirds of Hispanic-Americans will claim mixed ancestry by the year 2100. To the noted demographer William H. Frey, senior fellow at the Milken Institute and a professor at the State University of New York at Albany, all of this could mark "the beginning point of a blending of the races."

Nor are love and family the only areas where the old boundaries are eroding—it's almost everywhere in America, in culture and the marketplace and the images that construct our media reality. The authors Joel Kotkin and Thomas Tseng call it "post-ethnic America," a nation of blending and intersecting cultures and identities "in full bloom on American streets and in the marketplace, changing long-standing notions of ethnicity and race and reshaping interpersonal relationships in a manner that would have been unthinkable a generation ago." Using the proverbial white kid who buys hip-hop music, they argue that personal identity especially among younger Americans is shaped more by cultural preferences than by skin color or ethnic heritage, which means young people feel free to adopt and borrow and blend with a diversity of cultures and don't feel bound to any archetypal ethnic image of what they're supposed to be.

In music, art, advertising, media, cinema, and literature, we see a diversity of equals that draws on our various cultures but moves easily among them. All the more remarkable is the prominence of blacks and Latinos in this cultural stew, because only a few decades ago, in the Greatest Generation years, they were valued for producing little more than good dance music. Even the beauty ideal is expanding across ethnic lines—with the more ethnic lush lips and full bottoms replacing the prim and proper

WASP look that used to prevail. Boomers who intoned "black is beautiful" in the Sixties understood that ideal images have an impact on how we imagine and treat each other. How could it not be when white features were considered desirable and black features unappealing? So in a more egalitarian culture, with a more democratic notion of beauty, we're beginning to see the ethnic images meld. When Betty Crocker decided to revise its image of the ideal American woman in 1996, it used a computer-generated composite drawn from seventy-five women of different racial and ethnic backgrounds. Indeed our self-image as a nation is no longer restricted to the prototypical white American heroes of old. We're as much Freddie Adu as Mia Hamm, Derek Jeter as Curt Schilling, Tiger Woods as Phil Mickelson, Pete Sampras as Serena Williams. An America that used to see itself as exclusively Christian and white with a little European ethnicity thrown in is now partly black or Latino or Asian or Jewish or Muslim as well as Christian and white and ethnic, each distinctive but also mixed together. And while this giving and borrowing among our ethnic diversity remains a work in progress, and not all Americans are yet comfortable with it, what's clear is that there's no turning back from the multiculturalism that began in the Sixties when Boomers insisted on recognizing and respecting the diversity within the whole. Or as the author and former *Wall Street Journal* writer Leon Wynter observed, today's youth have "never known an America in which non-whites didn't occupy a disproportionately large space in . . . popular culture."

This free-trade zone among ethnic groups is also being replicated across the boundary of sexual orientation, with mainstream society beginning to accept that homosexuality is simply a part of life and slowly welcoming once-despised lesbians and gays into our community of cultural diversity. As the Yankelovich poll cited earlier shows, Boomers even in the early Seventies were deeply troubled by the way Greatest Generation society loathed homosexuals, and through a combination of Boomer tolerance and gay pride, the great bazaar of American diversity now includes lesbians and gays, no matter how anxious it makes more traditional Americans.

Our new willingness to travel between gay and straight worlds was perhaps best illustrated by two shows that aired the summer of 2003, *Queer*

*Eye for the Straight Guy* on Bravo and *Straight Plan for the Gay Man* on Comedy Central, one about gay guys teaching a straight guy to dress and cook with style, the other about straight guys showing gay guys how to shoot guns and act "manly," and in neither case were the straight guys threatened by their proximity to the gays, and by implication the viewing audience wasn't threatened either. The stereotypical images that used to divide heterosexual and homosexual men have begun to dissolve as well, with the "limp-wristed sissy" portrayal of gays giving way to muscle-bound gay guys who pump iron at the gym, and the aloof, laconic "real man" icon giving way to what one marketing firm has cleverly branded "metrosexuals," straight men who care about grooming and style and scent and express their emotions openly. This crossing of lines is also evident in contemporary literature, where gay characters joust with their straight friends, each advising the other about life. As one author wrote in a column about the demise of gay bookstores, "The line between gay and mainstream fiction is blurring. Heterosexual writers no longer omit gay characters from their universes; authors formerly categorized as gay writers are now reaching mainstream readers." In this Baby Boom culture of equal worth, homosexuals no longer must hide who they are, and as they brave the lingering bigotry aimed their way and move toward full inclusion in America's diversity, they become the sexual version of an ethnic group, giving and gaining from everyone else, mixing into our melting pot.

To critics of the Baby Boom, the likes of Robert Bork and Bill O'Reilly and William Bennett, all this diversity has gone too far. As they see it, Boomer culture has veered too far from their Norman Rockwell image of the "real America," and they complain that politically correct Boomers ever since the Sixties have imposed an ethos of group entitlement and victimization that has balkanized America into warring ethnic and identity communities. To be sure, it's easy to seize on the occasional excesses of some diversity proponents as evidence of an ideology run amok—as when an education task force from New York proclaimed various minorities "victims of an intellectual and educational oppression." But a corrective that goes too far at times doesn't mean a corrective isn't needed. To Boomers, diversity is not an ideology but rather a recognition of a reality that's been too long repressed—that many different people built and continue to build this country in large and small ways. So what Boomers want is quite simple: an acceptance and indeed embrace of this diversity. If Boomer culture sometimes emphasizes group rights, it's only to ensure a fair chance for those who would have gotten no chance just a few decades ago and whose fair chance today is still hindered by the lingering prejudice and bias against them. Only by validating the equal worth of once disdained and disparaged groups can we bury the old stereotypes and eliminate the excuses and rationalizations that have been used to diminish the individuals born into these groups.

It may well be that some critics of Boomer diversity are simply angry that their way is not the only way anymore—and that they can't pick and choose who gets added to the melting pot. In many unequal societies, the majority try to do the speaking for the minority, claiming to know the minority's thinking and aspirations, and often the minority nod their heads in agreement, not because they agree with the majority but because they fear what the majority will do to them if they disagree. And so the majority often think that their worldview is universal, that they had all the answers, and that minorities who disagree are uppity and presumptuous and simply don't belong. We saw this in the segregated South, as white politicians constantly told the nation what the Negroes wanted, and the black citizens back home often stayed silent, not wanting to arouse the wrath of angry whites. Even during the civil rights movement, white liberals felt most comfortable when making decisions, but once blacks said they wanted control of the organizations representing them, and once they started questioning the racial dynamics and power relationships within these organizations, many of these well-meaning whites left angry and embittered, demonizing their former civil rights allies.

But in more equal societies, in societies that respect diversity, members of the majority that claim to speak for minorities are often scrutinized to see whether they're accurately representing minority views or merely projecting their own interests onto the minority. And that scrutiny, that questioning of motives, often creates resentment among those in the majority most unwilling to accept that theirs is just one worldview, not the only worldview. So the more their preeminence is challenged, the more they view it as an attack—not simply as the creative tension of a more equal society sorting out its different perspectives. To them, diversity is an uncomfortable new reality, and the more they see it celebrated, the more they magnify their discomfort, and the more they magnify their discomfort, the more they see minority groups trying to unravel society and impose their will on everyone else. Typical of this complaint is what the talk show host Sean Hannity wrote in his book *Let Freedom Ring,* where he wails against "multicultural madness" and questions whether diversity and our culture of tolerance have gone too far. But only a few chapters earlier he describes with pride how his parents "never shied away from their Irish Catholic roots," and in fact "celebrated them," sending him not to public schools but to parochial schools "that would reinforce the faith, the heritage" of his family. "My parents' primary concern," Hannity writes, "was for us to know who we were, where we came from, and to be proud of it while learning how to pursue the American dream for ourselves." Now if an African-American or Latino or Asian or even a gay or lesbian wrote these words, Hannity might excoriate them for demanding special privilege or refusing to assimilate. Diversity for him—and for many of his conservative comrades—ended with the great European immigration of a century ago.

But even if diversity's critics don't understand it, most Americans of the Baby Boom era do. When asked in 1995 whether the growing number of minorities—and the decline of non-Hispanic whites to only about half the population by 2050—makes them uneasy about America's future, almost two-thirds said no. When asked in 2002 if creating a harmonious society means recognizing that "each ethnic group has the right to maintain its own unique traditions," 85 percent agreed or strongly agreed. When asked again in 2002 if "harmony in the United States is best achieved by downplaying or ignoring ethnic differences," only 38 percent agreed. A 1998 survey about higher education found majority support for required courses on both diversity and Western civilization. Americans today simply see no contradiction between diversity and being American. And as the children of Boomers grow into adulthood, acceptance of diversity will become even more widespread. In a 2000 survey asking whether the expected racial and ethnic changes over the next twenty-five years would be good or bad for America, almost a third of pre-Boomers said bad or very bad, a sentiment shared by only 16 percent of Boomers and those younger.

Perhaps even more telling than these attitudes is how our major institutions have internalized the diversity norm that Boomers initiated in the Sixties with the simple demand that we end prejudice and respect each other. In the Greatest Generation era, corporations and universities and even the military were simply the preserves of white men, and a minority in the ranks was considered an interloper lucky to be there, expected to defer and remain silent. Nowadays, it's increasingly common for major corporations to tie bonuses to how their managers meet diversity goals and to require a diverse slate of candidates for all executive searches. And these diversity goals are not merely about numbers or about kowtowing to some politically correct version of what's right. Businesses have come to understand a basic lesson of our diverse culture, that the majority can't always speak for the minority, and thus a homogeneous workforce may miss vital cues critical to gaining a market share that is growing more global and diverse. As Alcoa, Boeing, General Electric, Kellogg, Merck, Nike, Proctor & Gamble, Sara Lee, Shell, Xerox, and fifty-five other major companies wrote in a Supreme Court brief supporting diversity in college admissions, a commitment to diversity benefits their businesses because it uproots the subtle stereotyping that continues to stifle and demoralize minority employees, and because more diverse perspectives lead to better problem solving and therefore to better products and services for their varied markets. Such sentiments might as well have been written by a liberal Boomer college student in the early Seventies.

It's no different in our educational institutions, from grade school to graduate school, with inclusion and tolerance now central to the public school curriculum and more than two-thirds of colleges and universities requiring students to take at least one course dealing with cultural or ethnic diversity. High schools and colleges may not always be meccas of harmony, and black and white and Latino and Asian students don't always sit at the same cafeteria tables, but the media's need to report conflict sometimes overshadows the growing reality that for most of these students diversity is neither special nor unusual but simply a fact of life, and that the diversity message resonates with them at a personal and intellectual level.

In a 1998 survey of students at a large state university, more than 90 percent who had taken a required course on cultural diversity said they would have taken courses with diversity content even if they weren't required. Other evidence suggests that students in more diverse educational environments seek out more diverse social interactions and study groups. To conservative critics, it's the elites who impose diversity on a Main Street that prefers to be left alone, but as the education reporter Jay Mathews discovered, it may well be that Main Street is just as interested in diversity as the so-called elites. When Mathews asked *Washington Post* readers in 2003 which factors they considered most important in selecting a good school, he "was surprised at how many parents wanted to know the ethnic character of a school's student body." In the past, Mathews observed, "this might have indicated a sad desire to avoid race-mixing," and he expected the same today, but instead, the responses he got "made it clear they want their children to go to schools with MORE, not fewer, children of ethnicities other than their own." In the Baby Boom era the norm has simply changed, and we now expect our schools and colleges to promote rather than reject diversity.

Even more compelling is how the diversity norm has transformed the military, which was riddled with racial problems in the Vietnam era but now may be the most racially progressive institution in the country, embracing diversity rather than just dealing with it, further evidence that Baby Boom values have reached into corners of society that few would have expected. In the army, for example, promotion decisions are scoured for evidence of hidden or unconscious discrimination, and officers up for advancement are evaluated on how well they've created a bias-free climate. At Patrick Air Force Base near Cocoa Beach, Florida, the Defense Department trains equal opportunity officers at its Defense Equal Opportunity Management Institute, asking them for almost four months of soul-searching and education about prejudice and power and discrimination. "The Army is not race-blind; it is race-savvy," write Charles C. Moskos and John Sibley Butler in their book on race in the army, *All That We Can Be*. "Cognizance of race is used to further nonracist goals." It's not that the military has eliminated all ethnic tensions—not even the most tolerant institutions can do that—but it has created such a culture of ethnic equals that men and women who serve are far more likely to cross racial boundaries in all the realms of their lives, intermarrying at significantly higher levels than those who never served, and living in some of the most racially integrated neighborhoods in the country.

Diversity is so well rooted in Baby Boom America that its absence looks odd and resistance to it seems shrill. Newspapers that once ignored African-American life and buried hate crime reports now require photo editors to diversify the images on their pages. Ads that once excluded African-Americans or relegated them to the background now feature multiracial casts or African-Americans in key roles—with African-Americans now comprising 15–20 percent of the actors in television commercials. Promotional materials from companies and organizations and universities are a veritable United Nations of diversity. All of them are merely reflecting America's diverse reality—and not doing it, showing only all-white faces in a brochure, for example, seems odd and anomalous.

Just a generation ago it was diversity proponents who came off as strident, upsetting the settled order of the Greatest Generation years, but today diversity proponents represent the mainstream and the stridency is usually found in the deep recesses of conservative media, where angry talk show hosts complain that our shining city on a hill is being contaminated by demanding minorities. But as the Republican Party learned in the early Nineties, when more and more Americans began to perceive it as the party of intolerance—a party epitomized by the nativist rhetoric of Patrick Buchanan and the racially coded symbols of its campaign ads—such stridency only alienates mainstream Americans in the Baby Boom era, who increasingly reject the sky-is-falling view of a diverse America. George W. Bush certainly got the message when he crafted his "compassionate conservative" slogan for the 2000 campaign, reassuring voters that his tent is big and inclusive. And even when the policies of his administration veer from diversity goals, his rhetoric still hews to the diversity norm. "I strongly support diversity of all kinds, including racial diversity in higher education," he said when explaining why he opposed a college admissions diversity program that was before the Supreme Court in 2003. Flouting the diversity norm was just not in his political interest.

So ingrained is the diversity norm that xenophobic messages that once helped win elections are now treated as politically toxic, as in 2002 when the Iowa Republican Party repudiated a State Assembly candidate who wrote supporters an e-mail questioning whether her Democratic opponent, an immigrant from India who had lived in Iowa for thirty years and served two terms on the local school board, could truly represent Iowans. "How is this person adequately prepared to represent Midwest values and core beliefs," the Republican candidate asked, "let alone understand and appreciate the constitutional rights guaranteed to us in writing by our Founding Fathers? (Not her Founding Fathers.)" Perhaps even more revealing is how the Republican, in an effort to salvage her candidacy and undo the damage after the e-mail was made public, tried using Houdini logic to convince voters that it was she, not her opponent, who was the true defender of diversity. "Will a person raised to function in the upper caste of India, the most repressive form of discrimination on the planet, be able to shed such repressionist views and fully and effectively represent the citizens of House District 36?" The ruse didn't work: The immigrant candidate won in a landslide.

What may be the most convincing evidence that diversity and tolerance and inclusion have become the core values of Baby Boom America can be found in the growing acceptance of gays and lesbians in mainstream institutions and daily life. Even after it became inappropriate and indecorous to express any form of racial bigotry in public, many Americans continued to disparage and belittle homosexuals openly, and they did it with few qualms and too often with overt hostility, leading some to call gay bashing the last socially acceptable prejudice. Although racial bigots occasionally used religion and morality to justify their racism, such a rationale never caught on, perhaps because it was so blatantly contradictory, but those who hate homosexuals are quite fervent and unapologetic in claiming to represent religious tradition and Biblical law, professing righteousness without shame. In 2003, one school in suburban Little Rock even punished a gay student for discussing his sexual orientation by forcing him to spend hours listening to Biblical admonitions against homosexuality.

So it's all the more remarkable, given the religious and cultural hurdles, how acceptance of homosexuality has entered the mainstream of American life in the Baby Boom era. To religious and social conservatives, this acceptance has been forced on America through pressure from the "politically correct elite." But the real reason is that Boomers have simply changed the culture, creating a diversity norm built on tolerance, refusing to condemn or demonize people for being different. It's what Daniel Yankelovich found in a 1973 survey of college youth, when only 25 percent called homosexual relations morally wrong, an outlook diametrically opposed to the prevailing sentiment in the Greatest Generation era but one that represents a larger worldview that now predominates in Baby Boom America. And one by one our mainstream institutions have been opening themselves to lesbians and gays, showing how fully they've embraced the Baby Boom norm of equality amid our diversity.

Among Fortune 500 companies, more than two hundred and twenty-five offered health benefits to domestic partners as of October 2004, compared with only ten in 1993, and more than three hundred of these companies—including Wal-Mart, one of the most conservative corporations in America—specifically prohibit discrimination based on sexual orientation. Coors, once considered the bête noire of liberalism because its owners supported right-wing causes, not only provides domestic partner benefits but aggressively sponsors gay events—such as the Los Angeles Outfest, a gay and lesbian film festival—all part of a gay and lesbian outreach effort initiated in the 1990s by Mary Cheney, Vice President Dick Cheney's daughter. Not to be outdone, other beer companies compete for the gay consumer, worried little that it would alienate their macho male customers. And it's increasingly the same with sports, with major league baseball teams—among them the Phillies, Cubs, Athletics, Red Sox, Rangers, Mets, Pirates, and Giants—now holding gay community days at the ballpark. Some companies simply add gay themes to their advertising storylines, treating them as a non-issue, a matter-of-fact part of life, as when John Hancock insurance mentions who "came out" in a commercial about a twenty-fifth class reunion, or when Miller shows two women ogling a pair of guys who smile back but walk away, clasping each other's hands. Avis promotes its policy of including domestic partners as additional drivers, and local companies pressure their municipal governments to go after the gay tourist, with Philadelphia launching a three-year, one-million-dollar advertising and public relations campaign in 2004 to promote the city as gay-friendly. Even the home of NASCAR racing and muscle beaches seems comfortable with diversity. "Daytona Beach Promotes Summer Break for Gay, Lesbian Travelers," blares a headline in the *Orlando Sentinel*.

Slowly but surely our schools are also broadening the definition of diversity to include sexual orientation. As of October 2004, more than twenty-eight hundred schools around the country, even in the South, have active "gay-straight" clubs, which bring gay and straight students together to discuss their social lives and attitudes (up from sixteen hundred schools two years earlier). Schools are always cultural battlegrounds because of all the impressionable minds at stake, so we hear a great deal in the media about the occasional superintendent who shuts down all school clubs to keep one of these gay-straight groups from meeting. But what we don't hear is how students and parents in these twenty-eight hundred communities have accepted the clubs and the idea behind them. In the Greatest Generation era large majorities supported firing known gay teachers, but Americans today overwhelmingly reject that, the only exception being older Americans, a majority of whom still favor firing. And when Gallup asked adults in 1999 whether schools should teach "acceptance of people with different sexual orientations, that is, homosexuals or bisexuals," 55 percent agreed. It's even more accepted at college, where Boomer educators and their students share a common ground on diversity issues. Tolerance and acceptance are staples of dormitory programming, and most major colleges have gay and lesbian resource centers that are either run by administrators or sponsored by students. These programs simply reflect the tolerant majority among younger Americans: A 2001 poll of high-school sophomores, juniors, and seniors found that two-thirds supported giving gay marriage the same legal status as traditional marriage. Accepting homosexuality is just not a problem for today's youth—the children of Boomers.

The one institution that most visibly reflects the mainstreaming of homosexuality is mass media. "We don't expect any huge backlash," said the chairman of MTV Networks when he announced plans for a cable channel aimed at a gay audience, citing public opinion polls showing increasing acceptance of gays. MTV should know, as it saw nothing but rising audience numbers for its breakthrough reality show, *The Real World*, which featured a number of gays over the years and achieved its highest ratings when documenting the plight of a gay cast member dying of AIDS. Granted, it's young people that watch *The Real World*, but among shows targeted to all audiences, one of the most popular in recent years is *Will & Grace*, an NBC sitcom named after roommates whose gay and straight social lives collide, and one of the most widely watched shows in television history, *ER*, featured an ongoing storyline about Dr. Kerry Weaver's lesbian relationship. When the winner of the first *Survivor* turned out to be a gay man, viewers barely cared or noticed.

Until the 1960s, Hollywood was governed by a production code that prohibited the portrayal of gay or lesbian characters as well as any direct or indirect discussion of homosexual issues. And later, when TV producers tried showing gay relationships as normal and acceptable, the networks remained skittish, fearful of mainstream America's reaction, in one case forcing the drama *Picket Fences* to reshoot a scene so that viewers wouldn't see two teenage girls kissing, and in another case pulling a *thirtysomething* broadcast from the rerun lineup because of a scene with two men in bed. But today, with Boomer culture finally preeminent, with the American mainstream more accepting, with *Will & Grace* and *Queer Eye for the Straight Guy* and *Dawson's Creek* commanding large audiences and a cop show like *Law & Order* sympathetically portraying the transgendered issue and even World Wrestling Entertainment holding a mock gay wedding for its championship tag-team pair, complete with a gravy boat sent by the Gay & Lesbian Alliance Against Defamation—in other words, with gay issues woven so seamlessly into our culture, all of the old worries and concerns seem so preposterous, much ado about nothing except perhaps the bitterness, fear, and vindictiveness of a bygone value system. As the *New York Times* columnist Maureen Dowd noted when Madonna and Britney Spears French-kissed on stage at the 2003 MTV Video Music Awards, "it seemed more stale than shocking."

Indeed what used to be hushed up or guardedly discussed or treated with a dash of shame or embarrassment in the media is now out in the open, part of our public dialogue, increasingly covered with the same candor as any other part of American life. "Gay and lesbian issues are now so openly discussed in the mainstream media that it's almost as if gay literature were no longer niche publishing," a reporter who covers the book business observed. In news and feature reporting, some of the major daily newspapers are simply treating gay and lesbian families as just another household in the diverse neighborhood, as when *The New York Times* included a gay couple in an article on second homes, or when one of the four living rooms featured in *The Washington Post Magazine* came from a gay couple's home. As of 2004, newspapers in all twenty-five top media markets and in forty-eight of the top fifty—among them Dallas, St. Louis, Nashville, Salt Lake City, Montgomery, and Atlanta—were accepting same-sex union announcements, most of them on or next to their wedding pages.

Outside of organized religion, politics is typically one of the last institutions to embrace social change, with politicians often living in fear of angry backlash from those desperate to preserve the old ways. But as Baby Boom values continue to work their way through society, even politicians are moving toward acceptance of gays and lesbians into the American mainstream. We've certainly come a long way from the early Fifties when Wyoming senator Lester Hunt gave up his reelection bid and later shot and killed himself in his Senate office because he feared that Senator Joseph McCarthy would expose his son's arrest for homosexual behavior, or what was then called a morals charge. Nowadays, openly gay men and women serve in Congress, some even listing their domestic partners in congressional guidebooks, and even in the Bible Belt openly gay men and women have won local elections, including the remarkable story of a lesbian who in 2004 was elected sheriff in Dallas County, Texas. It used to be that district attorneys prosecuted gays and lesbians for lewdness and immorality, but when an acknowledged lesbian ran for San Diego District Attorney in 2002, no one in that conservative city made an issue of her homosexuality, and it mattered little to the voters, who elected her. Even in the Republican Party, the ideological home of the religious right, there's a Republican Unity Coalition led by former president Gerald Ford and former senator Alan Simpson, neither known for liberalism, and comprised of gay and straight politicians dedicated to rooting out homophobia and making homosexuality a non-issue in the party. When the culturally moderate congressman Richard Gephardt ran for president in 2004, he never shied away from the fact that his daughter was gay, sending constituents and colleagues a Christmas family photo that included his daughter arm-in-arm with her lesbian partner. Nor has Vice President Dick Cheney ever tried to hide or distance himself from his daughter's lesbianism.

Politicians rarely lead on an issue like this, so these ultimate public pulse-takers must be detecting a more tolerant and accepting worldview among their constituents. Boomer openness even seems to be spreading among rank-and-file Catholics, ostensibly one of the most socially conservative voting blocs, and this despite the Catholic hierarchy's staunch opposition to anything homosexual. According to a 2002 *Newsweek* poll, slightly more than half would attend a church with an "openly gay" priest, two in five would accept a gay priest in a committed relationship, and 56 percent approve of gays and lesbians adopting children. The sound and fury of conservative leaders and religious fundamentalists may delay full acceptance of gays and even lead to laws that restrict rather than expand the rights of gay and lesbian couples, but slowly and steadily the mainstream is embracing a diversity that includes gays, and the evidence suggests there's no turning back.

In fact to turn back may well be an economic catastrophe, according to a growing body of research that links acceptance of gays to economic creativity and innovation. It's not that gays themselves are singularly creative, but rather that our most talented, educated, and productive workers feel stifled amid conformity and thrive in more culturally diverse communities. According to Richard Florida, author of *The Rise of the Creative Class,* "studies controlling for a wide range of factors . . . show innovation and economic vitality closely associated with the presence of gays and other indicators of tolerance and diversity, such as the percentage of immigrants and the level of racial and ethnic integration." So openness to gays is like the proverbial canary in the coal mine, a sign that new and different ideas are welcome. Straight job-seekers are even known to ask if the company offers same-sex partner benefits, and it's not because they're secretly gay but because they prefer a company that values tolerance and diversity. The most productive among us simply don't want a return to the stifling norms of the Greatest Generation era. It's Baby Boom egalitarianism, Baby Boom diversity that animates our entrepreneurial and innovative culture today. Or as one of the gay makeover artists said in the show *Queer Eye for the Straight Guy,* "We're not going to change you, we're going to make you better."

The very fact that Boomers have made America better does not mean Boomers have overcome all the demons of America's past. Boomers have successfully changed the norm, and our country today is far more tolerant and accepting of its diversity than at any time in our history, but in too many cases the reality still lags behind the ideal, particularly regarding race, our nation's original sin. Blacks are disproportionately stopped by police when driving on interstate highways. Blacks are disproportionately searched and followed by department store security guards. Blacks are disproportionately discriminated against when trying to rent an apartment. One study found that it's easier for a white man with a felony conviction to land a job than a black man with a clean record. Another study found that employers were 50 percent more likely to interview job applicants with white-sounding names, such as Brad, Brendan, Emily, and Carrie, than those with black-sounding names, such as Jamal, Tyrone, Keisha, and Aisha. Perhaps most sobering is that the major metropolitan areas in the Northeast and Midwest are not much more residentially integrated than they were a generation ago, which is to say they're barely integrated at all.

Now if we turn these problems into a snapshot of society today, it would be easy to condemn Boomers for falling short of their diversity ideals, for talking a better game than they're playing. And too many, unfortunately, fit that profile. But such a snapshot would misrepresent the fact that Boomers have done more to implement these ideals than any generation before—opening cultural, economic, legal, educational, professional, social, and interpersonal doors that had been locked since the founding of our nation. And the continuing problems may have less to do with Boomers than with the racial divisions they inherited from previous generations, which have proven far more intractable than many imagined.

Saddest of all is that many of these problems could have been mitigated or avoided had Greatest Generation whites embraced at home the ideals they fought for overseas. In what may be one of the great missed opportunities in America's racial history, our suburbs—symbol of the American Dream in the Fifties—could have been integrated in the post-war years. But they weren't. Residential integration has been shown to improve race relations, turning black and white into classmate and class-mate, neighbor and neighbor. So perhaps, just perhaps, had Greatest Genera-tion whites not made the fateful choice to segregate the new neighborhoods and subdivisions of the Fifties and Sixties, our nation's racial script may have played out differently in the decades since.

According to the demographers Reynolds Farley and William H. Frey, there were "numerous opportunities to reduce segregation . . . after World War II" as America added twenty-nine million new homes and apartments between 1945 and 1980 and a newly empowered middle class settled in brand-new suburbs carved out of old farms and fields. "If blacks had been allowed to move into these new homes," Farley and Frey write, "the na-tion's racial history would have been quite different." But it was not to be. The moment a black family moved into an all-white urban or inner-ring neighborhood, "For Sale" signs sprouted faster than crabgrass, and some of these neighborhoods turned all-white to all-black in a matter of months. Whites fled for the suburbs, where restrictive covenants, physical harass-ment, police intimidation, and real estate redlining kept even the most solidly middle-class black families from moving in. "I have come to know that if we sell one house to a Negro family, then 90 or 95 percent of our white customers will not buy into the community," said William Levitt, builder of the famed post-war suburb, Levittown, New York, which even as late as 1990 had only 118 black residents. And in the Fifties there was no rising crime rate or low school test scores to justify this white resistance. No, it was simply a matter of prejudice and a willful refusal to transcend it. On the eve of World War II, 84 percent of whites believed that black peo-ple should live in "separate sections" in cities and towns. Through the 1960s, significant majorities of whites told pollsters that they should have the right to keep blacks out of their neighborhoods, and blacks should re-spect that right. As recently as the 1980s, before the Boomer voice began to predominate in polls, a majority of whites still supported a home-owner who refused to sell his home to a black. Even in 2000, with big-

otry repudiated and large majorities of Boomers and younger cohorts rejecting discrimination in any form, almost two-thirds of those born before 1943 still said that blacks shouldn't push themselves where they
weren't wanted.

So this is the racialized America that Greatest Generation Americans
bequeathed to Baby Boomers. But perhaps even more illuminating is
what Boomers have done when not burdened by the entrenched attitudes
and practices of previous generations. According to a Brookings Institution report based on the 2000 census, residential segregation is at its
lowest level since 1920, and a primary reason is that the fast-growing
metropolitan areas of the South and West "feature remarkably low and
declining segregation levels." The demographers Farley and Frey reached
a similar conclusion in a 1994 article, finding "that the lowest segregation
levels in 1990 and the largest percentage decreases in segregation scores
between 1980 and 1990 occurred in young, southern and western metropolitan areas with significant recent housing construction." And it just so
happens that these young metropolitan areas with the "low and declining
segregation levels" also happen to be the areas that Boomers—particularly
educated Boomers—populated and developed from early adulthood onwards. "Boomers reside everywhere, but their impact is especially pronounced in regions not thought to be particularly mature," writes Frey.
Indeed the four metropolitan areas cited by Brookings for low and declining segregation—Las Vegas, Phoenix, Austin, and Raleigh-Durham—
are precisely the four areas with the greatest growth in Boomer residents
throughout the 1990s. So when given the chance to start from scratch,
to build their own communities unfettered by the racial chains of old,
Boomers refused to recreate the rigidly segregated neighborhoods of
their parents and instead broke with the past, establishing communities
that welcome diversity and turn black and white into classmate and class-
mate, neighbor and neighbor. On race, America's central dilemma, the
Greatest Generation is far from the greater generation—at least in comparison, the Baby Boom is.

# Chapter Seven
# Do Your Own Thing

Whatever gets you thru your life, it's alright, 'salright
Do it wrong or do it right, it's alright, 'salright.
　　—*John Lennon, "Whatever Gets You thru the Night," 1974*

**W**eddings and funerals. One celebrates the promise of generations to come, the other honors the memory of a generation just passed. Often they are the only times extended families all gather together. We think of them as ritual events, steeped in religious tradition, sacred ceremonies with unchanging vows, prayers, rites, rules, and customs. In an uncertain world they are the hallowed sacraments that bind young to old, generation to generation. Even in modern times they've remained inviolate. At least, that is, until the Baby Boom era.

It's not that Boomers have forsworn weddings or put off plans for their final days—like any other generation, they take these events quite seriously. It's just that Boomers want to do them their own way, on their own terms, in a manner consistent with their values, and they don't like to be told otherwise. Boomers never felt comfortable amid the stifling conformity of the Greatest Generation years—the pursuit of conformity seemed a poor substitute for the pursuit of happiness. So they grew up determined to create a more expressive culture than the one they were bequeathed, a culture that would value individualism over traditionalism, spirituality over religiosity, free choice over blind loyalty, diversity over uniformity—a culture that puts a premium on the very American values of individual freedom and personal expression. As Boomers see it, if tradition can't accommodate this freedom, it's tradition that must change; just because something used to be a certain way doesn't mean it always has to be that way. And that's precisely how they've approached these most personal of life's events.

So when Boomers began writing their own wedding vows in the Sixties, refusing to say "man and wife" and weaving in spiritual themes that drew as much from Eastern religion and Native American custom as from the Judeo-Christian tradition, they were making a radical break from the matrimonial norm of the time, much to the chagrin of their elders. But in the process they created a new matrimonial norm, one that frees couples from what their elders expect and empowers them to express their own values and beliefs on their wedding day. And it's a norm that's becoming increasingly important to Americans, rivaling if not eclipsing the dictates of their religious faith. It's not that couples don't try to work this flexibility into their religious traditions—many do. But those who find their denomination too inflexible or their minister not at all accommodating simply choose to marry in a civil ceremony outside the church, which allows them as much latitude as they want to express their spirituality on this most important of days. So what used to be a trivial number of civil ceremonies jumped to about a third of all marriages by the early Eighties, when more and more Boomers were marrying, and today more than 40 percent of all marriages take place in civil ceremonies, a phenomenon that even reaches into the Bible Belt states. As *USA Today* put it, "Fewer American couples who marry today see the need for religion's approval." In the Baby Boom era, personal freedom overrides received authority, even that which is said to come from a higher authority.

It's no different as Boomers bury their parents and think ahead to their own goodbyes. Funeral services that were once scripted and structured around religion are increasingly giving way to more eclectic and nontraditional ceremonies that reflect individual character rather than religious ritual. One consultant to the funeral industry told *The New York Times* that the traditional chapel service and funeral home visit made up 90 percent of Christian funerals in the early Nineties but only 60 percent ten years later, and funeral home directors report a sharp rise in distinctive requests and ceremonies, such as a beach party to honor a Jimmy Buffett fan or a goodbye at sea or an "environmentally friendly" burial that places the deceased directly in the ground covered only by a cotton shroud. Rather than the grim and teary service of old marked only by grief and a trembling organ, it's not unusual to see a video celebrating the person's life or a wall of paper on which mourners can record their memories or a guitar player strumming the Beatles or a casket customized to express the deceased's passions, such as deep-sea fishing or rock 'n' roll music. *Time* magazine reports a growing trend among Boomers to write an ethical will, in which they describe the values and beliefs and memories they want passed along to successive generations. "It's not as if old rituals are evolving to absorb new needs," an Emory University theology professor observed. "It's as if we've broken with tradition and people make things up." Or as a financial analyst covering the funeral industry noted, "Boomers have changed every market they've come across. Why not death?"

The very fact that Boomers are willing to transform and take on even such cherished and time-honored rituals indicates how deeply individuality and personal freedom have taken root in this generation—and how profoundly different we are from the days when you never questioned God, father, the boss, or the preacher. What Boomers have done is to shake off the remaining Victorian restraints on our culture and give people as much liberty as they need to pursue their own happiness. Boomers have made it acceptable to do things differently—and not to feel guilty doing it.

This Boomer sensibility grew from a general unease over a Greatest Generation culture that exalted Ozzie, Harriet, Doris Day, and Norman Rockwell's Main Street as the archetypal American images. In the Greatest Generation years, to be different from the norm was to remain on the margins, and there were strict limits on acceptable behavior. If you were divorced or living together or sexually active or seeing a psychiatrist or into jazz or of any faith outside mainstream Christianity, you might be tolerated but only if you hid your deviation and stayed quiet about it. Almost half of adults in a 1940s poll considered premarital sex "wicked," and throughout the Greatest Generation era most associated it with degeneracy, opposing it even when couples knew they would marry. Even the mildest show of nonconformity evoked jitters of concern among the arbiters of mainstream culture—witness the 1954 Senate subcommittee that linked comic books to juvenile delinquency.

But Boomers were unwilling to be suffocated. Early Boomers gravitated to books like J. D. Salinger's *The Catcher in the Rye* and movies like James Dean's *Rebel Without a Cause* and comics like *Mad* magazine, which articulated varying degrees of discomfort with the prevailing norms of the Greatest Generation years. Rock music became an especially important outlet because it spoke directly to Boomers seeking to experiment with life, and it did so on radio stations they could call their own, without meddling and interference from parents and adults. In a culture that kept telling everyone not to express their individuality, Boomers kept asking why not, sensing that something was awry in this land of the free. From this sensibility arose the Sixties, when Boomers shed the ordered and manicured rules of the Greatest Generation years and in their stead ushered in an era of expansive personal freedom.

By 1971, pollster Daniel Yankelovich found Boomer college students renouncing the basic conformist tenets of Greatest Generation culture—outward conformity for the sake of a career, keeping one's views to oneself, living like everyone else—with large majorities saying they would reject them outright or accept them only reluctantly. Yankelovich also found Boomer students repudiating Greatest Generation morality, with most accepting premarital sex and only a quarter saying it was morally wrong. In a survey conducted a few years later, Boomers by a two-to-one margin said that young people should be taught to think for themselves rather than follow what their elders think—the exact opposite of what Boomer parents believed. Even the word "crazy," never a compliment in the Greatest Generation years, acquired an ironic charm to describe those willing to take risks or try something new. Greatest Generation America placed so many restrictions on so many things that Boomers could never be sure which restrictions made sense and which didn't, so when they decided to experiment with something verboten and the world didn't come crashing down—smoking pot, for example—Boomers could not but question the legitimacy of all the other moral judgments proclaimed by their elders. In fact a Nixon administration commission concluded in 1972 that the excessive fear of pot and the draconian laws against it—most "based more on fantasy than on proven fact"—actually worsened the generation gap because they undermined whatever else the authorities tried to say. "In an age characterized by the so-called generation gap, marihuana symbolizes the cultural divide," the report stated. Nixon squelched the report, but the message from Boomers was clear: We must err on the side of individual freedom, and that which is forbidden or sacred must be adequately justified and reasonably explained.

So what emerged from the Sixties was a Boomer ethos that it was okay to do your own thing—or in the cliche of the Seventies, that we should be free to be you and me. Rules are now meant to be questioned, traditions to be challenged and transformed, particularly those that seem arbitrary or outmoded. Today we expect groups to accommodate rather than suppress the individual. We prefer to break the mold rather than conform to it. Irreverence and nonconformity are assumed, even appreciated. And keeping up with the Joneses is no longer that important. Aspects of life stigmatized a generation ago, such as divorce and mental health and even impotence, are now accepted as mainstream and discussed rather openly, all without shame. Just imagine the scandal in 1960 if Ward Cleaver admitted to erectile dysfunction on network TV. It's all part of a culture so open and individualistic that even the army gets it, telling recruits that by joining up they can be "an army of one." We may look back on the counterculture as a quaint relic of the Sixties, but the values that animated it—express yourself, experiment with the new, find your own God, don't take anything for granted, appreciate nonconformity, feel comfortable in your skin, do your own thing—have permeated American institutions, families, and lives. No longer do Americans trust some anointed authority to define the truth and explain the meaning of life. We now seek it out on our own, finding what works for us, not worried whether our neighbors will disapprove, and the result is a freer, more vital America.

It's because of this Baby Boom ethos—because Boomers made it acceptable to enjoy the varieties of the American experience—that we've seen the proverbial thousand flowers bloom throughout our culture. Gone is the rigid social hierarchy of old that constrained people from pursuing their interests because it wouldn't look right. No longer do Americans fear social exclusion for doing the unique, the unusual, or even the eccentric. The pollster Daniel Yankelovich called it a "pluralism of lifestyles" in his 1981 book, *New Rules,* and what he meant was that Americans in the emerging Baby Boom era were breaking out of the old conformist mold and creating choices and opportunities unimaginable only a generation before. So today we have lifestyle choices, every type of music, artistic freedom, theater festivals, hundreds of television shows, and a variety of film genres from which to choose—and a marketing industry that's latched on to this pluralism, catering to our most personal of needs. Go to Broadway and see a wholesome Rodgers and Hammerstein musical one day and an award-winning play called *Urinetown* the next. Go out for a night on the town and dance to hip-hop or big band, electroclash or polka, country or rock, whatever captures your imagination. Express yourself through clothes and fashion, feeling no need to dress your age, status, or profession because those expectations don't really matter anymore. It's an era characterized by what the author Virginia Postrel calls "aesthetic abundance," where style is in the eye of the beholder and not determined by the high brows and bluebloods of taste. This democratic eclecticism is also seen in what we read. Every year publishers introduce hundreds of new magazines that indulge our whims and interests, even the most arcane—from snowboarding to pets to baseball statistics to model airplanes to Harley-Davidsons to lawn care to reptiles to video games to paganism, and so on. In the decade since 1992, magazine categories such as travel, music, health, and lifestyle have seen a 25 to 50 percent growth in titles, clearly reflecting the ferment of our interests.

Indeed in every corner of American life Boomers have refused to be tamed and restrained. Boomer culture has "fueled the constant trial of new things," wrote the authors of a 1997 book on generational marketing, *Rocking the Ages.* The travel industry credits Boomers who trekked through Nepal and joined archeological digs for launching the trend toward adventure and experiential travel, and now ecotourism is joining the list of Boomer-inspired vacations. Boomers may not backpack the way they did in college, but their zest for nature gave rise to the many outdoor activities flourishing today, from hang gliding to mountain climbing to parasailing to in-line skating.

The Boomer insistence on freedom and choice has translated into a commercial marketplace more interesting and diverse than ever before. Critics who deride Boomers as uncommonly self-absorbed consumers miss the point here—consumption became a national pastime ever since the first department store opened a century and a half ago, and by no means is it unique to Boomers. No, what made Boomer consumption different is the motive behind it—less about status, more about choice, less about acquiring, more about discovering, less to keep up with Jones, more to keep pace with one's desires, less about fitting in, more about experience and rejuvenation. The demographer Cheryl Russell notes the near five-fold increase in products carried by grocery stores since the mid twentieth century, with meat and potatoes now sharing shelf space with yogurt, tofu, tabouli, and frozen curry meals. There are stores and e-commerce sites that cater to every fancy and need, and retail analysts often note that it's Boomers—even in middle age, when previous generations settled into their lifelong habits—who are poking around and creating new market niches and snapping up products originally marketed to youth. As early as the 1970s, economists noticed that Boomers resisted the brand loyalty that characterized their elders, opting instead to try new products, explore different styles, and demand the highest possible quality for the best possible value. Having bought a certain brand does not mean Boomers trust that brand. Consistent with their generational ethos, it's choice and discovery that Boomers prefer, and that's now the tone of the American marketplace.

Critics also taunt Boomers for not letting go of their youth, for not growing up and leading a staid and settled life, for acting too much like their own kids, for abandoning restraint and doing too much of their own thing. But Boomers simply ask why they must playact the role of a traditional, conventional, prosaic, conformist adult. To them, youthfulness is a firewall against getting musty in spirit and set in their ways, which is the surest way to become outmoded and irrelevant in a rapidly changing America. As Boomers see it, there should be no statute of limitations on pursuing adventure, enjoying life, keeping current, and having fun— youthfulness does not mean immaturity, irreverence does not mean irresponsibility. Boomers also grew up with Holocaust images, the mushroom cloud, duck and cover, the Cuban missile crisis, and the pointlessness of Vietnam, all of which taught how life can be snatched from them even for the most senseless of reasons, so why not enjoy it while you can because no one wants to spend their final moments sitting behind a desk. *The New York Times* writes about a middle-aged Boomer who runs a design firm, wears a suit to work, lives in a nice house, and has a couple of kids, all the signs of a responsible life. But he also enjoys riding his bike, hanging with friends, playing in a rock band, "doing what I loved as a kid." As if speaking for all Boomers, he asks, "Why would I want to stop doing any of that?"

In fact Boomers since the Sixties have turned youthfulness mainstream, and as they head into their later years they are determined not to lose the generational spark that has remade America in their youthful image. In 1981 Daniel Yankelovich noticed that Boomers were much less willing than their parents to spend their lives in the rat race, to suppress themselves at work just to gain a promotion, and there's evidence that Boomers in mid-life are redoubling their effort to strike a proper balance, finding work that accommodates family life, choosing employers that offer flexible scheduling, downshifting from high-pressure jobs, quitting to start a new business, dropping their career for one that's more fun, following their dreams. The stories are legion, overheard at PTA meetings or found almost daily in the local paper or simply discovered in idle conversations with local store owners, the best source I've found because many of them have their own stories to tell. There's a lawyer who gave up her practice to open a pet shop, a lifelong dream. There's a high-powered couple, a lawyer and an MBA, who abandoned the corporate grind to start a bread-baking business. There's an accountant who gave it all up for his real passion, a design-build firm. There's a litigator who started his own Internet company, a pharmaceutical sales representative going half-time to become a pastor, a successful public relations executive who took a 75-percent cut in pay so he can write, teach college, and spend time with his kids. A 2002 survey of Boomers forty-five years and older found the vast majority looking to retirement as a time not to golf and relax but rather to "learn something new," "do something worthwhile," or "pursue something they've always wanted to do." Boomers will do their own thing until they are no longer able, and it would be hard to imagine future generations not following in kind.

Perhaps it's because Boomers are so free-spirited that they draw so many critics, but some of the same people who condemn Boomers for not growing up also charge Boomers with hypocrisy for inflicting a neo-puritanism on their kids that Boomers themselves rejected when they were young. These critics point to Boomer initiatives against tobacco and drunk driving and media indecency, suggesting that what used to be a live-and-let-live generation has morphed into a bunch of scolds intent on establishing a nanny state. The subtext, of course, is that the Boomer ideology of individual freedom is simply a cover for Boomer self-indulgence, that Boomers quite arrogantly enforce rules for others that they never would have enforced for themselves.

Yet once again these critics misinterpret Baby Boom culture. Boomers today remain as socially liberal as they were two or three decades ago, and if any generation wants to restrict individual freedom, it's those who came before the Baby Boom and their religious right progeny who share those views. Current surveys bear this out. When the National Opinion Research Center (NORC) asks about sex before marriage, most Boomers are unfazed by it, compared to only a quarter of those born before. When NORC asks about couples living together, once again Boomers fall on the side of freedom, with less than a third objecting compared to a majority of pre-Boomers who just say no. And while no one encourages teen sex, only the pre-Boomer group would deny sexually active teens birth control, whereas about two-thirds of Boomers and younger cohorts—many of them with their own kids now—would make it available to teens even if their parents didn't approve, and these numbers have remained fairly consistent over the years. In the Baby Boom era, concluded General Social Survey director Tom Smith, openness and acceptance have replaced the "restrictive, Puritanical" standard of the pre-Boomer years.

But the fact that Boomers believe in individual freedom does not mean they believe in individual license. Enough Boomers saw enough of their friends struggle with freedom's excesses in the Sixties and Seventies, and what evolved was a Boomer balance between doing your own thing and not doing something that would harm yourself or others. So big tobacco—which robs addicted smokers of their freedom, pollutes the air for nonsmokers, costs society enormous amounts of money, and markets to youth an image of cool—is a natural target for Baby Boom reformers, who say that smokers can smoke all they want as long as they pay for its costs and don't impose it on the rest of us. It's likewise with the NORC question on teenage birth control, which can be read two ways: Boomers accept that teens will experiment with sex, just as Boomers did when they were young, but Boomers also want teens to act responsibly when doing it and not to make a mistake that will haunt them for life. On marijuana, while most Boomers oppose legalization, Boomers are twice as likely to support it than older Americans, but perhaps more revealing is a 2002 *Time* magazine poll in which three-fourths of adults said that people caught with pot for recreational use should get off with only a fine, thus giving a wink and a nod to pot smoking as long as it doesn't get out of hand. So unlike their Greatest Generation elders, whose morality burdened individuals with restraints and arbitrary restrictions, Boomers accept and encourage personal freedom but layer it with an ethical component that defines limits based on consequences of the behavior. But as long as it remains a private matter, it's the Boomer credo not to condemn people for the choices they make, even if you wouldn't make them for yourself. Or as one columnist put it during the Clinton impeachment, as conservative moralists flailed in anger when most Americans rejected their grave jeremiads about moral decline, the public has "a more nuanced view of morality . . . than society's designated sages."

If there's a bellwether institution marking how our nation has changed in the Baby Boom years, it's religion, which is built so firmly on tradition and received authority that it would appear almost inherently resistant to the expansive Boomer values of personal expression and individual freedom—to doing your own thing. In the conventional media storyline about Boomers and religion, Boomers rebelled against their parents, pronounced God dead, found their lives wanting, dabbled in human potential movements, eventually grew up, and returned to the pews with family in tow, a nice happy ending that allows conservative pundits to proclaim how most Americans have returned to the fold and to portray anyone less devoted as outside the mainstream. So powerful is this narrative that news media, particularly after the 2004 election, are falling all over themselves to cover religious conservatives and evangelicals as the center of gravity in American life, as if to prove that the press understands America's religious impulse and doesn't harbor a cosmopolitan bias. But there's a problem with this storyline: It's misleading and inaccurate. It's misleading because Boomers never really abandoned their spiritual search in the Sixties, and it's inaccurate because Boomers have by no means followed a traditional path back to the pews and in fact have established a characteristically eclectic relationship with organized religion, one that is changing the nature of faith in America.

This isn't to say that Boomers don't claim a religious identity—most do, and ours remains a more religious society than Canada or Europe. But in the Boomer era we're simply not as traditionally religious as we used to be. According to numbers drawn from NORC's 1998 General Social Survey, only about 25 percent of those born from 1943 onwards call themselves extremely or very religious, which is mirrored by the 25 percent who in varying degrees call themselves nonreligious, with the bulk of this age cohort claiming to be "somewhat" religious, no ringing endorsement of traditional religiosity. It's likewise with a question from the 2000 General Social Survey, with only four in ten among Boomers and those younger saying they attend religious services once a month or more and only two in ten saying they go once a week or more, while six in ten—a substantial majority—attend infrequently, at most a few times a year if at all, almost the opposite of those born before 1943, 55 percent of whom attend once a month or more and 36 percent of whom attend once a week or more. And some scholars, using actual headcounts and time-use diaries, say these numbers may overestimate the number of weekly churchgoers—by as much as a factor of two—because survey respondents give what they think is the socially desirable answer, meaning that Boomers may attend religious services even less frequently than is commonly believed. Yet another indicator is the declining percentage of Americans who give time and money to religious organizations. According to Independent Sector, a group that studies trends in the nonprofit world, 53.2 percent gave money and 28.6 percent gave time in 1989, but a decade later, in 1998, those numbers fell to 45.2 and 22.8 percent, respectively. So with Boomers and younger cohorts increasingly less devout than their elders, the trend line suggests that traditional religious faith will play less of a role in American life as the years go by.

As for the much discussed religious conservatives, who have been emboldened and empowered by their recent media exposure, it is important not to mistake their outward zeal and talk show visibility with any leap in converts or as a sign that America is becoming more religiously conservative. Ever since Jerry Falwell and his Moral Majority quite publicly aligned with the Reagan White House, the press has largely accepted the story-line that evangelism and fundamentalism have been on the rise in recent decades. But the numbers suggest otherwise. "The common idea that more Americans are adopting fundamentalist beliefs and joining fundamentalist churches is not well supported by the available evidence," said a 1991 report by NORC's General Social Survey director Tom Smith, who blamed the media for hyping the rise of fundamentalism. In the 2004 presidential election, evangelicals were as motivated as ever to vote and more indeed voted, but their share of the electorate was no different from previous years. These religious conservatives may sound loud and aggrieved, and they may claim the mantle of Main Street, but as a number of scholars point out, they constitute a minority in the country, their percentage hasn't much increased, and in fact the fastest growing group of Americans in the Baby Boom era—according to the 2001 American Religious Identification Survey—are those who claim no religious identity at all, with their number now almost equal to the number who call themselves Baptists, the denomination most associated with American fundamentalism, a fact largely ignored by politicians and the press when discussing religion. To quote Smith, "the rise of fundamentalism has been much exaggerated."

But if Boomers aren't a particularly devout generation, it doesn't mean they're not a spiritual generation, which they are and always have been. There are times when their spirituality will mesh with organized religion, and there are times when it won't, but the key is to understand that Boomer religiosity is personal, not institutional, and thus reflects the characteristic Boomer values of individual freedom and self-expression. The impact on American religious life has been dazzling.

Growing up in the Greatest Generation years, it was simply assumed that Boomers would follow their inherited religion. According to the sociologist Wade Clark Roof, a leading authority on Boomers and religion, most Boomers were raised in a religious tradition—Protestant, Catholic, or Jewish—and nine in ten attended Sunday school or had some type of religious training when young. It also was a time when two-thirds of American adults believed the Bible was the literal word of God, when most Americans had confidence in organized religion, when it was a civic duty and sign of respectability to attend church functions, contribute to the building fund, say grace before meals, and profess one's religiosity. As Will Herberg put it in his 1955 classic on religion in the Fifties, *Protestant— Catholic—Jew*, it was a time of "religious conformism."

But as with every other institution in America, religion couldn't escape the cultural riptide of the Sixties, and within a decade, the same generation that sang Sunday hymns in crew cuts and pigtails began to see organized religion as yet another expression of a hypocritical, hierarchical, status-seeking culture, the religious equivalent of a labor union or government bureaucracy or corporate boardroom or university administration or political system that mouthed the words of love, peace, and justice but too often acted otherwise. Increasingly to Boomers, religion seemed to divide rather than include; churchgoing seemed an act of duty rather than faith; sermons seemed platitudinous rather than meaningful; clergy seemed uncompromising rather than open-minded. There were exceptions, of course, but those most religious seemed most resistant to social change. Boomers saw the most pious Americans, the Bible Belt, bomb black churches and justify racial segregation in the name of God. Boomers also heard precious little from the mainstream pulpit about civil rights and Vietnam. They also saw how most religions deemed women second-class parishioners, good enough for bake sales but not to lead prayers. Clergy were also among those most vociferously opposed to Boomer individualism, not welcoming it in the name of a beneficent God but instead chastising it in the name of a wrathful God, denouncing sexuality and homosexuality and women's liberation as sins, and even condemning rock 'n' roll to eternal damnation, some burning Beatles records and other trappings of Boomer youth. After a while, some Boomers simply grew accustomed to being labeled godless Communists. And always in the background were gruesome images of the Holocaust, a constant reminder that religions of love also could hate.

These accumulated impressions led Boomers to view religious authority as increasingly empty, too full of misplaced piety, too worried about its place in society, too concerned about church attendance and not enough about social justice, far too unwilling to challenge the status quo, act on conscience, and speak truth to power. To Boomers in the Sixties and

Seventies, the gap between religious word and religious deed seemed gaping. Being seen on Sunday seemed more of a virtue than doing good. Or as Barry McGuire sang in "Eve of Destruction," a popular protest song from the mid Sixties, "hate your next-door neighbor, but don't forget to say grace."

So Boomers began to flee organized religion. "Young people have abandoned their churches and temples in the past," wrote Wade Clark Roof, "but rarely in such large numbers." According to Roof, more than 60 percent of Boomers have dropped out of church or synagogue at one time or another, most taking the step during their adolescent or young adult years, a majority of them never returning, and it was during the Sixties and Seventies that Boomer confidence in organized religion began to plummet. Yet in rejecting religion Boomers were by no means rejecting spirituality. The Sixties was a time of dreams and ideals, when changing the world seemed like a not-too-distant possibility, and in that sense the mood of the times was quite spiritual, even apocalyptic. Writing in the spring of 1969, the Catholic writer Andrew Greeley found college students fascinated with the sacred but exploring it in nontraditional ways, Eastern mysticism being one of them, and in the late Sixties, enrollment in religion courses had risen on many campuses, with students showing particular interest in archaic religions. The social critic Paul Goodman, also writing in 1969, found Boomers engaged less in a political movement and more in a spiritual quest to remake society. "In the end it is religion that constitutes the strength of this generation." Tom Wolfe's famous Me Decade article was actually entitled "The Me Decade and the Third Great Awakening," a reference to the Boomer search for spiritual values, and after surveying the many gurus and encounter movements Boomers tried during the Seventies, he concluded, "It is entirely possible that in the long run historians will regard the entire New Left experience as not so much a political as a religious episode wrapped in semi-military gear and guerrilla talk."

Boomers were turning away from "the rote religion of our childhood," wrote Baby Boom chronicler Annie Gottlieb, but in its stead Boomers were fusing various religious traditions from every part of the world. They made bestsellers out of Hermann Hesse's books, which drew from

Eastern religion to guide readers through a process of self-discovery, and Carlos Castaneda's, which told of his mystical experiences with an Indian wise man, Don Juan. Open the popular *Whole Earth Catalog* from 1970 and there are pages upon pages featuring books and booklets about meditation and Zen and Hopi philosophy and Buddhism and African proverbs and yoga and the I Ching. What these Boomers were doing was finding their spiritual fulfillment outside established religion—they were seeking a direct relationship with their God without someone else interpreting it for them. To Boomers, God was far from dead, but he wasn't always found in a church. Indeed to many Boomers in the Sixties and Seventies, the church and its rules not only were extraneous but actually were obstacles in their spiritual quest. Whereas their Greatest Generation parents sought affirmation by belonging to a church, as Herberg describes in his book, Boomers found belonging at times antithetical to their journey and instead sought truth through exploration and experimentation. It was especially troubling for Boomers to see religion turned into a social obligation, which made a mockery of the spiritual quest behind it.

This was the religious sensibility Boomers developed when young—this weaving of individuality, spirituality, and religiosity—and it has become the template for religious life in America today. Americans now see no contradiction between identifying with a particular religion and practicing it as they wish. Roof writes that "the pressures of religious conformity have greatly weakened," and not just in the cosmopolitan centers of the East and West Coasts but "increasingly in cities across the country." Nor are liberals the only ones who think this way. The talk show host Bill O'Reilly, a conservative who supports putting the Ten Commandments in government buildings, mocks "the ridiculous stuff that sometimes rolls off the tongues of overzealous clerics." O'Reilly may shudder at the thought that he has any connection to the countercultural religious sensibility, but when he talks about religion his words may as well be coming from a Sixties Aquarian. "I go to church, but I'm an independent thinker. For me, religion is primarily a way to examine my conscience and spend some time thinking about things more important than my own existence."

As for Boomers who have returned to organized religion, it's often less out of a commitment to a particular religion and more out of a desire to find a comfortable place where they can hang their spiritual hats. Of the more than 60 percent of Boomers who have dropped out of organized religion, about a third have returned to religious activities, particularly those with children, but for many of them their faith is more individual than institutional. According to Roof, Boomers within religious institutions are "retraditionalizing" their faith, abandoning outmoded perspectives and customs that no longer make sense and replacing them with alternative practices and "ethical formulations" much more consistent with their values and lifestyles. Boomers are not simply revising or modernizing old traditions but instead are developing new approaches to their religious beliefs. "Here the emphasis is not on reinterpreting words or symbols embedded in a religious narrative," Roof writes, "but on the fact that new traditions arise and should be recognized as serious alternatives." In other words, we shouldn't serve the church—the church should serve us. And what happens when the synagogue or church is nonresponsive or incompatible with our spiritual needs? We simply switch to another. In 1958, only one in twenty-five Americans left the religious denomination of their upbringing, but today more than one-third of Americans switch denominations. Or as an article in *American Demographics* magazine put it, Americans are busy "mixing and matching" their religious practices and beliefs.

What Boomers have done is infuse what used to be a staid and hierarchical institution with a democratic sensibility built on the core Boomer values of individualism and choice. We now have a pluralism of beliefs, a complete acceptance of different perspectives, a respect not only for religious diversity but for spiritual diversity, yet at the same time we are united in a common search for answers and an appreciation of those who seek them. A generation ago, most Americans believed that the Bible told the absolute truth, but today, barely 10 percent say that truth can be found in just one religion and almost 90 percent say there are basic truths in many religions. A generation ago, most Americans believed in the Biblical God, but today, according to some scholars, up to a third of Americans who believe in God don't imagine a Biblical God but rather a higher consciousness or power or a sense of the divine drawn from Eastern religion. A generation ago, most Americans believed in moral absolutes, that we should abide by the word of God as translated through our priests and ministers, but today, the vast majority say that morality is a personal matter, that our priests and ministers should guide but not tell. A generation ago, we imagined a stern, unforgiving, autocratic God thundering his absolute commands and laws from high above, the old Hollywood God epitomized in the 1956 film *The Ten Commandments,* but today God is a friend, a spiritual advisor, a force to help us lead ethical lives, the new Hollywood God of the films *Bruce Almighty, Dogma,* and *Oh, God!,* and the television shows *Touched by an Angel* and *Joan of Arcadia.*

It's largely because of this Boomer reformation that we've seen such a remarkable surge in religious activity and experimentation over the past few decades. According to Roof, more alternative religious groups have been established since 1960 than during all the previous years of American history. A report done for the Episcopal Church in 2003 found that members want a spiritual but not an institutional religious experience, one grounded more in the grass roots and less in the hierarchy. Young people today—much like the Boomers before them—do not feel beholden to church structures that are "rigid, central, authoritative, business-minded, controlling, and very unidirectional," as one self-proclaimed independent Christian thinker described it, so there's an underground movement afoot to establish their own groups and autonomous churches, what some call "emerging" or "postmodern" churches, many of them linked by the Internet and most of them welcoming different perspectives and rejecting the hierarchical, uniform, absolutist character of organized religion. As a T-shirt sold at Christian rock festivals put it, "Religion Is Dead. Jesus Is Not." One 2002 study of Americans in their twenties found them blending different traditions, harboring skepticism toward organized religion, and forming "highly individualized" belief systems. Religion has metamorphosed from a received set of teachings to a voyage of spiritual discovery, with Americans from all religious backgrounds seeking spiritual enrichment and meaning through a smorgasbord of New Age, Eastern, therapeutic, as well as Judeo-Christian ideas.

So nowadays the Dalai Lama does a multi-city U.S. tour to sold-out audiences, and his *Ethics for the New Millennium* and *The Art of Happiness at Work* have become business bestsellers. There are leading corporations that bring in urban shamans who run Native American talking circles for their predominantly white Christian executives. Football players now do yoga, leading celebrities promote Taoism and Zen and the mystical Jewish cabala, and according to one estimate, 20 percent of Americans are sympathetic to New Age ideas. Today there are about 20 million Americans who attend yoga studios, which approaches the combined number of Boomers and younger adults who go to church at least once a week. Americans now spend well over $100 million a year on New Age books, and in any bookstore there are shelves upon shelves of books dealing with the soul or the spirit or the self-help, with subjects ranging from Eastern mysticism to the Tarot to the Gospel of St. Thomas, and titles that include mainstays like *The Road Less Traveled* and *Chicken Soup for the Soul.* Among Jews, a rapidly growing denomination is Humanistic Judaism, which asks for spiritual discovery but doesn't insist on faith in God. There are Christian clerics who explore the religious message in *The Simpsons, The Matrix, The Lord of the Rings,* and the music of U2, and others who market their churches with ads featuring Elvis Presley and images of the crucifixion with a tagline welcoming "people with pierced body parts." Increasingly popular are Internet sites that list religious retreats, some of which get hundreds of thousands of hits per month. Americans are simply following the eclectic religious path that Boomers blazed in the Aquarian Sixties and Seventies—finding their own God, creating their own traditions, seeking their own meaning, searching their own soul, and doing their own spiritual thing.

Even the Catholic Church, the largest denomination in America and also the most resistant to change, has been forced to reckon with the Boomer reformation. In 2003 the Church released "A Christian Reflection on the 'New Age'" that acknowledged how "the search which often leads people to the New Age is a genuine yearning for a deeper spirituality," one the church hopes will lead Catholics back to the pews. But the real challenge for Catholicism in America is not New Age but rather the Baby Boom age with its cultural cornerstones of individual freedom and personal expression, both fundamentally at odds with the institutional philosophy of the church.

While the priest sex scandal may have garnered the most headlines recently, the real storyline for Catholics in the Baby Boom era has been their widespread rejection of church hierarchy and teachings and their willingness to pick and choose among church doctrine. No longer will most American Catholics accept the old model of "pay, pray, and obey." Since the 1950s, the percentage of Catholics attending Mass weekly has fallen precipitously, from 75 to about 33 percent, with younger Catholics at about 25 percent, and even these declining numbers may be a bit inflated, according to some scholars. Among Catholic Boomers and those younger, only 26.5 percent label themselves traditional, compared to 43.8 percent among pre-Boomers, and religious liberals now exceed traditionalists in the Boomer and younger group.

It used to be that Catholics accepted church teachings without question, but today, with almost cavalier indifference to church authorities, American Catholics now see no contradiction between being a "good Catholic" and deciding for themselves which church teachings make sense for them. Almost emblematic of the Baby Boom era, most Catholics simply feel at odds with church authority over their personal behavior and individual worship. Not even a majority of the most devout and committed Catholics see church leaders as having the final say on various moral issues. The church says no to artificial methods of birth control, but polls show that three-fourths of Catholics disagree, and most Catholics simply ignore the ban. The church says no to married priests, and again three-fourths of Catholics disagree. To the church prohibition on women as priests, two-thirds of Catholics disagree. On abortion, an issue the church has elevated to its highest priority, only 32 percent of Catholics in a May 2002 CBS/*New York Times* poll say that abortion should not be permitted, no different from what the rest of America thinks, and most estimates suggest that Catholics obtain abortions at the same rate as other Americans. Growing numbers of Boomer and younger Catholics also believe you can marry outside the church and still be a good Catholic, and in fact about a third of younger Catholics do just that. And despite the church ban on divorce, the percentage of Catholics separated or divorced in 2001 is right at the national average. As the editor of a Jesuit journal observed, if the church ever requires complete agreement with these issues, "I'm afraid we're going to have nobody taking Communion."

Nor are Catholics discontented only with church teachings. In what is a typically Baby Boom critique, many are troubled by the lack of church democracy, by the top-down hierarchy of church authority. According to one study, large majorities of Catholics support "more democratic decision making" in the church, and another study found 95 percent of Catholic Boomers rejecting the hierarchy's sole authority and favoring lay involvement in the development of church teachings. Roof found in his research that while more than 80 percent of Catholic Boomers say you can be a "good Catholic" and not obey church teachings on divorce and remarriage, only 19 percent say you can be a "good Catholic" without being concerned about the poor, the implication being that the hierarchy should stop meddling in individual lives and start listening to its parishioners, which reflects the larger moral sensibility of the Boomer generation. Other scholars find that Catholics have lost so much faith in what many consider to be the hidebound traditionalism of the church that they increasingly rely not on church teachings but their individual conscience to make ethical decisions and sort through contemporary values. And to make their voices heard, there's been an upsurge of Catholic lay groups challenging church traditions, with grass-roots activity growing in parishes and communities throughout the country. The group Voice of the Faithful, a lay organization established during the priest sex scandal, attracted 150 affiliates around the country in just a year. The Association of Pittsburgh Priests, a group of clerics and lay people, initiated a petition drive in support of making celibacy optional. Even the local parish priests are expressing their discomfort with church rules: More than 160 in the Milwaukee Archdiocese signed a letter calling on the church to allow married men into the priesthood.

What's going on in the Catholic Church reflects the overall religious ferment of the Baby Boom era: Confidence in religious institutions is low, but spiritual yearning is high; outmoded rules are rejected, while modern values are embraced; distant authorities are diminished, and individual choice is celebrated. Even this most traditional of institutions is emerging as more democratic, responsive, expressive, equal, and free, and when religious authorities fail to accommodate the Boomer spirit of personal freedom, we no longer cower under their gaze but instead find our own spiritual voice and take matters into our own hands. Roof believes that Boomers may well be remembered "as a spiritually creative generation," one that refused to conform, rejected an easy institutional identity, grappled with a larger vision of life, and in the process "reclaimed something fundamental to the American religious experience."

And as religion goes, so goes the rest of American culture. For what Boomers have reclaimed is something fundamental to the American experience, a passion for experimentation and enterprise that drove our forefathers to reinvent themselves, conquer frontiers, and chart out new lives, and they've combined it with a modern sensibility not tied down to outmoded beliefs and value systems. Have there been excesses along the way? Yes. Did we sometimes mistake license for liberty? Yes. But any break with tradition is messy. That some can't handle the new freedom doesn't mean the freedom itself is invalid, any more than the malfeasance of some executives invalidates free market capitalism. America was born challenging tradition and promoting individual freedom, and Boomers have rescued it from the jaws of lockstep conformity and willful authority. In the choices we have and the way we lead our lives, the Baby Boom era has made it acceptable to do our own thing. And we're a more free, equal, expressive, and democratic country because of it.

# Chapter Eight
# Meet the New Boss

If you ever get annoyed
Look at me I'm self-employed.
—*Bachman-Turner Overdrive, "Taking Care of Business," 1974*

In this storied age of high-tech firms and fast-paced media companies, a manufacturing plant in southwest Ohio would probably be the last place to look for evidence of the way Baby Boom values have reshaped and revitalized the American workplace. But all it takes is a peek at the Osborne Coinage Company and its subsidiary, Doran Manufacturing, based in Cincinnati, to see how the Baby Boom sensibility has enlivened the shop floors and offices where most Americans spend their days. The way that Osborne and Doran have embraced Baby Boom egalitarianism—and shed the entrenched ways of old—can tell us a great deal about the very real and tangible ways that Boomers have changed and indeed improved our daily lives.

To say that Osborne and Doran are emblematic of Baby Boom values does not mean their workers and owners munch granola and walk around in tie-dyes and Birkenstocks, a Rust Belt clone of Ben & Jerry's. No, Osborne and Doran are no-nonsense manufacturing companies that together employ sixty-five people and generate about seventeen million dollars annually in sales. Osborne, the nation's oldest private mint, was founded in the 1830s to make a form of scrip that facilitated trade back then, but now it manufactures coins and tokens used in arcades and casinos as well as collectibles, medallions, and key tags. Doran, which Osborne acquired in 1971, currently makes school bus and other vehicle safety products, and over the years has adapted to challenges from changing markets and competition from overseas. Both companies are nimble, scrappy, and profitable.

But they weren't always that way. During World War II, Osborne found a profitable little niche manufacturing ration tokens used for gasoline, food, and nylons, but after the war it fell on some hard times and was bought out by an executive, Clifford Stegman, who kept the company afloat and then in the late Sixties handed it over to his two Greatest Generation sons. Yet this generational handover meant little change in the way things were done. Osborne and Doran were both built on the traditional manufacturing structure—the old compartmentalized, hierarchical factory floor model, with separate production, sales, purchasing, accounting, and customer service departments each with specific portfolios and little interaction between them, all with their own boss and workers. When an order came in, it was the supervisor who scheduled the work and told people what to do. Any and all ideas came from the top down, and any shop floor needs or customer concerns had to work their way up the hierarchy till they reached the owners, who would then make the decisions that would filter back down again. So much was so tightly controlled that if the owners walked through the plant and someone looked up, it must mean they were loafing. And woe to those front-line workers who spoke up because they saw something wrong with the process—how presumptuous to think they know more than their supervisors and owners, they're just causing trouble and we better keep an eye on them.

It's not that Osborne and Doran were hostile or unfriendly companies. Far from it. The owners organized company picnics, they paid their workers well and took care of them on holidays, and overall they projected the warmth of a family-run company. But to them the workers were still just workers—they needed to be kept in line, they were expendable—and there was no need to deal with them at any interpersonal level beyond signing the paycheck and wishing them a merry Christmas. And so it went for two decades until the late Eighties, when the bottom began to fall out.

"It was then that we started to remake the company in our own image," said Baby Boomer Jeff Stegman, who with his brother Todd would soon become the third generation of Stegman owners. "As Boomers we came in with a different sensibility." What they faced were serious signs of trouble at Osborne and Doran, a story not much different from what other old manufacturing companies were going through at the time. Production was bogging down, business was going abroad, profits were declining, workers were demoralized, and there were growing questions as to whether the company could remain viable—and yet the old guard continued to resist change, figuring that they were still making money so why tinker. Eventually, things got so bad that the elder Stegmans, under pressure from their Baby Boom kids, agreed to bring in a business consultant who tried to sort through some of the family issues and conflicts, and that began a process which would eventually result in this new generation taking over. But unlike the last generational handover, when little changed, these new Boomer owners would do to Osborne and Doran what Boomers at large have done with society: cast off the outmoded, undo the hierarchy, reduce barriers to communication, and respect people not for their rank or title but for their individuality and ideas. The companies are now back on their feet and thriving.

Upon taking over the company in the mid 1990s, Jeff and Todd immediately challenged the old nostrum that workers should work and bosses should order. What they did was empower their workers by giving them more responsibility—and trusting them to get the job done. To that end, they flattened the hierarchy, eliminated the compartmentalization of work, cross-trained workers in all facets of the production process, gave teams full scheduling authority, and entrusted them to troubleshoot directly with their customers without seeking approval from any bosses or superiors. If the old way meant supervisors keeping information to themselves and telling workers only what they needed to know, the new way involves sharing all the information so that everyone in production can contribute and claim ownership of the process. "Everybody doing ANYTHING on an order MUST know what we are promising to the customer on that particular order," writes Jeff in the company newsletter. That all workers have a say is clear the moment a new order comes in, when those doing the job—not just their supervisors—determine among themselves the work and scheduling requirements. That all workers have value is demonstrated daily in brainstorming and negotiating teams that include everyone from owners to accountants to the guy in the tool shop who repairs the machines. That all workers have potential is demonstrated by the emphasis on getting an education—and the promise that Osborne and Doran will pay for it. "We welcome more well-rounded and autonomous workers," said Jeff, who spins story after story about workers who translate their learning into company improvements.

True to the Boomer way of thinking, the Osborne and Doran workers

have as much freedom and the company culture is as equal as any manufacturing business structure will allow. Unlike the old days, when worker
suggestions were treated with suspicion, Jeff and Todd now urge their
employees to take risks, offer solutions, and come up with new ideas—
and they make clear that taking the initiative will be supported and rewarded, even if the idea doesn't work out in the end. So even new hires
working the most rudimentary jobs have confidence that their ideas
won't get them penalized. One in particular, a low-level worker buffing
coins, identified problems in the coin recycling process and offered some
ideas to change it; Jeff and Todd empowered him, the solution worked,
and now this worker is responsible for key areas of Osborne's overall production. In the case of an employee whose solution didn't work, he was
rewarded for stepping up and simply moved to another position of responsibility. When a production team needs more money than is allocated
in the budget, they're authorized to approve the purchase order and spend
it—says Jeff, "Just do it, don't ask me, I trust you," a clear contrast to the
old way when the owners and supervisors signed off on everything. Jeff's
primary portfolio at the company is to develop new markets and products, but he freely admits that much of his inspiration comes from his employees, and he publicly recognizes them for it. "Most of the ideas come
from the plant—we even have a huge backlog of ideas to think about and
see how they fit."

The Stegman brothers may own Osborne and Doran, but they're far
from the old style of owners who exercised their power and remained
quite protective of it. Rather it's more like a balance of powers at Osborne and Doran, quite in line with the Baby Boom's deep suspicion of
unchecked authority. Indeed Jeff and Todd could never imagine themselves claiming to know all the answers or telling workers they were
lucky to be employed there. As much as the workers must prove their
value to the owners, the owners must prove their trust and respect for the
workers.

Jeff quite candidly admits the gut temptation to exercise power and
lash out when workers doubt him, but the Baby Boom part of him keeps
that very human temptation in check. If there's a problem, he looks first
at the structure of the job or the position description before finding fault

with the worker—unlike the old days when workers were blamed for structural problems that the owners were too supercilious to admit. Jeff also knows that manufacturing workers in particular remain wary of management, so any reversion to the old command-and-control style would not only backfire but reinforce every suspicion among his workers. In fact one of his greatest challenges is to bring around gun-shy workers who come to Osborne and Doran after spending years at old-style companies—"One worker took four years to get over it, but he's now trustful because we showed our trust in him." These are often the workers who complain that "they're working me too hard"—to which their peers respond that it's not "they" but "we." As Jeff describes it, you can see the difference when a machine isn't working properly. The old-style worker might complain to a foreman and sit around waiting for someone to fix it. The Osborne or Doran worker will try to troubleshoot it him- or herself—checking the air pressure in an automatic screwdriver, for example—and then seek out a maintenance expert in the tool and die shop before going to a supervisor to get something done. It's all about respect and trust, says Jeff.

So when Jeff or Todd are caught up in other work and aren't walking and talking on the shop floor, everyone wonders where they are. And when they do walk the shop floor, they hold conversations and seek input and don't see it as a sign that someone is loafing, the way their elders used to do. Jeff just wants to do his job well the way everyone else does, and at every opportunity he tries to minimize the distance between himself and his workers, so much so that he downplays his CEO title as merely being "for outside consumption, we never use it in the plant." As to the ultimate test of whether the Stegmans put their money where their values are, two facts tell the story: For 2003, not a single Osborne or Doran plant worker suffered any hearing loss as recorded by OSHA, and in a manufacturing culture that rarely rewards workers beyond their hourly wage, Jeff and Todd typically give 25 percent or more of their profits in bonuses to their workers.

The Stegmans have certainly remade Osborne and Doran, and they deserve all due credit for their innovation, inspiration, and intelligent transition from the old manufacturing model to the new. But as much as they've done personally, as much as they may be agents of change, it may be more fitting to see them as part of something larger, part of a script their generation sketched out in the Sixties and Seventies, personifications of the Baby Boom's unfolding history.

As early as 1971, Daniel Yankelovich found Boomer college students extremely uneasy with the top-down, hierarchical, "organization man" work culture, with almost two-thirds saying they would reject outright or accept only reluctantly the power and authority of a boss at work. And there was good reason for that. Work as organized then seemed antithetical to the emerging Boomer worldview. Most companies offered their workers few rewards for risk-taking or creativity. There were clear lines separating superiors and subordinates, and managers saw no reason to question the status quo because it seemed to be working well for them. It was a workplace that valued yes-men, rang a bell for coffee break, and prohibited clerks from going to the bathroom without permission—a well-oiled machine in which everyone knew their place and no one dared throw a wrench in the gears. In his book *The Fifties,* the historian David Halberstam describes it as a "corporate culture in which the individual was *always* subordinated to the corporate good." Intellectuals at the time—such as William Whyte, who wrote the 1957 classic *The Organization Man,* and Sloan Wilson, author of the 1955 novel *The Man in the Gray Flannel Suit*—skewered the American workplace for its stifling conformity, but it wasn't only intellectual critics who saw it that way. The dominant management theories back then taught that workers needed strict rules to function and were motivated primarily by job security and wage incentives. Almost no one talked about giving workers a voice in production decisions, and when a few brave souls started floating that as a better way in the Seventies and Eighties, most managers scoffed at the idea, saying that managers were there for a reason and workers need to be told what to do.

Though this entrenched corporate culture seemed resistant to change, it did not keep Boomers from pushing their concerns. By 1974, Yankelovich found Boomers almost universally rejecting the old model—not only Boomer students, but non-college youth as well. Most Boomers simply recoiled at the idea that they could spend the rest of their lives in this work environment. But they weren't merely rejecting the old. They also were developing a vision of the work culture they hoped to create when their turn came around. As Yankelovich wrote back then, Boomers were "inclined to take 'less crap' than older workers. . . . Nor are they as awed by organizational and hierarchical authority." What they wanted was the opportunity to "participate in decisions that affect their work," and while money was indeed important, equally important was "interesting" or "meaningful" work that allowed them self-fulfillment and self-expression. As Yankelovich summed it up, what appealed to Boomers were "nonfinancial rewards, participation in decision making, tolerance of varied styles of dress and outlook, and an effort to make work interesting and meaningful." Though written back in 1974, with most Boomers still a few years away from their eventual careers, it quite presciently shows how the earliest Boomer values would provide the blueprint this generation would use to remake the American workplace.

But it wasn't just their egalitarian sensibility that sowed Boomer discontent and motivated them to upend the organization at work. To Boomers, the old way was unsustainable, wrongheaded, and falling apart. In the Seventies, at the precise moment a critical mass of Boomers were entering the workforce, it became painfully clear to them that the economy was collapsing under the weight of shortsighted management decisions that protected the status quo at the expense of investments needed to keep our economy a step ahead. As Boomers saw it, the dinosaur organizations their parents embraced stifled not only creativity but fulfillment on the job. Just look at the automobile industry, Boomers said, and their obsolete, gas-guzzling cars, the products of bureaucratization rather than imagination. Or look at our declining electronics industry, shamed by the Germans and Japanese. One University of Michigan study in the late 1970s found that 27 percent of American workers were so embarrassed by what they made at work that they wouldn't buy it for themselves. Another survey in 1977 found more American workers unhappy with their jobs than at any time in the previous twenty-five years, with most concerned about a "hierarchy gap" between managers and workers. Boomers even saw how some companies rewarded the loyalty of their parents' generation—by laying them off in the Seventies. So even the old social compact—loyalty in exchange for security—seemed to be coming un-done. Increasingly, Boomers began to perceive the vaunted prosperity of the Fifties as more an illusion than a triumph, the result not of American vision and ingenuity and creativity but rather the lucky by-product of our post-war dominance. By the Seventies, Boomers found few redeem-ing qualities in the work world of their fathers.

So the Baby Boom set out to reshape the way Americans work—and to make it consistent with Boomer values. Individuality, innovation, and greater workplace democracy would reign. Breaking the rules would be almost as important as following them. Organizations would be flattened, bureaucracies would be streamlined, and front-line workers would be sought out for advice and ideas. Work would become meaningful and challenging. Merit would trump cronyism. The organization chart no longer would rule. Quality would improve and the "mass" would be de-emphasized in "mass production." Social responsibility would be valued. The only obstacle would be the stubborn resistance of the old regime.

And that's precisely how the economic story of this generation has unfolded. Unfortunately, it's a story rarely told in the media, which prefers the stereotypical storyline about Boomers, that they rejected capi-talism in the Sixties and then sold out to become grasping yuppies in the Eighties, so they're not really a generation of reformers but a generation of self-inflated narcissists. Yet the truth is that most Boomers never really rejected capitalism in the Sixties and most never bathed in its excesses in the decades since—from the Sixties onwards they've simply wanted to make our system more responsive and humane, which is precisely what they've spent the past two decades doing, and it's a perspective they've fairly consistently held since their youth. All the media tales juxtaposing hippies and yuppies obscure the truth and amount to little more than me-dia typecasting brought about by journalists in search of a good news hook. More accurate is what Yankelovich observed in 1974 about Boomer college students. "One of the most interesting aspects of students' views is their continued respect for the right of business to make a profit, but because of their growing conviction that business strikes a bad balance between profits and public responsibility, they feel that business requires fundamental reform."

In fact anyone willing to look beyond the yuppie stereotype would have found the contours of this Baby Boom reform quite clear as early as the 1980s, when Boomers were beginning to make their economic mark. *Business Week* in particular caught it in a 1984 cover story, avoiding the Yuppie storyline and instead offering a clearheaded portrait of the way Boomers were remaking the world of work. What was emerging, the magazine wrote, was a "greening of management" that seemed to be "a direct outgrowth of dealing with the '60s generation of workers." As *Business Week* put it, "The manager of the 1950s, whom William H. Whyte wrote about in *The Organization Man,* slowly worked his way up the corporate ladder by fitting in. He is the antithesis of the baby boomers." Under Boomers, *Business Week* wrote, the new corporation will increasingly be built on participatory decision making, workplace flexibility, worker autonomy, and a respect for personal growth on the job. Boomer managers interviewed by the magazine spoke of how "their 1960s experience affects how they manage," particularly in their emphasis on openness in decision making, interpersonal contact, and an awareness of social concerns. It will be a work culture "very different from old-line, hierarchical American companies," *Business Week* concluded. But that wasn't all. The magazine also noted how Boomers won't turn themselves into organization men just to get ahead. "Old-style autocratic management angers the baby boomers," the magazine said, so much so that Boomers put off by organization charts and hierarchies were opting out of corporate America and heading for what was then "the economic frontiers of high technology and personal services." So coupled with the greening of management inside corporate America was "a whole new wave of entrepreneurs . . . being born out of this generation." As *Business Week* concluded, this surge of high-tech start-ups was changing the economy, providing jobs and growth, and it was in many ways "a baby-boom phenomenon—a timely matchup between new technology and a new generation."

Other observers have cut through the Yuppie clutter as well. Landon Jones, whose 1980 book *Great Expectations* stood for years as the standard history of this generation, observed later that decade how the Boomer resistance to sclerotic organizations would spawn successive waves of technological innovation. "It's the idea that you can do it in the garage and wag your finger at IBM and get away with it. And then when the company gets too institutionalized and oppressive, you start over." The economist Robert Krulwich wrote in 1986 that "companies want to hire [Boomers], but once hired, they are hell on managers and, if managers don't handle them right, they leave." *Megatrends* author John Naisbitt has drawn connections between the grass-roots political networks Boomers created in the Sixties and the more participatory, egalitarian business culture they've created since then. J. Walker Smith, co-author of *Rocking the Ages,* a book on generational trends, credits Boomers with focusing on worker fulfillment and fighting the depersonalization of work. "The whole concept of meaningful work is a baby boomer concept," wrote Smith. There are books by economists and business school professors and public opinion experts—books such as *Not Like Our Parents: How the Baby Boom Generation Is Changing America* and *The New Individualists: The Generation After the Organization Man*—that describe how the Boomer values of personal freedom and participatory democracy have filtered throughout our economic institutions. Just look at some of the core tenets of our high-tech economy today—work is personal, break the rules, create networks, not hierarchies—and the Boomer pedigree becomes clear, almost exactly as Yankelovich described it more than three decades before. Or look at surveys and studies of information technology and knowledge workers, who seek autonomy and responsibility and participation in decisions as much as they seek stock options and financial rewards.

Much has been written about the success of our free market economy in creating new jobs, technology breakthroughs, entrepreneurial energy, and the remarkable economic renaissance of the last two decades. But perhaps the credit belongs as much to the generation that came of age in those years, a generation that refused to cower in a hierarchy, a generation that balked at conforming to clotted organizational structures, a generation not afraid to speak up and share its ideas, a generation that replaced the manager and yes-man with the entrepreneur and individualist as the dominant ideals of American economic life. No one will ever know whether the Greatest Generation would have been able to break from its conformist culture to seize the reins of the new economy, and it's unclear how much the Boomer sensibility actually created the elements of our new economy or whether Boomers simply catalyzed economic variables already in place. But it would be hard to deny that the core Boomer values of equal worth, personal expression, individual freedom, cultural diversity, and social responsibility dominate America's shop floors and offices today, and it was Baby Boomers who put them there.

Indeed evidence of the Boomer worldview can be seen just about everywhere in the economy. You can see it in office designs, which are now more open, with hubs for impromptu meetings and shared spaces where employees can congregate to brainstorm and create, emblematic of the Boomer resistance to hierarchy and artificial barriers. Some companies are completely open and have no walls, others use desks with rollers so they can be moved around to other pods, still others keep posterboard and rolls of paper in conference rooms so project teams can spontaneously write down their ideas. In many companies the imposing corner offices once reserved for managers are now meeting rooms open to everyone. And among industry leaders—most notably AOL and Microsoft and others in the technology sector—the office complex is now giving way to the corporate campus, complete with little neighborhoods and campus centers and dormitory-like buildings where workers are told to go off and create, facsimile colleges designed to encourage inventiveness and free thinking.

It's evident as well in the growing number of companies that are asking their employees—not just their supervisors—for suggestions and initiatives and ideas, respecting their insights and empowering them to participate in company decisions in a way no front-line worker in the Greatest Generation years ever would have imagined. From their earliest days in the workforce, Boomers made clear that they wanted a voice in company decisions, but they ran into a culture clash with their more senior managers who fought it and resisted—or as one academic article from the Eighties put it, listening to workers "conflicts with traditional management-worker relations." But Boomers never gave up. They made clear that decisions imposed from above were enervating, but that they could accept change more easily if they had a say in it. And as they themselves moved into management, they stayed true to their ideals.

By the early 1990s, according to a book entitled *The New American Workplace,* a large majority of Fortune 1000 companies were experimenting with employee-involvement practices, and at least a quarter of American businesses with at least fifty employees empowered half or more of their workers in self-managed teams. There are companies that hold "fishbowl sessions" in which managers must listen to recommendations and criticisms gathered by employee task forces. Other companies ask employees from different departments to meet and fertilize each other with suggestions and ideas. Southwest Airlines created a Culture Committee that comprised a cross-section of employees tasked to brainstorm on a broad swath of company issues. Bristol-Myers Squibb, the pharmaceutical giant, employs an "idea searcher" whose job is to tap employee ingenuity and creativity for use in the company's marketing campaigns; a typical year might see twenty to thirty of these idea searches, some of which generate thousands of suggestions, many via e-mail or in town hall meetings or even in response to something as campy as an employee walking around the office in a sandwich board asking for ideas. According to the 2002 General Social Survey conducted by the National Opinion Research Center (NORC), 73 percent of American workers say they have "a lot of say about what happens on my job," and when asked if they take part in decisions that affect their work, 43 percent say they often do and another 35 percent say they sometimes do, meaning that almost eight in ten Americans now do exactly what Yankelovich described as an essential Baby Boom reform back in 1974, letting workers "participate in decisions that affect their work."

Workplace hierarchies also have flattened in the Baby Boom era, confirming yet another of Yankelovich's 1974 insights that Boomers, unlike their elders, would not be "awed by organizational and hierarchical authority." It used to be that workers would do only what their supervisors told them to do, but as the 2002 General Social Survey reports, most Americans now say they are "given a lot of freedom to decide how to do my own work," with 57 percent calling that statement very true and another 30 percent calling it somewhat true. To be sure, Boomers haven't turned the workplace into a food co-op, and there are still plenty of managers with full responsibility for business decisions. But it's a different type of managerial relationship today, one built not on paternalism or intimidation but on collaboration, motivation, respect, and teamwork.

Communication and decision making no longer move vertically down the hierarchy but horizontally among workers and across functional lines. If the old way was to distrust workers and give them information only on a need-to-know basis, the new way is to equip them with the details that only supervisors used to have. If the old way was to make the employee conform to the organization, the new way is for the organization to value the contributions of the employee. "Hierarchy might work well for control purposes, but it doesn't work well when you're trying to respond to the type of change our industry has seen," said one banking executive with an implied criticism of what the organization man of old deemed important. Or as one software company employee said about his firm's non-bureaucratic culture, "The people here enjoy the entrepreneurial spirit, the style, the pace, the lack of bureaucracy, the chance to make decisions. You're not baby-sat around here. You're not hand-held." In fact a look at most work teams illustrates the end of rigid hierarchies quite vividly: Whereas the managers of old never would be seen collaborating and consulting with what used to be called "young upstarts," today's team members might include fifty-somethings and recent college graduates sharing responsibilities and quite boisterously developing ideas in free-for-all meetings.

That Americans are more casual at work is yet another product of the Boomer reform—another sign that Boomers have rejected rigidity and embraced flexibility—and again Yankelovich foresaw it in 1974, when he noted that Boomers wanted more "tolerance of varied styles of dress and outlook" on the job. By the 1990s, Boomers rid most American offices of dress codes—one survey of human resource managers found nine in ten companies allowing workers to wear casual clothes regularly or on special occasions. But clothing is only the most visible expression of the new flexibility at work. When the 2002 General Social Survey asked Americans if their employers allowed them to change their starting and quitting times, 33 percent said yes, often, and another 22 percent said yes, some of the time. "People come in when they want," explains a twenty-something employee of a company that develops Web sites. "If there's work to be done, you'll stay and do it. No one I know would ever work for anyone where there's a premium on face time." Such a perspective would have been deemed near blasphemous in the Greatest Generation workplace. But with employee relations increasingly built on mutuality rather than rules, this new freedom is only to be expected. Companies that used to instill fear in their organization men now conduct focus groups to figure out how to accommodate the work-life balance, and wired workers find that their companies trust them to get the job done without showing up at the office. Control is no longer the managerial mantra that it was in the Greatest Generation years—nor could it be, because Boomers and everyone after them wouldn't allow it.

And if any workplace gets too unbearable, Boomers don't swallow it the way their elders did. They either change jobs or venture out on their own. Today we have more entrepreneurs and small businesses per capita than at any time in our recent history. Small businesses, considered in the organization man era to be "woebegone and backward, even static and dull," according to *The Wall Street Journal,* are now "a hot destination for job seekers," who find them more nimble, flexible, and entrepreneurial than larger and more bureaucratic companies. It's an outlook even institutionalized in the staid world of business school, with about fifteen hundred colleges and universities now offering courses in entrepreneurship, compared to only sixteen such programs in 1970. But it's perhaps better symbolized by eBay, which in 2004 had more than four hundred thousand individuals and small businesses making their living entirely on that site. In small businesses today we see the embodiment of the Boomer spirit—question hierarchy and authority, assert personal expression and individual freedom.

Nor is the work culture the only part of our economy Boomers are changing for the better. They're also beginning to imprint their social concerns on the American corporation. The media, of course, focus only on the self-consciously progressive companies that are out front with their politics—Ben & Jerry's with its Peace Pops; Kenneth Cole with its AIDS and homeless campaigns; The Body Shop with its ban on animal testing; Timberland with its support for AmeriCorps and paid week off for volunteer service; Starbucks with its generous healthcare benefits for part-time workers; Working Assets with its "Styles Change, Values Don't" slogan and its 1-percent donation to human rights, environmental, and children's advocacy groups. But as much as these high-profile cases make for good news copy, the movement for corporate social responsibility reaches far more broadly and deeply than the activities of a few individual businesses would indicate. For what more and more companies have found is that they can do well by doing good—that in the Baby Boom era Americans gravitate to companies that take their social responsibility seriously. It's yet another reform Yankelovich predicted in 1974 when he noted that Boomers wanted something to be done about the "balance between profits and public responsibility." One recent study found that nearly half of Americans form an impression of a company based on its social behavior, and when price and quality are equal, more than three-fourths of consumers would switch to a brand or retailer associated with a good cause. Another study, from 2002, found that 39 percent of Americans reported boycotting a company because of concerns about its business practices, particularly when labor or environmental problems are involved, and while that number may seem high and inflated, it nonetheless reflects an emerging norm about corporate citizenship. It's not that these Americans expect corporations to forego their profits and bottom line—that would be naive and unrealistic. All they want is some social responsibility added into the equation.

And that's exactly what's been happening over the last couple of decades. The more Boomers talked about social responsibility, the more corporate America began to listen and respond. As of December 2004, more than five hundred American corporations have issued "sustainability reports" that assess their record on the environment, safety, community service, and social responsibility—fewer than ten companies had issued such reports as of 1990—and that number is expected to increase by about fifty to seventy-five reports every year. Nor does that include the thousands of smaller reports companies regularly put out on social and environmental issues. One 2002 survey of 140 American companies found that 73 percent already publish or are planning to publish sustainability reports. The corporate accounting firm PricewaterhouseCoopers has even established a new practice to help companies find avenues for social responsibility and to audit these reports for accuracy. McDonald's, for example, issued a forty-seven-page report in 2002 documenting the company's progress in using recycled packaging materials, building energy efficient restaurants, creating sustainable agriculture guidelines, improving animal welfare, employing people with disabilities, giving back to the community, and a whole host of other initiatives. It's not that McDonald's or any other company all of a sudden becomes socially responsible by issuing a report. The report itself acknowledges that it's a "roadmap," that "the road to being a socially responsible corporation is not only long, but it's one that requires constant attention." But the very fact that these companies are now holding themselves publicly accountable shows how far these Baby Boom values have spread in a single generation.

And they're likely to spread farther because more and more investors are refusing to buy stocks in companies associated with tobacco, environmental problems, labor violations, and human rights concerns—a movement rooted in the campuses of the Seventies when Boomers opposed to apartheid urged their colleges and universities to divest from companies with holdings in South Africa. There's a flip side as well, as an increasing number of Americans are putting their investment money into socially responsible companies and mutual funds. According to Lipper Inc., which tracks mutual fund investments, assets in funds that call themselves socially responsible—funds like the Calvert Social Investment Fund, the Ariel Fund, and the Parnassus Social Fund—rose more than 6,000 percent between 1988 and 2003, compared to less than a 2,000 percent increase in all other funds. The Social Investment Forum, a nonprofit group dedicated to socially responsible investing, estimates that in 2001 more than $2.3 trillion in assets were controlled by portfolios that screen for environmental, ethical, and community criteria—an amount equal to 12 percent of all investment assets in the United States. And if offered a socially responsible fund in their employee retirement plan, two-thirds of Americans would choose it, a recent Harris poll found. The end result of this money flow is in increased shareholder pressure on companies to consider changing their practices. As the Social Investment Forum wrote in its 2001 report on socially responsible investing trends, "through resolutions and dialogues with executives, investors have played a substantial role in changing corporate behavior regarding the environment, workplace issues, health, equality, and human rights." So a number of supermarkets and drugstores no longer sell mercury oral thermometers because investors raised concerns about mercury pollution and health hazards. And Coca-Cola has increased the amount of recycled plastic it uses. And General Electric adopted stronger efficiency standards for washing machines, which then influenced the entire industry. These social investors, predominantly Baby Boomers, are grinding out changes behind the scenes, doing exactly what Yankelovich predicted in 1974 by creating a better "balance between profits and public responsibility."

Finally, it's not only as workers and investors that Boomers are remaking the economy—it's as consumers as well. The early consumer economy in America was a one-way street—managers developed products and assumed the rest of us would happily consume them without asking many questions. It was crystallized best by Harley Earl, the fabled General Motors designer known for tail fins and pastel color combinations, who rather cynically observed that it was his job to "hasten obsolescence." Said Earl in the 1950s, "In 1934 the average car ownership span was five years; now it is two years. When it is one year, we will have a perfect score." That the corporate ethos at the time seemed not about producing quality goods but about selling us as many goods as possible was not lost on Boomers, who in the Sixties—in rhetoric if not in deed—rejected the mass-produced, caveat emptor norm of the marketplace back then.

So Boomers began demanding products that worked well and served their needs, becoming what Yankelovich called "strategic consumers," unwilling to trust what the corporation told them. Salesmen girded themselves for the prototypical Boomer purchaser who came armed with the latest *Consumer Reports* and every possible write-up of the product. Boomer parents demanded better quality cars for their families and more durable and educational toys for their kids. And when Boomers didn't get the quality they wanted, they either returned the product—something Greatest Generation consumers rarely did, perhaps out of a misguided sense of honor—or they abandoned American manufacturers and bought better-made products from overseas. Boomers also energized the consumer movement, not only as members of various watchdog groups but also as regular readers of consumer magazines. Today this Boomer consumer ethos is on display most vividly in what cyber wags call the "word of mouse"—on-line product ratings that can sink a product with the click of a mouse. Manufacturers have gotten the message, using focus groups and market research to find out what consumers want, how they want it, and how much they'll pay for varying levels of quality—creating what the authors of the generational marketing book *Rocking the Ages* called "mass customization," which may sound like an oxymoron but makes perfect sense with the Boomer consumer who wants quality, value, and accountability in the marketplace.

Perhaps the main reason Boomers don't get credit for reshaping the way we work, invest, and buy is that the media remain too fixated on the Boomer sell-out caricature—the storyline about Boomers abandoning the Sixties but still using the style and rhetoric of the Sixties to hide the fact that they've sold out. Critics on the right enjoy this caricature because it trivializes Boomers and their accomplishments—every three-dollar latte and visit to a Whole Foods market becomes grist for conservative ridicule. And critics from the left see corporate slogans like "Think Different" or "Think Outside the Box" and draw the conclusion that Boomers are simply exploiting the Sixties for their own corporate gain but want everyone to think they're hip and cool. But the reality is more like what the Stegmans have done at Osborne and Doran—and any critic who bothers to look past his or her ideological blinders would see thousands of Stegmans at every level of our economic life, making real changes for real Americans. It's far from perfect, and there are still many more businesses that need owners like the Stegmans and many corporations that could internalize more socially responsible values. But the Boomer economic genie has been let out of the bottle, and there's no way to push it back in and return to the old days of organization men and rigid controls. In the Sixties, Boomers sang about giving power to the people. With no small dose of irony, it's Baby Boom capitalism beginning to do exactly that.

# Chapter Nine
# The Greening of America

They paved paradise
And put up a parking lot.
　　—*Joni Mitchell, "Big Yellow Taxi," 1970*

Welcome! Sulphur dioxide
Hello! Carbon monoxide
The air, the air
Is everywhere.
　　—*"Air," from the 1968 Broadway musical* Hair,
　　*a song that ended with the cast coughing*

**I**t wasn't only the lamp fixtures made from recycled aluminum lawn chairs that made Austin Grill, a Tex-Mex eating place, seem slightly different from other restaurants in Washington, D.C. Founded in 1988 by Baby Boomer Rob Wilder, seven Austin Grills now operate in the Washington area, but success hasn't dampened the spirit behind the lawn-chair lamps and the other recycled material used throughout the restaurant. From its earliest days, Austin Grill has donated a third of its sales from the first Monday of every month to a local charity, and for two months in 2003 the company offered diners a chance to give money to a local environmental group, the Chesapeake Bay Foundation, by adding it to their bill in exchange for an Austin Grill gift certificate of equal value, which yielded almost $30,000 in contributions. But what really put Austin Grill on the map was its 2003 decision to scrap its reliance on traditional electrical energy and instead power its restaurants entirely by wind energy, making it the first restaurant group in the country to do so. Making that change was neither an affectation nor a whim—it would cost the company real money, about $40,000 more per year. But as the company's chief operating officer, Chris Patterson, said, it was well worth the cost because "the air's going to be cleaner, the bay's going to be cleaner, and I really hope that others would look at it and say, if they can do it, I can do it."

Not everyone has the means to spend thousands of dollars on alternative energy sources, but in a wave of environmental activity never before seen in our country, millions of Americans in big and small ways are doing their part for the environment, making the era of Baby Boom ascendancy the most environmentally active period in our nation's history. Most of these deeds garner few if any headlines, in part because they're not controversial and in part because the people behind them don't conform to the cynical media stereotype of tie-dyed tree huggers or yuppie poseurs in pricey hiking boots or shrill suburbanites shouting "not in my backyard." No, they're simply the good and virtuous deeds of everyday people who believe that caring a little about the environment is a good and virtuous thing.

Consider a little-noticed item from 2002, when the office supply store Staples heeded the call of various environmental groups and agreed to phase out the paper it bought from endangered forests and to increase the amount of recycled fiber it uses when making paper, from less than 10 percent to about 30 percent. Or there's the New Belgium Brewing Company in Fort Collins, Colorado, whose employees voted unanimously to start buying wind power as a way to offset high carbon dioxide emissions that result from its brewing and fermentation process. Or there's the city of Portland, Oregon, whose residents roundly rejected an initiative pushed by developers to weaken rules that restrict urban sprawl. Or there's the Virginia organic lawn care company that's seen a ten-fold growth in business since the early 1990s, or the well-trafficked Maryland garden supply store that with the support of its customers eliminated almost all chemical lawn treatments from its shelves. Or there's the Navy League of the United States, whose new national headquarters uses rainwater to flush its toilets, or Ford Motor company, whose new factory in Dearborn, Michigan, has a "living roof" made of vegetation and soil designed to suck up carbon emissions, both of them on the cusp of what's known as the "green-building movement," which represents an emerging trend in the construction industry to design and construct buildings that save energy, minimize pollution, use recycled materials, and accommodate the ecology around them.

Both in word and in deed, environmental awareness has permeated almost every part of American life in the Baby Boom era. How deeply Americans have adopted the environmental norm can be seen in public opinion surveys, which consistently show a well-developed and growing green conscience, particularly among Boomers and everyone younger. According to RoperASW, a market research firm, about a third of American adults can be persuaded to consider the environment when making a purchase, and another 16 percent already do it. In a 1999 Gallup poll, 40 percent said that they or another household member avoided buying a product because it wasn't recyclable. Almost a third, 29 percent, also said that they've boycotted a company's products because of its record on the environment. In 1994, the razor company Schick found that two-thirds of adult women aged eighteen to forty-nine said that a recyclable package or one made from recycled materials was very or somewhat important in deciding which brand to buy. Nor is this simply an elite or coastal sensibility. Rice University surveyed Texans in 2000 and found that 26 percent often avoided and 35 percent sometimes avoided buying or using environmentally damaging products, such as non-biodegradable plastics or high phosphate detergents. In a 2002 RoperASW poll, almost half of potential computer, printer, and scanner buyers said they would pay more for a product that used one-third less energy.

Over the years the National Opinion Research Center (NORC) has probed a number of environmental issues in its General Social Survey, asking rather pointed questions about how much people would sacrifice to protect the environment, and again the pattern is clear: Environmental protection is the norm for a critical mass of Americans. Do we worry too much about the environment and too little about the economy? Only a third of Boomers and those younger say yes (compared to half of those born before the Baby Boom). Should natural environments that support scarce or endangered species be left alone, no matter how much one's community might benefit economically from developing them? About two-thirds of Boomers and those younger say yes. Should I do what's right for the environment even when it costs more money or takes more time? A healthy majority of all Americans agree. Almost half of Americans would pay "much higher prices" to protect the environment, about a third would pay "much higher taxes," and three in ten even would accept cuts in their standard of living.

This developing new consensus is so powerful that politicians who openly flout it quickly backtrack when their policies are labeled anti-green. It's something President George W. Bush learned early in his first term when he renounced the Kyoto treaty to cut greenhouse gas levels, reversed a campaign pledge to reduce power plant emissions, and then tried to weaken standards limiting the amount of arsenic in our drinking water, a proposal that generated so much public outcry that he promptly withdrew it. Environmental issues "are killing us," his communications director Karen Hughes said at a White House meeting she called in 2001 to contain the damage, which is precisely what the Bush administration tried to do. Republican consultants advised the White House to use words and phrases like "balance" and "common sense," to proclaim its commitment to "conservation" and "environmentally responsible" policies. Bush began to counter his resistance to tougher auto fuel efficiency standards with a call to develop a hydrogen-powered "Freedom Car" sometime in the future. He then wrapped some of his more controversial proposals in the language of environmental protection, using names like Healthy Forests or Clear Skies. To be sure, public relations is no substitute for environmental protection, and so the Bush administration set out to prove its credentials by implementing some small but significant initiatives that showed a degree of independence from industry and developers, such as rules to reduce diesel emissions and protect some wetlands, and his administration also ordered a corporate ally, General Electric, to undertake and pay for a massive clean-up of PCB-contaminated sediments in the Hudson River, which the company polluted for many years. Even an administration considered hostile to environmental protection understood the political risk in blatantly violating our new environmental consensus.

The greening of America is also reflected in the growth of environmental organizations over the past few decades. In the 1990s, according to one study, the number of environmental groups relying primarily on membership dues grew from about nine hundred to more than seventeen hundred, a 90-percent increase in that decade alone. Other research suggests that there are as many as thirty-eight thousand environmental or wildlife organizations in the United States, some big and national but many more small and grass-roots, some focused on advocacy but others involved in education, conservation, and animal protection. Still other research, by the Census Bureau, estimates that the number of environmental groups specifically dedicated to political advocacy has grown to about three thousand, employing almost twenty-eight thousand green activists. Indeed environmental activism percolates all over the country, in cities and towns and states and communities. Just look at the Clean Water Network, an alliance dedicated to tough water pollution laws, which numbers more than one thousand diverse and affiliated organizations nationwide, most of them local grass-roots groups such as the Cahaba River Society of Birmingham, Alabama; the Ozark Society of Little Rock, Arkansas; Residents Against Local Landfill Expansion of Harrison, Ohio; and, Pennsylvania For Responsible Agriculture of Annville, Pennsylvania.

Among the major environmental groups, membership growth has been breathtaking in the Baby Boom era, and it tracks almost exactly the Baby Boom's emergence as adults with the financial means to support these groups. The Sierra Club numbered a little over 100,000 in 1970, nearly doubled its membership by 1980, and has since grown to 700,000 members. The Nature Conservancy went from 99,000 members in 1980 to about 1 million today. The World Wildlife Fund grew from 172,000 in 1980 to its current 1.2 million. Greenpeace didn't exist in 1970, but now has 250,000 dues-paying Americans. According to a 2000 Gallup poll, 43 percent of American adults say they strongly agree with the goals of the environmental movement, with another 40 percent saying they somewhat agree, and even more telling, 19 percent told Gallup in 2002 that they actively participate in the environmental movement—which translates to nearly forty million American adults—with another 51 percent saying they were sympathetic but not active. The extent to which those one in five Americans actually participate is certainly open to question, but at a minimum most are opening their wallets and giving money. Independent Sector, which follows trends among nonprofits, estimates that one in eight households regularly contributes to environmental groups. But there's also evidence that members do a lot more than simply write checks. One researcher looking behind the membership numbers found local chapters around the country bustling with activity, from the political legwork of door-to-door canvassing to the monthly lecture on conservation issues to the hike up the mountain or the bird-watching expedition.

But even if they don't belong to a group, most Americans still feel they can make a difference by themselves: According to the 2000 General Social Survey, a healthy majority rejected the notion that "there is no point in doing what I can for the environment unless others do the same." Indeed it doesn't take a poll to show what Americans are doing on their own—how environmental action has crept into our lifestyles and homes. Recycling barely existed a generation ago, but nowadays nearly ten thousand communities have curbside collection programs, serving half the country's population (much more if the South kept pace), and there are about 13,000 drop-off centers for recyclables and 3,800 yard-trimmings composting programs. According to the General Social Survey, 57 percent of Americans report that they always or often recycle cans and bottles, with another 22 percent saying they sometimes do. Altogether, according to government statistics, Americans now recycle 30 percent of all household and work-related trash, up from 6.6 percent in 1970 and 9.6 percent in 1980, which translates to some sixty-four million tons of newspapers, junk mail, soda cans, office paper, milk cartons, wine bottles, yard trimmings, rubber tires, and plastic containers recycled every year.

Americans are also greening their kitchen tables, buying an increasing amount of organic foods because of their health and environmental benefits. Organic farming, which uses no pesticides or antibiotics, began as "a fringe movement in the 1960s," as *The New York Times* put it, with its customers drawn mostly from food co-ops and farm stands, but by 2003 sales of organic foods and beverages had burgeoned to $13.3 billion, with whole foods stores the fastest growing segment of the supermarket business and the entire organic industry growing at a rate of 20 percent a year. All it took were savvy businesspeople like Mark Ordan, a Baby Boomer from Brooklyn who understood the power of Sixties culture and in the Eighties founded one of the first whole foods grocery chains in the country, Fresh Fields. By 2000, half of Americans were telling a Roper poll that organic foods are worth the extra money, and a 2002 Department of Agriculture analysis of survey research found that as many as two-thirds of shoppers say they purchase organic foods at least some of the time. And it's a trend that will likely expand and grow, as large food producers and distributors—who won't risk their money unless they see the potential for real market growth—are starting their own organic lines or buying out successful organic companies. Horizon Organic, whose black-and-white cartoon cow adorns the company's dairy products, was purchased for $216 million in 2003 by Dean Foods, the nation's largest milk producer, which plans to expand the market reach of Horizon's products into more mainstream supermarkets and warehouse clubs. If the 20-percent growth rate continues, organics that once sold exclusively at storefront co-ops with names like Sam's Belly could soon account for one out of every ten or fifteen dollars that Americans spend on food.

Of course to critics who enjoy nothing more than calling Boomers hypocrites, all the Birkenstocks and green rhetoric and Fresh Fields and even the Boomer-led surge in gas-electric hybrid car sales can't hide the fact that it's been Boomers who have driven the market for gas-guzzling minivans and sport utility vehicles over the years, which has left the fuel economy ratings for the average new car no better than they were two decades ago. Boomers perched high in their eleven-mile-per-gallon Hummers, Expeditions, and Yukon Denalis, these critics say, are only deluding themselves into thinking they're any better than their Greatest Generation suburban parents in their eight-mile-per-gallon Grand Torinos and Vista Cruisers. The only difference is in the SUV's off-road imagery, styling, and name, which exploit the Baby Boom's generational vanity by giving them the illusion of communing with nature as they drive to the shopping mall.

There's certainly merit to these criticisms, and all the Boomer protestations that they and their families feel safer in SUVs sound a bit self-serving. But as tempting as the hypocrisy charge may be, to hoist Boomers on a four-wheel-drive petard is to caricature the Baby Boom's environmental sensibility and to trivialize how far we've come in such a short time. We have to remember that Boomers grew up in the Greatest Generation era, which as the author Jon Margolis describes it, meant sitting

through endless "public school filmstrips celebrating how DDT had con-
quered malaria and how TVA dams controlled flooding and brought cheap
power to impoverished farmers. Altering nature was culturally progressive
and politically liberal." What Boomers imbibed from their earliest years
was the civil religion of progress, an ethos that taught how technology
brought nothing but benefits and blessings. It also was an age of gadgetry
and devices, and Boomers were raised to enjoy them without guilt. Those
who worried about consequences, who spoke for nature, were deemed
backwards, almost superstitious, harboring ideas that impeded the forward
march of civilization. So we were told—and believed—that we would live
better through chemistry. We were told—and believed—that technology
would set us free. We were told—and believed—that gadgets could make
us happy. Today we might smile at the gung ho naiveté of this industrial
era worldview, but there was always plenty of evidence to support it, and
even among the most die-hard back-to-nature Boomers it was still hard to
find more than a few who disavowed the progress and technology that
brought us such wonders as life-saving medicine and space exploration.

So it wasn't really progress or technology or even gadgetry that bothered Boomers back in the Sixties and Seventies. No, what's always troubled Boomers are the by-products of progress and technology, and it's
when those by-products turn toxic that this generation draws the environmental line. Boomers who never read Rachel Carson's *Silent Spring*
still understood how pesticides could poison the food chain. Boomers
who didn't live near the Great Lakes or Hudson River still knew that tox-
ins were blighting the waters and killing the fish and keeping the kids
from wading in. Boomers who didn't live in Los Angeles still could feel
the choke of smog. Boomers who didn't surf the California coast still saw
how the 1969 Santa Barbara oil spill coated birds and beaches. Boomers
who didn't fight in Vietnam still knew that DuPont and Dow made
chemicals that boiled the skin off of innocent peasants. You didn't have
to be a hippie to know these things and to recoil when hearing them. In
fact most Boomers never became hippies—at most half a million hung
their bandanas at rural communes in the Sixties and Seventies—but this
litany of environmental hazards and the Love Canals and Three Mile Is-
lands that followed certainly left Boomers open and predisposed to the

counterculture critique. And Boomers showed this predisposition en masse during the first Earth Day in 1970, when students from two thousand colleges and universities as well as ten thousand high schools and junior highs constituted the bulk of the twenty million Americans who participated. "We were totally unprepared for the tidal wave of public opinion in favor of cleaning the nation's environment that was about to engulf us," recalled President Nixon's cabinet secretary almost two decades later. By 1971, when the pollster Daniel Yankelovich asked college students if they would be willing to devote a year or two to a social problem of greatest concern to them, more students (34 percent) chose reducing pollution than any other issue, ahead of fighting poverty and even bringing peace to Vietnam.

Faced with the mounting evidence of environmental damage, the Baby Boom did what no other generation had done before: They not only demonstrated that progress came at a cost, but they also forced a national reckoning about it. In their emerging commitment to the environment, it wasn't technology Boomers rejected but rather blind faith in technology. Boomers began to speak about trade-offs, about the harm to nature, about the moral and spiritual consequences of our unfettered pursuit of wealth. The same technology used to harness nature was harming nature instead, so somehow we had to strike a balance. "Our responsibilities are to separate the promise of technology—its creative potential—from the capacity of technology to destroy," wrote the grass-roots environmental group Ecology Action East in 1970, typical of the rhetoric at the time. It's not that Boomers were the first American generation to fear the machine and yearn for simpler times. Almost every generation has worshiped the pastoral ideal, the more so as our country grew increasingly urban and industrial. But often this worship of nature served to conceal our exploitation of nature. So we read Thoreau and Emerson as if they and not the train or the factory at the edge of Walden Pond represented the real America at the time. Or we live in prefabricated suburbs but call them Forest Hills and Live Oaks. The pastoral ideal, as historian Leo Marx wrote in *The Machine in the Garden,* "enabled the nation to continue defining its purpose as the pursuit of rural happiness while devoting itself to productivity, wealth, and power." It was a nice fiction that let us obey the logic of progress and still believe it wasn't corrupting us. But then the Baby Boom unmasked it. The issue had been forced. Putting nature on a pedestal was not sufficient anymore—we now had to integrate it into our policies and our lives and the technology that so defined the character of our nation.

And that's what Boomers have attempted to do ever since they injected life into the modern environmental movement more than three decades ago. "When John Kennedy assumed the presidency in 1961, an environmental movement was nowhere to be seen at the general public level," wrote the late Everett Carll Ladd, who ran the Roper Center for Public Opinion Research. "By the mid 1970s, however, it was in full bloom." Boomers revived the environmental sensibility, creating aggressive new organizations such as the Environmental Defense Fund and Friends of the Earth, and invigorating the older, more established groups, shifting their agenda from simply conserving resources to fighting polluters. The result is an environmental awareness that now serves as a brake on progress, a balance against excess, an alter ego to the favored sibling technology that makes sure the costs of progress don't outweigh its benefits. So by incorporating environmental considerations into our common outlook, Boomers have recast the national norm. No longer is it possible to embrace progress and growth without thinking about the quality and consequence of that progress and growth. We now have a little more control over what the machine does and how it does it.

Today it's hard to imagine just how bad the air and water were decades ago. The thick, brown, malodorous, sooty smog that blanketed Los Angeles bronzed foliage, damaged crops, and caused pedestrians to wheeze and cry. In 1954 it effectively shut down schools and industry for a month, and in 1958 the city suffered through 219 Stage-1 smog alerts. By 1999 those smog alerts had been eliminated. Cleveland's Cuyahoga River actually caught fire in 1969 as a thick brown oil slick floating under a bridge ignited from sparks thrown by a train overhead, and it became an emblem of a water quality so poor that two-thirds of our nation's lakes and rivers were unsafe for fishing and swimming. Today two-thirds are safe for those purposes. In 1948, twenty died, six hundred were hospitalized, and many more took ill when weather conditions trapped smoke, soot, and particulate matter for five days in the industrial valley town of Donora,

Pennsylvania, and similar weather conditions in the two decades since would lead to periodic killer pollution fogs in New York and other cities, resulting in hundreds of deaths. These disasters just don't happen anymore in the United States.

Before the first Earth Day in 1970, according to an Environmental Protection Agency (EPA) publication, there were just six laws on the books dealing with environmental issues, most of them toothless and written to accommodate business, but in the three decades since, Congress has passed a flurry of new laws and amendments to old laws that range from the Endangered Species Act to the Safe Drinking Water Act to the Toxic Substances Control Act to the Clean Air Act to laws dealing with asbestos, lead, medical waste, shoreline erosion, toxic cleanup, ocean dumping, energy-efficient appliances, and marine protection, and that list doesn't include hundreds of executive orders and dozens more laws dealing with national parks and wildlife preservation and various other environmental issues outside the EPA's jurisdiction. The EPA itself, created in 1970, now employs eighteen thousand workers, and since the early 1970s it has banned or eliminated more than two hundred thirty pesticides and twenty thousand pesticide products. And it's not just government doing the work: The industry that makes air pollution control equipment now employs more than one hundred thousand Americans. In the Baby Boom era, Americans have institutionalized environmental awareness and made it a permanent part of our lives.

Now the fact that people aren't choking and dying doesn't mean the air is completely healthy and our job is done. It's not, and there are still far too many days when the Pollution Standard Index exceeds 100, signifying unhealthy air. Nor should we celebrate our improving water quality when a third of our lakes and rivers remain unsafe for fishing and swimming. But despite our continuing environmental shortcomings and challenges, the gains we've made these last few decades have still been considerable. We drive twice as many cars more than twice as many miles per year, but air pollution has declined by nearly a third since the first Earth Day. We still use a disproportionate share of the world's resources, but while our gross national product almost doubled between 1980 and 2000, our total energy consumption increased by only 26 percent and our oil consumption went up only 12 percent. We may like our air conditioning blasting cool air in the hot summer, but as the U.S. Green Building Council reports in 2004, more than 150 new buildings constructed since 2000 qualify for certification under a green-building rating system, and 1,700 more are already in the pipeline. And yes, we enjoy shopping malls and brand-new housing developments, but in the ten years since 1996, we've voted for more than one thousand local and statewide ballot measures in forty-three states, most by large margins, to provide nearly thirty billion dollars in taxpayer funding for land conservation and open space protection. America may never become a nation built in the Green Party image, and we may not want it to be, but we are now an environmentally vigilant country seeking practical solutions and determined never to let the bad old pollution afflict us again.

What makes all of this so tricky and difficult to balance is that Americans see environmental protection and technological progress as dueling positive goods, both deserving our loyalty. When asked in a recent survey if developments in new technology helped make society better, 85 percent of Americans said yes. Americans like their goods, want their comforts, and find pleasure in cars and Jet Skis and off-road vehicles—and they're not at all defensive about it, nor should they be. But when Boomers and younger cohorts were asked if almost everything we do in modern life harms the environment, nearly twice as many agree as disagree.

Where much of this ambivalence gets played out is in the business world, which creates most of the progress but also most of the pollution. Americans appreciate and often idolize business, seeing it not merely as an economic institution but as an expression of our values and aspirations—indeed the entrepreneur has become the narrative locus of the American Dream. But when it comes to the environment, Americans don't trust business to be much of a custodian. When the General Social Survey asked whether government or business should decide how to protect the environment, a resounding nine in ten Americans voted for government, with the Baby Boom and younger cohorts registering even slightly higher numbers. When asked who they trust to give accurate information about the causes of pollution, business and industry finished dead last among six institutions, with universities and environmental groups at the top and the government and media in between. When asked whether many businesses will cut corners and damage the environment unless strong government rules and regulations are in place, two-thirds say yes.

So one of the more fascinating developments in recent years is the way American companies have tried to wrap themselves in green and present themselves as friends of the earth—something unheard of just a generation ago. No doubt concerned that their hostility or indifference to environmental protection was harming their reputation in an increasingly green society, many companies have launched public image campaigns designed to show how they're searching for solutions to accommodate both progress and nature. "Profits and Principles. Is There a Choice?" is how Shell Oil posed the question in an ad that appeared in *U.S. News & World Report,* answering that it's possible to have both.

Some companies burnish their credentials by highlighting programs and initiatives—Boeing touts its management of hazardous waste, Raytheon details its stewardship of Narragansett Bay, Cargill Dow shows how it makes plastic from corn, Alcoa describes how it reduced carbon dioxide emissions 25 percent while still increasing production, Intel reports its success in exceeding recycling goals for solid and hazardous waste, Hewlett-Packard prides itself on innovative recycling programs and state-of-the-art reclamation plants that process 6.5 million pounds of computer hardware per year, much of it containing lead and other toxic materials, and not to be outdone, Dell offers to pick up old printers free of charge from customers who buy its new ones. Other companies prefer to highlight their partnerships with environmental groups—such as McDonald's work with the Environmental Defense Fund to create more environmentally friendly packaging, Anheuser-Busch's partnership with The Conservation Fund, which the company claims will lead to more than two hundred thousand acres of new wildlife habitat sites, and Pepco's agreement with the Nature Conservancy to protect a wetland in southern Maryland. A few companies even stake their entire reputation on environmental stewardship, most notably BP, which calls itself Beyond Petroleum and whose logo evokes a bright yellow sunlight wrapped in a burst of green; the company backs up its image campaign with hundreds of millions of dollars invested in renewable energy and with its early adoption of mandates from the Kyoto environmental treaty.

To some environmentalists these companies are merely greenwashing— putting a coat of green over unrepentant corporate practices, with the sole goal of improving their public relations and nothing more, no different from pro-business politicians who use photo opportunities at lakes and mountains and soaring rhetoric about forests and skies to mask environmentally dubious policies. So yes, there's plenty of reason to be skeptical. General Motors sends its customers newsletters highlighting the company's many environmental partnerships, yet GM also has been at the forefront of fighting tougher emissions and fuel efficiency standards, and it belatedly adopted the energy-saving hybrid technology for its vehicles only after seeing the huge demand for hybrids built by other manufacturers. The National Mining Association runs warm and fuzzy ads featuring reclamation professionals in flannel shirts talking about restoring landscapes and reintroducing wildlife, yet behind the scenes the mining industry has undercut regulations for cleaner coal-fired power plants and fought limits on sulfur dioxide emissions. On the *New York Times* op-ed page, ExxonMobil frequently buys ads proclaiming its support for mom-and-pop conservation projects like the Bermuda Biological Station for Research, yet the company continues to drag its feet over responsibility for the 1989 *Exxon Valdez* oil spill incident.

Perhaps the push and pull between profit and principle is best illustrated by the case of William Clay Ford, Jr.—Bill as he's known to the public—the Boomer great-grandson of Henry Ford who became chairman of the Ford Motor Company in 1999 and CEO in 2001. Here was a guitar-strumming vegetarian, an outspoken advocate for measures to address global warming, and when he became chairman he pulled Ford out of a group that was fighting emissions restrictions and then vowed to improve the fuel efficiency of Ford's SUV fleet by 25 percent over five years. He seemed the prototypical CEO for the Baby Boom age, seeking profits and pollution control at the same time. But then he began to backtrack, citing a money squeeze to hedge on his SUV pledge, and in what many environmentalists claimed was a breach of faith, he personally led a lobbying and advertising campaign against a Senate bill that would increase fuel efficiency standards. One environmental group ran a caustic advertising campaign depicting him as Pinocchio and telling people to buy neither his environmental rhetoric nor his cars. But not too long after, he fulfilled a promise to manufacture the first gas-electric hybrid SUV, the Ford Escape, which came on the market in 2004 with a fuel efficiency rating of nearly thirty-five miles per gallon, twice what the typical SUV gets. At about the same time he reopened an old Dearborn plant with its "living roof" and green design. So once again his environmental star began to rise. "I would be lying to you if I said I wasn't kind of hurt by it," Ford told *The New York Times* when asked about attacks on his credibility, "because to be singled out, when for many years I felt I was a lone voice in the wilderness, surprised me."

The Ford saga may be typical of the environmental bargain Boomers have struck in society today. For much of the twentieth century, before the environmental movement gained traction, Americans accepted only the privileges of progress without looking at the costs. Boomers have righted the balance, perhaps not to the liking of environmental activists, though certainly not to the liking of those who remain wedded to the old ways, to a progress unfettered and unregulated. But with our culture torn between our dueling passions for technology and environmental protection, this may be the only workable solution available right now. Even if some of the corporate claims of green are overblown and driven by public relations motives, the very fact that companies are staking their reputations on environmental responsibility may mean that the public relations efforts designed to appease our increasingly green majority may in the long run transform corporate business practices and make them more green—or as a student of mine put it in a thesis on the subject, the tail of environmental public relations may end up wagging the dog of corporate decision making. Indeed it should not go unnoticed that a growing number of American companies—even energy, chemical, automotive, and forestry companies—now issue reports on their environmental performance, most of them verified by accounting firms or other third parties, which means that companies once hostile or indifferent to environmental considerations are now willing to be held accountable for their environmental goals, and as Bill Ford understands, it could be a public relations nightmare if they fail to meet them. And ultimately there's no turning back: The more we expect environmental performance, the more they'll have to deliver.

Considering that environmental protection barely registered as an issue before 1970, and that companies cavalierly created hazardous waste dumps and toxic runoffs with little regard for the consequences, the change in priorities in the Baby Boom years is rather historic and remarkable. In a mere three decades, Boomers have permanently altered our way of thinking—from unfettered progress regardless of costs to a progress that considers the cost to future generations. "It's a start," BP says in one of its ads. Given the history, it's more like a leap.

# Chapter Ten
# Power Corrupts

Power to the people.
—*John Lennon, "Power to the People," 1971*

I'm *as* mad as hell, and I'm not going to take *this* anymore.
—*Anchorman Howard Beale, from the 1976 movie* Network

**M**aybe we don't need to know whether a presidential candidate wears boxers or briefs, or whether he inhaled or not, or whether he got high enough scores on his college entrance exams. Maybe not. But a Baby Boom generation that grew up amid cover-ups, dissembling, stonewalling, and secrecy would prefer to err on the side of openness and transparency in every area of government and politics. The cost of not knowing—symbolized by Vietnam and Watergate—is just too high.

There's plenty to criticize about our political system these days—the negativity, the media manipulation, the inordinate power of moneyed interests. But whatever ails our democracy today pales in comparison to the problems that riddled it just a generation ago. We tend to forget what it was like before the Sixties protests and post-Watergate reforms pried open the inner sanctums of government. We tend to forget how hard it was to get information out of our elected officials. We tend to forget how entrenched committee chairmen ruled Capitol Hill and turned Congress into their own private fiefdom. It was only a few decades ago that influence in Washington meant being part of a coterie of well-connected power brokers who sat up nights drinking bourbon, playing poker, and smoking cigars—and who doled out unregulated and under-the-table wads of cash that politicians turned into walking money for their campaigns back home. It was only a few decades ago that urban bosses like Chicago's Mayor Richard Daley held an iron grip over their cities, delivering goods and services to precincts and blocks loyal to their machine. As for those who asked discomfiting questions, who refused to play along, they were routinely shut out of deliberations and debates. Reformers were shunned, distrusted, rarely given a platform unless the ruckus they caused could not be ignored. That's not to say there weren't a number of public-spirited officials who got elected and tried to defy the powerful and connected—there were. But we remember them precisely because they were the exceptions to a closed, clotted, and too often self-serving system.

Nor were the media much better. Far from challenging the status quo, the press too often helped perpetuate it. Today we see journalists unafraid to take on the influential and powerful, but back then much of the press operated under the assumption that politicians always said what they meant and meant what they said, that they acted only in good faith. "Governments, official agencies, and politicians got most of the ink," wrote *Washington Post* editors Leonard Downie and Robert Kaiser in their book about American journalism, *The News About the News,* and it was ink that usually told only their side of the story. In Washington, journalists often got so cozy with the politicians they covered that they rarely investigated abuses of power and typically reported official statements and proclamations at face value. To Russell Baker, the legendary newsman from *The New York Times,* the White House press corps looked like a bunch of "courtiers" in the royal antechambers, preening themselves in the company of important people, gaining their status not through their reporting but through their association with power. It was all an insular political culture that bred insular logic and insular policies, the most egregious of which—as America would soon learn—was the fateful decision to escalate the war in Vietnam.

To Boomers who were taught the values and virtues of our system, who were told how much better we were than the rest of the world, the reality of our political system belied its promise, and the more layers Boomers peeled away, the more dishonest and deceitful it looked. Almost every prominent public institution—political parties, labor unions, local governments, corporate suites, Congress, the White House, and the military— seemed rife with cronyism and corruption, not accountable to the public and not willing to listen. Boomers never doubted that the American way was far better than the alternatives, and indeed Boomers have always fought for more participation and more speech and more challenges to power, each of which is the quintessence of American democracy. But in practice it seemed like a democracy in name only.

So as Boomers came of age in the Sixties and Seventies, they saw crony politicians, not voters, choose candidates. They saw senators filibuster against simple justice. They saw dissenters labeled disloyal and segregationists reelected. They saw a military-industrial complex—a term coined by President Eisenhower—impel us to war. They saw officials shade the truth about nuclear fallout from atomic tests in Idaho and Nevada. They saw unions, defenders of the little guy, discriminate against blacks and advocate only their own parochial self-interest. They saw moneyed interests block environmental, health, and safety legislation, even something so sensible as airbags for cars. They saw corporations pollute and pay no price for it. They saw the military lie about body counts. They saw the Nixon administration threaten espionage charges against *The New York Times* for publishing the Pentagon Papers, the classified history that documented the official lies and duplicity that led to the Vietnam War. They saw Watergate.

These were the facts and impressions that shaped the Boomer political worldview. By the early Seventies, according to the pollster Daniel Yankelovich, a significant majority of Boomers—both college educated and high-school graduates—were rejecting the blind faith of their parents and harboring a deep and abiding skepticism toward politics and politicians. "They do not believe that our system of American democracy functions in practice as it is supposed to in theory," Yankelovich wrote in 1972. "They believe that 'special interests' run the political machinery of the nation, with little true participation by the mass of American citizens," he wrote two years later. Political parties, corporations, unions, the military, the institutional pillars of the Greatest Generation years—Boomers found them too closed, too insular, too self-serving, in need of "drastic reform."

Boomers certainly don't agree on all political issues, but what united them politically in the Sixties and still unites them politically today is a rejection of this old style of politics and any accommodation of it. And in its place Boomers have created a culture of political openness and transparency that insists on scrutiny and levies a heavy toll on politicians and institutions that try to hide something or keep it from the public. Our politics today may be far from perfect, and at times the cacophony of pundits and opinions can reach an unpleasant and discordant din, but underlying it is a healthy rejection of secrecy, a repudiation of back-room deals, and a belief in as much openness and disclosure as possible in every area of politics and society. That, more than anything else, is the Baby Boom's permanent imprint on our political culture.

Consider the 2004 race for the Democratic presidential nomination, when former Vermont governor Howard Dean initially electrified voters by promising an archetypally Boomer campaign that would speak truth to power, a campaign of belligerent candor that reminded some of a Sixties revival. But then it came out that this self-styled establishment rebel tried to seal all off his records and correspondence from his six terms as governor, that he wanted no one looking into them for ten years, that he appeared to have political motives behind it, and when he steadfastly refused to open his papers, voters began to wonder what he had to hide, whether he was just another politician—and it was about then that his candidacy began to deflate. Or consider when Bill Clinton asked his wife, Hillary Rodham Clinton, to head his administration's task force to provide affordable healthcare coverage to everyone in America. Initially, according to the polls, the country welcomed her as a leader who could seize the moment and reform the system. But then she closed the task force meetings to the press and kept the deliberations out of public view, which made Americans wonder what she was hiding and why she needed such secrecy, which in turn fostered an image of her as just another calculating, Machiavellian politician, an image from which she has never fully recovered. Or consider the public's leery relationship with Vice President Dick Cheney, whose high negative poll ratings derive partly from concerns about the veil of secrecy he wraps around all of his work—a veil so imposing that it's made strange bedfellows out of liberal and conservative groups that have joined forces to challenge the secret proceedings of his White House energy task force, which he has steadfastly refused to disclose despite concerns that the task force was closed to all but the most favored corporations and industries.

This distrust of back-room politics has become the defining characteristic of public life in the Baby Boom era. What was commonplace years ago—the old insular political clubs and machines, the smoke-filled rooms and crony nominees—has all but disappeared in recent decades, lurking only at the margins of our political life, and any attempt to maneuver behind the scenes is usually met with a glare of suspicion and media scrutiny. Almost daily there's a newspaper story putting the spotlight on a politician or government agency that tries to operate in secret or avoid the sunshine of public scrutiny, all with the implication that something sinister is going on. "Closed WSSC Meeting Draws Criticism," headlined a 2004 *Washington Post* article about a public utility that tried to restructure its operations at a closed-door meeting called on less than two hours' notice. "Scandal Develops into Challenge for Mayor of Frederick," ran another *Post* article detailing allegations of cover-up directed at "a mayor who came to office pledging to stop the backroom deals that defined the city's politics for generations."

What Boomers have tried to accomplish—imperfectly but earnestly—is to weave a thread of transparency through our many political institutions, to open up proceedings and deliberations and to give citizens the opportunity to place a check on the officials they've entrusted with power. So it's in this context that we must view the cascade of laws and initiatives that have reshaped public life in America since the Sixties and Seventies— the proliferation of open government laws, freedom of information acts, conflict-of-interest rules, watchdog groups, investigative reports, reporting requirements, even the widespread use of political primaries to select candidates at all levels of government, which has replaced the old way of wheeling and dealing among cigar-chomping cronies. It's not that special interests don't continue to hold undue power—it's just that more of it is out in the open and exposed to public inquiry. Even the military, which tried to cover up and evade responsibility for its mistakes and misjudgments during Vietnam, now scrutinizes everything it does, frequently in public, and often its internal investigations—on such issues as bias in promotion or sexual harassment or prisoner abuse in Iraq—are more incisive and thorough than any congressional oversight report. Sunlight is the best disinfectant, Justice Louis Brandeis once wrote, and it's a sentiment that Baby Boom America has internalized and taken to heart.

So what's emerged in the last three decades is a national consensus that the public has a right to know almost every detail of what their government is doing. From the school board to the mayor's office to the White House, Americans want to know what decisions are being made, how they're being made, who holds power, and how they're exercising it—and we object when this information is not disclosed. It was Ralph Nader and his youthful band of Boomer raiders who first pushed for open government laws in the 1960s, and it's been a generational mantra ever since.

Typical is a Boomer couple from Woburn, Massachusetts, who in 2001 wandered near a landfill that had been reopened without public notice. So they started asking questions, but when city hall refused to provide answers, the couple began filing state and federal freedom of information requests that led to the horrifying disclosure that the landfill was not properly lined and that medical waste, oil, construction debris, and coal ash were seeping into the watershed below. Typical too is a Kansas district attorney who in 2002 charged seven local school board members with making official decisions about a plagiarism case behind closed doors, which violated the state's open meetings law. Also typical are the 76 percent of Florida's voters who in 2002 passed an amendment to their state constitution making it tougher to dilute the state's Sunshine Law ensuring open government records and public meetings—and this vote came only a year after September 11, when proponents of secrecy in government had a stronger case to make than at any time in the previous three decades. In recent years some states started requiring advance notice of all legislative meetings, other states began challenging the secrecy of legal settlements involving defective products or toxic wastes, yet others passed laws forcing officials to disclose all gifts, including such old crony perks as golf club memberships given free to governors and powerful legislators so they could hobnob privately with their state's corporate elite. We also now have whistleblower laws that protect civil service workers who report the wrongdoing, waste, and fraud they witness first-hand—in 2003 alone the federal government reviewed nearly one thousand cases raised by whistleblowers, and in the press whistleblowers are treated as heroes. It's all part of a Baby Boom culture of institutional openness that evolved from widespread disillusionment after Vietnam and Watergate and mutated into a generalized suspicion of power and its ability to corrupt almost anyone entrusted with it.

It should be no surprise that a primary engine behind this culture of transparency is the news media. The press is far from perfect, and too often its default storyline follows hackneyed formulas, overused cliches, and herd–like thinking, examples of which we've discussed in this book. But as formulaic, predictable, and unimaginative as the media may be at times, it would be hard to deny that there are more individual journalists sniffing out more truths and writing better investigative stories than at any time in our history. You see it in gritty newspaper exposés of nursing home abuse and magazine pieces uncovering political duplicity and in the many reports on government waste that even the much-maligned broadcast news brings our way. Barely a day passes without stories on corporate malfeasance or abuses of power or executive sleight of hand or official corruption. Columnists regularly flay public officials for their hypocrisy and broken promises. A news media that only decades ago covered the doings of well-respected white men now does in-depth reporting on women's issues and minority concerns and immigrant dreams and hip-hop culture. American journalism has effectively become an expression of the Baby Boom sensibility, unafraid to question motives, determined to speak truth to power, unwilling to accept what the authorities say at face value, and committed to a diversity of images, opinions, and perspectives. For most mainstream reporters, that's about the only bias they ever bring to the news.

It's important to remember that the press didn't just evolve this way on its own. Boomer journalists have been a driving force ever since a number of them tried to answer the failings of the mainstream press by creating their own alternative news sources in the Sixties. With little money but a grand passion for truth, they wrote and staffed magazines like *Ramparts, Washington Monthly, Rolling Stone,* and *Mother Jones,* newspapers like Chicago's *Seed,* Berkeley's *Barb,* New York's *Rat,* and Los Angeles's *Free Press,* even wire services with names like *Liberation News Service* and *Dispatch News Service,* some still around, most long gone, some often puerile but others daring to break news that the mainstream press wouldn't touch back then, including the My Lai massacre, the use of Agent Orange in Vietnam, and the CIA's infiltration of student organizations. Today it's hard to imagine how different these publications seemed back then—there was nothing similar in the Fifties, except perhaps the *Village Voice,* New York's hipster paper, and I. F. Stone's muckraking weekly, which only a select few read. What emerged in the Sixties were media with an attitude—they held nothing sacred; they questioned assumptions; they gave voice to growing doubts about the official versions of truth. And eventually the mainstream media began to listen. Inspired by this Boomer ethos and empowered by the daring dispatches from Vietnam and *The Washington Post's* intrepid Watergate reporters, the press no longer felt duty bound to report news solely from the perspective of power brokers and political leaders. It wasn't long before journalism would become a preferred profession among educated Boomers, and as the mainstream media grew more combative, many Baby Boom veterans of the alternative press moved on to senior positions at major papers, magazines, and broadcast news. And as the World Wide Web increasingly became a central resource for information, Boomer doggedness would shape the culture of that medium as well, turning it into an investigative tool for any citizen or consumer seeking the truth about the policies and products they were asked to consume. Much of what motivated the alternative press of the Sixties has long passed, but its spirit and attitude—its insistence on official candor and transparency, its reflexive suspicion of power—live on in America's newsrooms and media today.

Always central to the Boomer political worldview is the radically democratic notion that power is meant to be challenged, not revered. Back in the Sixties, Bob Dylan and other generational troubadours exhorted Boomers not to follow leaders, and Boomers responded by questioning parents and administrators and authorities who tried to harness them and tell them how to lead their lives. A key phrase of the decade was "participatory democracy," which in practice meant that no one leader could accumulate too much power without being suspected of undue grandiosity or egoism. Boomers became an irreverent bunch, and everyone in authority was fair game. One result has been the rise of political humor as a way to keep our leaders in check. Boomers have always been attracted to humor that lampoons pretense and authority—the Three Stooges reached their peak of popularity in the Sixties. And who better to lampoon than the politicians whose foibles and desperate attempts at image-making appear via television in our living rooms daily? Boomers certainly didn't invent political satire—witness the angry nightclub rants of Mort Sahl and Lenny Bruce in the early Sixties—but it's the Boomer sensibility that has made political humor mainstream.

So from *Mad* magazine to the Smothers Brothers, from George Carlin to Richard Pryor, from *National Lampoon* to *Saturday Night Live,* and from *Politically Incorrect* to Leno and Letterman and Jon Stewart and all the irreverent heirs to this humor now on the Internet, Boomer culture has spared no hypocrisy or affectation or attempted cover-up, rationalization, and spin. George W. Bush does a photo op in a classroom full of African-American kids? That's more black people than voted for him in the election. John Kerry enjoys windsurfing near his home in Nantucket? Even his leisure depends on which way the wind blows. How about all the delegates who got patted down, frisked, and groped during the 2004 Republican Convention? That's just by Arnold Schwarzenegger. George W. Bush landed his Mission Accomplished jet on an aircraft carrier? The last time a president landed on something that big, he got impeached. Florida chose election observers to keep the vote fair? Too bad they're the Olympics gymnastic judges. Recent studies by the Pew Research Center for the People and the Press have found that nearly half of Americans under fifty learn at least something about presidential politics from comedy shows and late-night TV. What it says is that we measure our candidates by the level of their hypocrisy, and we want our most trenchant observers—our comedic wits—to fillet right before us the characteristics and shortcomings that might get our country into trouble. The scrutiny of humor is yet another way Boomer culture holds its politicians accountable.

Some critics say our free-for-all public culture has gone too far, that it's penetrated beyond a healthy distrust of power and a vigorous discussion of issues into an unnecessary fixation on the character of our political candidates and elected officials. And indeed there are downsides to our public focus on character issues—it can get deeply personal, meanspirited, and partisan, much like what happened to John Kerry in 2004 when his Vietnam service was challenged, and as a result it can divert attention from policy issues and discourage future public-spirited citizens from running for office. But as enervating as character questions can be at times, for Boomers there's no choice but to raise them, and for good reason: Boomers too often have seen character flaws drive policy decisions that have fateful consequences for our country. Seared into the Boomer memory is the combination of hubris and insecurity that drove Lyndon Johnson's deference to the military and his decision to escalate Vietnam. Equally haunting and unforgettable is how Nixon's paranoia and resentfulness led to Watergate. Bill Clinton may have survived politically only because our need for transparency exposed his shortcomings early and voters accepted them as the price of his brilliance. Of course Boomers are not the only force behind the rise of character politics—television by its very nature is an intimate medium that thrives on the personal and devours stories of human interest. But it's all part of a larger culture of full disclosure that defines our public life today. Figure out what makes our leaders tick, Boomers argue, and we may get a better sense of just how far we can trust them.

One consequence of this generational distrust is to pry citizens away from the strong political party affiliation that was characteristic of previous generations. By the early Seventies, pollsters looking at the first wave of Baby Boomers were detecting a seismic shift away from party loyalty, with as many as two in five saying they had no interest in calling themselves a Democrat or Republican. Statistics since then show an 800-percent increase in officially registered independents nationwide, and even in Massachusetts, considered the most Democratic of Democratic states, about half of voters shun party affiliation. There's even a core of voters who split their ballots between the two parties as a way to divide government and keep one party from accumulating too much power.

What started this dealignment among Boomers was a near universal disgust over the bipartisan lies and quagmire in Vietnam, which led them to conclude that no party had a corner on virtue or truth. Boomers who grew up believing in racial justice also wondered how our parties could still tolerate the continuing power of Southern segregationists. Watergate certainly compounded their misgivings, and before long Boomers simply assumed that politics was rife with special interest influence and sweetheart deals and crony handouts and official dissembling and environmental cover-ups. With their growing distrust Boomers then began to ignore what party leaders had to say and instead found alternate sources to help them make sense of the world—television news and alternative publications and university classrooms and now the Internet and political humor—which further unhinged them from any tendency to see events through a party prism. Boomers also contrasted party and institutional sclerosis with the vigor of advocacy groups that brought change from outside the government—the civil rights marchers, the anti-war activists, the women's groups, the environmental organizations. Caring passionately about an issue seemed worthy and admirable; caring passionately about a party seemed unappealing and impure. So this estrangement from the parties began to take on a life of its own, to the point that by 2000, according to NORC's General Social Survey, only 12.5 percent of Boomers and those younger identified themselves as strong Democrats and only 8.9 percent called themselves strong Republicans. In its place is a political standard defined by the Boomer worldview, that votes must be earned, power must be balanced, leaders must be candid, principles must be articulated, and government must be approachable. "Don't waste your vote on politics as usual," was the slogan former wrestler Jesse Ventura used in his successful 1998 run as an independent candidate for governor of Minnesota, and it resonated with voters throughout the country. Nothing in politics can be taken for granted anymore.

Conservatives and even some liberals interpret this distrust of power and privilege to mean that Americans don't like government and therefore have become more conservative over the years. But to read conservatism into this is to misconstrue the political tea leaves of the Baby Boom era. If anything, the political center of gravity has clearly moved toward Boomer liberalism in the last generation, and even conservatives now frame their agenda in a Sixties context. Women's rights, diversity, consumer rights, environmental protection, civil rights, gay rights, religious diversity, personal freedom—all except the most paleo of conservatives at least give lip service to these Boomer era norms, and those who don't pay a price for it. George W. Bush may not support gay marriage, but he's quick to add that he wouldn't object if states allowed gays to enter into civil unions, which would give gay couples many of the legal benefits that married couples enjoy, a viewpoint unimaginable for a conservative politician a decade or two ago. It would be well nigh impossible to get elected today as an opponent of family leave policies and civil rights laws and diversity initiatives and environmental regulation. Senator Trent Lott showed how out of touch he was when he made comments unsympathetic to civil rights, and within weeks he lost his powerful post as Senate majority leader. When the Republican Convention veered hard right in 1992 with its talk of culture wars and religious battles, they got less than 40 percent of the presidential vote. So for their 2000 and 2004 conventions the Republicans hid their right wing and instead offered the nation a picture of moderation and racial diversity, effectively conceding that they couldn't win without kneeling before the Boomer norm. For most Americans the social advances of the Baby Boom era are simply a done deal, and now it's just a matter of working out the details.

What gives the impression that conservatives are gaining ground is perhaps the greatest irony of politics in the Baby Boom years, and it has everything to do with the Boomer suspicion of power and the success of Boomer social liberalism. In the often topsy-turvy world of political warfare, conservatives now fashion themselves as prototypical Boomer rebels, as insurgents fighting the establishment, but in this case it's the establishment put into place by Boomers to protect the social gains and personal freedoms that Boomers themselves fought to secure over the last generation. Conservatives portray today's courts, institutions, and bureaucracies in much the same way Boomers portrayed the military-industrial complex and the power structures of old—as legalistic, closed-minded, arrogant, and imperious, or in the lingo of the conservative movement, as oppressively politically correct. The author Dinesh D'Souza describes how he and his conservative college comrades in the 1980s struck a pose as "social guerillas" to fight what they called the liberal establishment. "We realized something the left realized, that there's an importance in being exhibitionist and in being lively, and in being anti-establishment." Conservative students today portray themselves as "the new counterculture," and their rhetoric reeks of resentment and anger, a rage against the system. So the Boomer establishment is now in the unusual position of defending a progressive status quo against an angry minority of conservatives who use the language and spirit of progressive empowerment that Boomers formulated a generation ago. And conservatives are able to gain whatever traction and followers they have not because of what they believe but because of their anti-establishment way of expressing it. What it all suggests is that the Boomer sensibility—the distrust of entrenched power—has become the natural language of politics in America today. It's the reason why Senator John McCain is considered such a political folk hero— because he commits himself to "straight talk" and shows no fear going after big money, big tobacco, and big polluters, all of whom prefer to keep their influence hidden and quiet. Americans do not dislike government; what they distrust is power.

There's a classic Sixties story about a bunch of long-hairs who asked Greatest Generation adults to sign a petition supporting the Bill of Rights—and the adults turned them away, calling it a communist document. What these long-hairs were trying to show was that they, not their elders, were the generation that stood in the patriotic tradition. Thump your chest and salute the flag all you want, these Boomers said, but it's our commitment to ideals that makes us a genuinely American generation. Indeed the very founding of our nation was built on the idea that power corrupts, an idea central to the Declaration of Independence and the writings of Tom Paine and Thomas Jefferson and the crafting of our Constitution and Bill of Rights—indeed central to the political development of our country. The Revolutionary generation, writes the historian Bernard Bailyn, was warned again and again "of the folly of defying received tradition, the sheer unlikelihood that they . . . knew better than the established authorities." A century ago another great generation—the Progressives—infused fresh blood into our political system by taking on the trusts and advocating for workers and exposing corporate misdeeds and abuses through their muckraking journalism. They too challenged the entrenched interests—the Robber Barons of the Gilded Age—and they too wove a narrative that power corrupts.

So the Baby Boom follows this historic American spirit of shaking up the power structure and advocating openness and transparency and greater rights for the underdog. To Boomers, the same Greatest Generation that fought unchecked power abroad fell silent at home as our government and many of our institutions stifled dissent, deferred rights, misled the public, and found the accumulation of power more appealing than candor and honesty. So Boomers spoke up. They protested. They doubted official-dom. They demanded openness and accountability. Theirs was a politics rooted in the ideas and impulses that created our country. Back in the Six-ties they cited the Founding Fathers, quoted from the Declaration of Inde-pendence, studied the Bill of Rights and its protection for individuals against the majority. Their literature was full of these references—and full of plaintive questions about why America wasn't living up to its ideals. There may be drawbacks to the Boomer distrust of power—it can cer-tainly keep government from running as efficiently as possible. But after Vietnam and Watergate and the countless other secrets and deceptions that we learned about only years later, recapturing this distrust was a healthy response for our body politic, and it places Baby Boom America right at the center of a great American tradition. It's better for democracy to be too boisterous than too ordered, Boomers believe. We all gain when our politicians and government are held accountable before the American people.

# Chapter Eleven
# Take Over the Administration Building

> One of the dangers of going to college is that you learn things.
> —*James Simon Kunen, from* The Strawberry Statement, *his 1969
> book on the student protests at Columbia University*

**R**ead almost any conservative author today and you'd think that the most dangerous place in America is the college or university campus. Forget the fact that colleges are graduating the most talented, tolerant, and well-educated students in our nation's history. Forget that American higher education is seen as the envy of the world. Forget that colleges now offer more academic options and expose students to greater diversity than ever before. No, higher education, as these conservatives see it, has been taken over by tenured Baby Boom radicals intent upon turning this next generation into a politically correct version of the Stepford wives, programmed to embrace the Sixties values of multiculturalism, feminism, and cultural relativism. "Political Indoctrination Supplants Education in Nation's Universities," goes the headline for a George Will column. "Today, thought control is the dominant theology on campuses, often hiding behind the mantras of diversity and multiculturalism," writes the conservative activist Phyllis Schlafly. "Intellectual integrity comes in a distant second to political correctness," proclaims Robert Bork, the former judge and failed Supreme Court nominee. The worms in the apple, of course, are Baby Boom liberals who latched on to the one institution they could control—the university. They were barbarians at college in the Sixties, Bork says, "only now they are tenured barbarians." Or as the conservative author Dinesh D'Souza bemoans, "the generation of the 1960s is fully in charge" of the campuses today. This is a generation reliving its college radical highlight reel and imposing it on the future of America.

Like Captain Queeg's maniacal obsession with stolen strawberries in *The Caine Mutiny,* these critics seem fixated on finding categorical proof that the predominantly Boomer faculty are politicizing education and undermining what higher learning ought to be. Almost desperately they ferret out any course that studies lesbian writers or the pop star Madonna or sex in literature or black nationalism or the films of Oliver Stone and offer it as evidence to prove their case. And the news media, always looking for a good fight, amplify the charges and leave the impression that there's a battle over the heart and soul of higher education, with steadfast proponents of Western culture struggling against the trendy and politically correct curriculum of Sixties liberals.

From the news clips and jeremiads it's not hard to get the impression that Shakespeare is out and Toni Morrison is now a graduation requirement; that courses on race and gender have replaced the study of European culture; that American history is taught only as narrative of white men oppressing Native Americans, blacks, and women; or that our colleges and universities are simply out of touch with the mainstream. "Most English departments," writes the critic Robert Brustein, "are now so completely hostage to fashionable political and theoretical agendas that it is unlikely Shakespeare can qualify as an appropriate author." They study "such rap artists as Ice-T in equal proportion to William Shakespeare," says another. "Only literature professors now believe in socialist revolution and centrally planned economies," says yet another. Of particular concern are African-American and women's studies programs, which the critics dismiss as little more than academic propaganda mills. "Women's studies programs make few pretenses of concern with academic rigor, openly insisting on their political aims, as if all scholarship were simply politics by other means—as it was, of course, in totalitarian societies like the old Soviet Union," declares the conservative scholar Jeremy Rabkin in a piece called "Feminism: Where the Spirit of the Sixties Lives On." And the state of scholarship today? It's not really scholarship, the critics say, but rather obscurantism dressed up as knowledge, all driven by a leftist political agenda designed to blame America for all the world's ills. As one author famously put it, it's not a college education—it's "the closing of the American mind."

You almost have to feel sorry for these critics because they're so angry and bitter toward one of our nation's greatest institutions, higher education. But you also have to wonder how many of them have actually spent any time on campus or in a classroom recently—beyond, of course, parachuting in for an evening to pick up a tidy lecture fee—or whether the professors among them have ever stepped beyond the threshold of their musty offices to explore the intellectual plenitude unfolding before them. For the college culture they describe is so completely unlike what most students, graduates, and faculty experience that there has to be a reason why these critics are so intent upon distorting it through their embittered looking glass.

Perhaps the only thing these critics get right is that Boomers have indeed taken over and transformed our colleges and universities. Simply by virtue of demography and age, they're now the professors and administrators who teach the courses and develop the curriculum and create the programs to meet the needs of today's student body. And as Boomers have done throughout society, they've made our campuses more open, more diverse, more interesting, more conducive to personal freedom and creative expression, more egalitarian in function and spirit. Far from demanding lockstep conformity, colleges today allow and indeed encourage students to pursue their intellectual interests, and to do it with a rigor forged by a blend of traditional and innovative pedagogy. Students are no longer taught to accept things as they are and ask why, but to look at things the way they could be and ask why not. Does race or gender or language or culture or social class influence an event or work of art or sociological study or healthcare practice? Does the world look different through the eyes of an African journalist or an El Salvadoran farmer or a Chinese factory worker or a slave's great-granddaughter or a Wall Street bond trader? Does power shape the way we perceive society and culture and economics and the environment? Today there are more courses that cover Shakespeare than at any time before, but there are also more courses that discuss race and sex and women's rights and poverty and economic disparities. True to the mission of higher education, students are exposed to a wide range of perspectives, pedagogies, and subjects, more so than any previous generation. The world is no longer a black-and-white picture but rather a three-dimensional holograph, and students are asked to inspect it from every angle. And that may be what riles these conservatives so about higher education and indeed the rest of Baby Boom culture today—that their authority is no longer the only authority, that their learned perspective is no longer the only learned perspective, that the contemporary world has simply passed them by. Colleges in the Baby Boom era are opening minds, and these critics don't like it.

What may be the most telling evidence of how much higher education has changed for the better can be found in the types of dissertations and theses American students have written over the years—which tells a lot about the intellectual interests of professors and what they teach in the classroom. Take black history. It would be difficult today for even the most conservative intellectual to deny that race relations and the black experience are central to understanding our nation's history. Yet according to the *Dissertation Abstracts* database of more than two million theses and dissertations, only two theses were written under the black history category in the entire 1950s—one for an M.A., the other for an educational degree, neither for a Ph.D.—and not a single black history thesis was written in the 1960s. To be sure, the database categories aren't foolproof, and there are probably a few more black history theses sprinkled throughout other subject categories. But a search of all 96,000 doctoral dissertations written in the United States from 1955 to 1964—in every possible subject ranging from economics to education to literature to anthropology to agriculture to the sciences—found only 255 in which the commonly used words "Negro" or "Negroes" were included in the title. So of all dissertations written back then, less than 0.3 percent appear to be on topics related to African-Americans. Think about the very rich record of black life in America, and only a handful of theses done on it during those years. Now fast forward to the 1990s, where 1,405 were written on black history. To conservatives, that number might signify that racial issues now dominate academic circles. But wait: Medieval history registered more than 1,200 theses during the same decade, Germanic literature almost 1,600, and classical literature about 1,300, each about the same as black history and not one of them having much to do with questions of gender and race. In the Baby Boom era university, African-Americans have simply gotten their seat at the seminar table, nothing more, nothing less. The intellectual diversity is palpable and real—it's the opening of the American mind.

Nor is it much different with women's studies—a field that rescued the lives and dreams of half the world's population from academic obscurity and indifference. It may not interest the conservative critics that women have struggled with economic dependence and wrestled with sexual prohibitions and carved out lives separate from the traditionally male domains of power and commerce, but if academia is at all true to its mission of understanding the whole cloth of society and life, it's a field whose prominence was long overdue.

According to the *Dissertation Abstracts* database, there was not a single doctoral dissertation under the women's studies category written in the entire United States during the 1950s and 1960s, and only one thesis at the MA level, not surprisingly about a home economist. Let's allow that "women's studies" is a term of recent vintage that came of age in the Seventies, so it may be that most dissertations on women were filed under different categories back then. But a search of all 96,000 doctoral dissertations written between 1955 and 1964—on every possible subject—found only 292 with the word "women" in the title, a meager 0.3 percent of all dissertations. Consider that: Women's lives were not deemed worthy of serious scholarly study during those years. By the Seventies, the number in the women's studies category jumped to 164, fewer than the 607 in medieval history for that decade but certainly better than zero or one, and the word "women" made it into the title of about 1,975 dissertations, 0.7 percent of the 280,000 dissertations written that decade. It was only when Boomers began to fill up the ranks of tenured faculty—and only when Boomers pried open the professoriate to include more women—that universities finally began to meet the pent-up demand for understanding female narratives and lives. During the 1990s, American graduate students wrote more than 12,000 doctoral dissertations under the rubric of women's studies—on such varied topics as Virginia Woolf, sexuality in older women, the differential in male and female medical care, and female athletic accomplishments, among many others, all quite fascinating and critical to our cumulative understanding of who we are and how we got there. Now to put that number in perspective, about 360,000 doctoral dissertations were written at American universities during those years, meaning that women's studies accounted for only about 3 percent of all dissertations. As with blacks, it's a seat at the seminar table, nothing more, nothing less. And again the custodians of traditionalism need not fear: There were as many dissertations in English and American literature as in women's studies, and if romance, comparative, modern, classical, and all the other literature categories are added in, the canon beats women hands down.

Even the most alarmist jeremiads against academia today unwittingly confirm that universities are opening rather than closing minds—which may be exactly what our conservative critics fear. Back in 2000, a conservative group called the National Association of Scholars (NAS) created quite a media stir with a study showing that among college course descriptions, the percentage featuring Shakespeare and Chaucer declined significantly between 1964 and 1997, Shakespeare by a third and Chaucer by half. Just as troubling, the study found, is that such venerable authors as William Faulkner and Henry James now rank below Nobel laureate Toni Morrison among author mentions in course descriptions. The study generated a feeding frenzy among conservative pundits who cited it as conclusive evidence that literary standards are under siege from politically correct academics. What have we come to, they asked, if Toni Morrison gets more attention than an English poet like Alexander Pope?

The problem with this report, and what NAS hides in its appendix, is that courses covering Shakespeare, while declining as a proportion of the whole, still doubled during the time period studied, and Chaucer likewise went up by nearly 60 percent—and they still remain the top two assigned authors by a wide margin. In fact most of the authors whose declining proportions are decried in this study—Wordsworth, Donne, Keats, Swift, Whitman—actually saw substantial increases in the number of courses that featured them, typically by 50 percent. Indeed the only way these proportions wouldn't decline is if the 1964 curriculum remained frozen in time, which would mean the near complete exclusion of contemporary greats, female authors, and minority writers from the classroom— thus no Baldwin, Woolf, Stowe, Hurston, Rushdie, Nabokov, Ellison, Gordimer, and Heller, to name just a few. That would be a bit like saying the Olympic games have deteriorated because men's track and field is a smaller percentage of the competition now that women's sports have been added, so let's go back to the old way to make it better. Moreover, any look at a college catalog will show few if any courses dedicated exclusively to Toni Morrison, but a fair number dedicated to Shakespeare and Chaucer and the English authors, which shows that Morrison is typically included in survey courses designed to expose students to different perspectives and genres, whereas Shakespeare and Chaucer are often treated as greats on their own. So peel away the veil of ideology from this NAS study and what you find are more courses offered, more authors read, more attention to the major authors, and more students exposed to the variety of literary voices that enrich our world. Isn't that what higher education is all about?

In fact this flowering of perspectives is a core characteristic of higher education in the Baby Boom era, and for good reason. Boomers were the first generation to confront the nascent media age, and they understood as long-haired students that higher education was no longer a privilege but rather a pillar of the modern world and economy and information culture—and that the stodgy, constricted, upper-crust university of old was simply obsolete in an era of constant change and dissolving borders. Back then Boomer students understood that something at college was out of synch—that the traditionalist worldview didn't have any answers for ethnic diversity and cross-cultural conflict and misguided wars and overcoming a past stained by injustice and a present riddled with inequities and discrimination—that in fact the traditionalist worldview too often reinforced these problems. Boomers saw what later studies confirmed, that those who attended college before them and received a more traditional education showed little interest in or awareness of racial issues or sex roles or foreign cultures beyond what they could find in London and Paris. Civil rights, Vietnam, and women's liberation were especially eye-opening because they forced Boomers to reckon with the deficiencies in the education they were getting, how it left huge gaps in preparing them to understand and examine different lives at home and cultures abroad—indeed a 1992 U.S. Department of Education report concluded precisely that about the higher education most Boomers received.

To many Americans back in the Sixties and Seventies, it may have seemed impudent and brash for Boomers to have shut down their universities and demand more attention to minority and women's concerns. But whatever righteousness and conceit they showed at the time doesn't mean their critique of the old-style university was misguided or wrong. For however they articulated it, they were right to point out that the rigid university curriculum was becoming increasingly irrelevant in our transitional times. To read what the conservative author William Buckley said in 1967 is to be reminded of just how stale, stifling, and entitled the old worldview was and how appropriate it was for Boomers to challenge it: Yale, Buckley lamented, was no longer the "kind of place where your family goes for generations," that it had regrettably been turned into a school where "the son of an alumnus, who goes to a private preparatory school, now has less chance of getting in than some boy from P.S. 109 somewhere." You went to chapel, studied your Latin, memorized your Homer, and all was well, wasn't it?

So Boomers set out to rebuild the academy—first as students, now as professors—and to turn it into an institution that reflects the diversity of challenges, traditions, pedagogies, and peoples that brought us to this point in time and will lead us into the future. Students can still study the classics, but now they also can study the lives of women and African-Americans as well as mass media and environmental science and cross-cultural communication. A student today can just as easily study the Bible as the Koran, or read Jonathan Swift as readily as Gabriel Garcia Marquez, or gain as much support for a thesis on sex in Shakespeare as one on sex in the media—and each topic would be welcomed equally and appreciated for its value. What Boomers have done is recognize the necessity of preparing students for a world far more complex and intricate than what was covered in the traditional Western Civilization course of old—a world built on information, images, new technologies, communication, clashing values, different perspectives, regional politics, religious hostilities, ethical dilemmas, power relationships, economic imbalances, and a wide diversity of people. So yes, study European history, but also study global conflict. Study the American founders, but also study how some of them held slaves and how that influenced our national culture. Or study the American Dream and its widespread appeal, but also study the obstacles to achieving it.

Critics of higher education believe there's something vaguely un-

American for professors to challenge the traditional narrative of our history and the prevailing assumptions about power, culture, race, gender, and class—that it's all part of a liberal Boomer political agenda foisted on this next generation. "Promoting multiculturalism," writes the conservative talk show host Sean Hannity, "really means demonizing Western civilization." Robert Bork fumes that "hatred of America and the West is seen most clearly in American universities." There's even been a resolution introduced in Congress criticizing professors for one-sidedness and urging universities to adopt a so-called "Academic Bill of Rights." But like so many other conservative concerns about the academy, this one is wildly exaggerated and mistaken. As much as they'd like to, conservatives can't wish away the fact that race and gender and culture and class are simply part of life, that faculty would be negligent not to address them, and that the only thing political about these topics is when the critics try to deny their significance. To appreciate freedom we need to know how freedom can be subverted. To understand democracy we need to know what undermines democracy. To grasp equality we need to know both the subtle and explicit ways it can be and has been thwarted. Indeed to sanitize America is to deny our rich history of facing flaws and, however painfully, surmounting them. Today's students will be tomorrow's decision makers, and they need to know what we've overcome, how we've overcome it, and what remains in their way. And they need to know it not merely as a general philosophical statement but as a tangible, ongoing part of daily life that shapes how we as individuals think and behave.

But it's also important to note that using race and gender as interpretive tools does not mean they're the only tools professors use in class. According to a recent survey of college English professors, a majority say it's important to teach about race and gender—but a majority also say it's important to teach about the enduring ideas of Western civilization—and of all the possible teaching approaches used in class, the most popular is to study texts the traditional way. Another survey of undergraduate teaching faculty nationwide found that 57 percent thought Western culture and civilization should be the foundation of a college curriculum and 58 percent said that colleges should enhance a student's knowledge and under-

standing of other racial and ethnic groups. In the overheated world of talk
show media, these approaches may stand in conflict, but in an open college
environment there's nothing mutually exclusive about them.

My own university, American University in Washington, D.C., is as
representative as any of the intellectual fermentation and cross-pollination
that goes on in college classrooms today. The core of AU's education is
called the General Education Program, which is designed to give students
a grounding in the five curricular areas considered essential for a well-
rounded, modern education—creative arts, Western traditions, global and
multicultural perspectives, social institutions, and the natural sciences.
Students must take courses in each area, and any look at the curriculum
will show that both the canon and the cutting edge are well represented.
So under the creative arts, students can study the classics of literature, the
history of art, the masterpieces of music, Shakespeare, poetry, and opera as
portrayed on stage and film—and they also can study African-American
influence on the performing arts, cinema studies, visual literacy, modern
art, and the African writer. In other words, they're exposed to the best of
the old and the most interesting of the new. The other areas do precisely
as they say: Courses under the Western traditions rubric explore European and American history, philosophy, law, religion, and literature, with
such specialty courses as Jewish civilization, English literature, women in
the West, and American ethnic literature spiced in; under the global perspectives curriculum, students study comparative politics, Third World
literature, international media, economic development, multicultural societies, Asia, the Middle East, Africa, Latin America, Islamic culture, and
women in developing countries; and for social institutions, the courses
cover mass media, education, the legal system, cities, families, finance, and
the way ethnicity and gender weave through them all. By the time they
complete this program, AU's students receive a broad and rigorous education that steeps them in both tradition and diversity and empowers them
to understand the past, wrestle with the present, and prepare for the
future. It's neither politically correct nor politically incorrect—it's simply
broad-based learning consistent with the Boomer vision of an educated
society.

And it's no different in each of the individual departments, which again show a blend of the traditional and the new, the consensus and the diverse. History majors must take survey courses in American and European history; at least one course in ancient or medieval history; at least one in Asian, Middle Eastern, Russian, or Eastern European history; at least one in African, African-American, Latin-American, or Native-American history; and at least one upper level course in both American and Western European or British history. That's a fairly balanced set of requirements, and if biased at all it's in favor of Western culture. Altogether a little more than eighty courses are offered, and most cover the core subjects of American, European, Latin-American, and Asian history. There are also the typical courses that concentrate on certain periods—the Renaissance and Civil War, for example—and specific countries—England and Russia, to name two—as well as seminal topics in human history—the Holocaust, immigration, and the American Revolution. Nothing unusual there. But now hold on to your hats because a closer review of the catalog reveals three courses on African-American history, three on women in America, one on Native-American history, one on the nuclear age, one on Americans and their environment, and sit tight now, one called "Oliver Stone's America," which teaches about the relationship between Hollywood and history. Heaven knows what these tenured radicals will come up with next. Let's be generous to the critics and add to this list a course on the history of medicine in the United States because it includes a section on the role of race. That's eleven courses that might not make it into the 1964 curriculum. Eleven suspect courses out of eighty—assuming, of course, they're suspect. The politically correct have taken over this department, haven't they?

It's likewise in the literature department, with more than sixty courses offered during the academic year, and while there are two every term exclusively dedicated to Shakespeare, each with multiple sections, as well as two a year on Victorian literature and a host of others on the classics and the Romantics and the European greats, it's hard not to notice the infiltration of nine courses that never would have made it into the 1964 curriculum—one on African-American literature, one on Asian-American literature, one on ethnic literature, one on the African writer, one on Third World literature, one on gender in literature, two on cinema and literature, and one on

American realism that spends some time studying "self-expression by those who were marginalized, including African-Americans, Native Americans, and women." To be sure, there's no course dedicated to Toni Morrison, the Nobel laureate; in fact there's only one mention of her in the catalog. But nine out of sixty courses—my goodness, the politically correct have taken over this department as well, haven't they? As for the government department, we better man the barricades because among the sixty-five courses on Congress, the presidency, political parties, public policy, and political thought are four on women in politics, three on gender and politics, one on feminist political theory, two on civil rights, one on minority politics, one on dissent, one on federal Indian policy, one on environmental policy, one on Third World politics, one on politics in Cuba, and one on politics and the cinema. What are we doing to our students? How dare they stray from tradition like this?

Please pardon the sarcasm, but it escapes me how anyone could ever accuse these departments of rampant radicalism or indoctrination. And to think that someone might call these new courses illegitimate or politically correct seems absurd and bizarre as well. What students are getting is a full view of the many issues and variables that make up our history and culture and institutions and world—and they're getting a wide range of intellectual tools to make informed judgments about them. A student influenced most by Adam Smith will still be exposed to Thomas Hobbes and Malcolm X and Thomas Jefferson and Shakespeare and Simone de Beauvoir and Marshall McLuhan and Karl Marx—and vice versa. That's what a liberal arts education is all about, isn't it? Of course, conservative critics may seize on a course about Oliver Stone, but doesn't a course like that teach more about the popular historical imagination than any traditional history course ever could? Or they might say that the history of medicine course has succumbed to politically correct thinking by including a section on race—but shouldn't such a course cover the ignominious Tuskegee experiment, in which blacks with syphilis were left untreated so that medical researchers could track the full impact of the disease, an experiment that wasn't halted until 1972? Or they might target a course on women in American history, or gender in literature, or minorities in politics. But under what criteria would these topics lack rigor or credibility?

Is it because they're on women and minorities? Is it because Alexander Pope is more important? Is it because students shouldn't be thinking about the role of race and gender? Is it because students should look at history only from the standpoint of the powerful, not the powerless? The bottom line is that our universities are enriched by these topics and inquiries, just as they're enriched by Alexander Pope, and neither is exclusive of the other. The result is a better education for our students and a more ebullient and lively democracy.

The breadth, energy, and diversity at AU is no doubt a mirror of university classrooms across the country. One nationwide survey asked faculty to rate the priorities of their institutions, and by a wide margin the most important was to promote the intellectual development of their students—whereas one of the least important was teaching students how to change society. There may be some faculty members with political agendas, liberal and conservative, but most professors today—like their more traditionalist predecessors of a generation ago—see their role as teaching students how to think, not what to think. As for courses about diversity or gender or any of the other areas maligned as politically correct, only the most narrow-minded and embittered would say these have nothing to do with the intellectual growth and development of students. For in today's world it would simply be an act of academic malpractice for students to graduate without examining the full texture of American and global culture—especially so because too many students grow up in isolated enclaves knowing far too little about people unlike themselves yet with dreams of getting jobs that will depend on and influence these same people unlike themselves. Whatever universal knowledge Shakespeare might teach, there's still room for learning about women in the Middle East or the great black migration to the North during World War I—and to figure out how these lessons help us understand the society we've created and the world we confront. That's why more and more universities, almost two-thirds at last count, either have some sort of diversity course requirement or are in the process of developing one, with most—like AU—giving students an opportunity to choose among a variety of courses. And there are no pre-fabricated molds or politically defined formulae for such classes. They vary from institution to institution and faculty to faculty, and they reflect both intellectual rigor and the academic interests of faculty who create them—and anyone who suggests otherwise hasn't been on a campus lately and is probably just reading a few contentious news clips.

In fact the Boomer ethos on campus has translated into a veritable renaissance of curriculum development and course creation on topics that illuminate what were once neglected and disregarded subjects in the classroom. Universities now teach courses on Hispanic cultures in the United States—courses that can be considered politically correct only by ignoring the fact that people of Hispanic heritage will comprise a quarter of the population later this century. Or there are courses that compare race relations in various countries—the United States, South Africa, and Brazil—which give students an international perspective on how our own nation has dealt with its original sin. Then there are courses that ask students to look at things from a vantage point different from their own—for example, a course that examines immigration issues not from the mainstream American point of view but from the perspective of Mexicans and other immigrant groups. There are also courses that explore images of disability in American society—what it means to call someone an invalid, spastic, cripple, or monstrosity—or homosexuality and its tangled relationship with mainstream culture. There are occasional courses on gay and lesbian literary voices or on the culture of sexuality or on interracial and interfaith relationships or on national identity in a multiethnic society, and there's even a hip-hop culture course at Texas A&M that serves as a gateway for discussion of race, gender, and ethnic influence on art and society. The point of all these courses is to probe our diversity, to explore the tensions and opportunities inherent in a pluralistic society, to teach about the varieties of our American and global experience.

Do courses like these enhance the curriculum? Of course they do. Are they representative of all courses in higher education? Of course they're not. Have they replaced Shakespeare and the other greats? Of course they haven't. Because they're different, because they buck tradition, they get a disproportionate share of media attention and media caricature, but the reality is that they're still only a small minority of course offerings, and their role is to fertilize, not dominate, the traditional and mainstream curriculum—which is clearly evident when looking at the courses my own university teaches. As to the well-worn criticism that these courses teach identity politics, demonize white males, and pull us all apart, the truth is that we never were completely together, and the best way to promote inclusiveness is to understand the unspoken assumptions that shape and divide us. What seems to rile the critics of academia is a lot like what angered the old Southern whites who accused the civil rights movement of agitating blacks and causing so much trouble down South—when in fact blacks were already agitated and trouble had been smoldering long before a single civil rights worker ever went South. It's the same with diversity courses, which aren't creating divisions but trying to confront and address divisions that for too long had been ignored or suppressed. What Southern whites really resented was how civil rights challenged their power, threatened their privilege, and forced a public reckoning over the society they had for so long dominated. Isn't that exactly what makes these critics of academia so dyspeptic today?

Nor is teaching the only academic activity these critics attack. To them, today's universities have abandoned scholarship standards and have rewarded professors for researching the most obscure and trivial topics, particularly on the usual suspects of gender and race and popular culture. Academics today, according to the critics, produce not scholarly works but rather "a moated scholasticism of many-footnoted obfuscation," and to prove it they'll trot out conference papers on the semiotics of rap music or sexuality in Emily Dickinson's poetry or Woody Allen's comic use of gastronomy. Sure, some of these might sound amusing, and they may drill down into subjects that seem overly pedantic and not all that significant. But it's worthwhile asking whether scholarship was any more edifying and broad-minded back in the old days. So consider a sampling of dissertation topics from the 1950s. In medieval history you could learn about the court of Champagne under Henry the Liberal and Countess Marie, or about the English Episcopate during the reign of Henry I with an account of the Welsh dioceses. In American history you could learn about the story of Galveston on the eve of secession, or about the life of David Gouverneur Burnet, the first president of Texas, or about what YMCA boys did between 1900 and 1925, or about the seventeenth-century fur trade in

New Netherland. Now look at today's topics and behold, they're equally esoteric, with the one difference that many dissertations in American history now include explorations of race, ethnicity, gender, and sexuality, themes largely missing from the topics done in the Fifties. So there will be a thesis on the gay and lesbian migration to San Francisco from the Forties to the Sixties, or one on male army nurses, or one on the Tulsa race riot of 1921, or one on visual images of Jim Crow laws, or one on American women artists from 1820 to 1880—along with the more traditional topics such as the Civil War in West Virginia, medical education in nineteenth-century New England, and artisan workers in antebellum Virginia.

The truth is, much of scholarship has always been bereft of grand themes and ambitious topics. Academics have always bored into little topics searching for illuminating truths—some succeed, some don't. But knowledge is cumulative, and as any professor will testify, that little and seemingly trivial nugget of research discussed at a conference or found in a journal can all of a sudden have meaning and value in a larger and more significant scholarly project, not to mention in the classroom. As to the criticism that there are more papers and books on popular culture these days, that's true, but what it signifies is nothing more than the fact that scholars today are plumbing every part of the world around them, that the text of our culture is as worthy of study as an archived box of documents. It's simply no different from what scholars of the medieval era do, which is to probe every possible corner of that period in history. For critics to say that medieval history is more important or worthwhile than mass media studies—and to disparage any exploration of popular culture—is to imply that European society as it unfolded eight hundred years ago is more deserving of study than the culture that materializes before us today, which is a dubious conclusion at best. Just because a field is new doesn't mean it's any less legitimate than a field that's been around for years. Shouldn't we be encouraging our scholars to explore all aspects of the human condition?

Furthermore, to say that academic scholarship can be narrow and trivial doesn't mean that all academic scholarship is narrow and trivial. In fact it's been quite the opposite in the Baby Boom era, notwithstanding what the critics say, with many scholars churning out relevant studies that have a real impact on our public culture. We've learned a lot from recent research exploring the way people communicate by e-mail, or how inheritance affects racial economic disparities, or how classroom culture favors boys, or how beauty and appearance influence status and pay, or how women negotiate less aggressively for starting salaries and pay raises. Historical research helps us understand why certain immigrant groups act in similar and different ways, why the black family faces pressures the typical white family has never faced, and why some metropolitan areas have housing segregation patterns different from others. Media research helps us understand the appeal of advertising, the shortened attention span, and why the political sound bite has declined from forty-five seconds in 1968 to only about seven seconds today. Political research helps us understand who votes, who doesn't, and why. From research on religion we gain insight into churchgoing, denomination switching, and cultural values. From international research we better understand why our nation is admired and hated by many of the same people. From legal and social research we know more about barriers to full civil rights and about continuing inequities between men and women. From medical research we see how medicine has given short shrift to illnesses afflicting minorities and women.

As these examples show, so much of our public discourse and policy is seeded by academic research and insights that we take them for granted and barely notice anymore. But the impact is tangible and real. Those newspaper articles that analyze the role of race when a star African-American athlete is accused of rape? Typically they're shaped by long interviews with academics who have studied all sides of the issue. Those classroom practices designed to get more girls interested in math and science? They too derive from academic research. Certainly there were many conservative critics who ridiculed gay and lesbian scholarship as an exercise in politically correct solipsism with relevance only in the academy—until they saw how Supreme Court Justice Anthony Kennedy relied on this scholarship in his landmark 2003 decision overturning sodomy laws and upholding sexual privacy. Indeed what's so breathtaking about academic scholarship in the Baby Boom years is how so much of it reflects the core Boomer values of rooting out inequality and exposing hypocrisy and examining the unexamined and holding society up to its ideals and values. That racial and gender studies constitute such a growing field should be seen not as a threat but rather as an opportunity to better understand our culture and society—and to make us a more inclusive and democratic country. Scholarship can be trivial, but it also can be meaningful, and when it is we all benefit greatly.

The end result of all this fermentation is an extraordinarily dynamic higher education culture that is producing some of the most provocative research and open-minded students in American history. What was once a static, ossified, privileged world on campus has been unbuttoned and freed to engage the compelling questions of society and history. The available research shows that students graduating from college today are far more tolerant of others and aware of different perspectives than any previous generation of graduates. One study of Harvard and University of Michigan law students found that exposure to diversity in their classes helped to deepen their understanding of civil rights and criminal justice issues. Other studies show that women's studies courses stimulate more debate among students than other courses do, and actually enhance women's attitudes toward men. But we don't need surveys to tell us what is evident every day, that universities are asking the questions and seeking the answers for the dilemmas and problems and ethical questions we face daily at work and at home and in the community. Race, religion, sex, power, injustice, the limits of science, the morality of commerce—we shouldn't be running from them, as the old system did, but rather addressing them and confronting them and understanding them, which is precisely what universities do today. There's a reason why students from around the world are flocking to American universities for study, and that's because the Baby Boom has reinvigorated higher education to prepare young people for economic innovation, cultural diversity, global engagement, and the real challenges of a rapidly changing society and world.

All of this doesn't mean that Boomer era universities are free of drawbacks and problems and their share of pompous and self-righteous faculty. Certainly not. Universities throughout history have been characterized this way, and remember, universities are institutions like any others, made up of people with their virtues and flaws and idiosyncracies. The most educated are as prone as anyone else to say silly things, and like anywhere else in society today, the academy is not immune to the egregious and ridiculous, which is what gives the critics ammunition for their accusations. How about the professor who said that "no aspect of twentieth-century thought and culture can be understood well without asking how it's intersected with issues of homosexual/heterosexual definition"? Or the professor who said that Shakespeare's play *The Tempest* was all about the rape of the Third World? Or the professor who called marriage "an instrument of oppression"? Such statements would be legendary for their foolishness even if the press never reported them, and on their own they would simply sink under the weight of their own absurdity. And students themselves have a baloney detector for ridiculous statements, professorial posturing, and ideological spin, and are not afraid to say so. But do these excesses justify the conservative movement's effort to discredit higher education? Certainly not. That would be the equivalent of rejecting capitalism because of misdeeds at Enron and WorldCom and the other cases of corporate malfeasance. To blow out of proportion a few high-profile cases is to misrepresent what's really happening on campus and to do precisely what the traditionalists supposedly reject—take things completely out of context and see them only through an ideological prism.

As for the much-debated speech codes that try to prohibit offensive speech on campus, these too are wrong and misguided—textbook cases of good intentions gone overboard, and it's not only conservative critics who have every reason to denounce them. For a college to determine what's offensive, who's offended, and who should be charged is messy enough in a culture that values free expression—particularly when so much is left to interpretation. Even worse is when administrators go a step further and try to insulate anyone vulnerable from anything offensive, as when some tried to outlaw "inconsiderate jokes" or "lookism," defined as discrimination based on appearance. No matter how well intended, these administrators couldn't have created a better caricature of the politically correct Baby Boomer.

Thankfully, action against alleged speech code offenders is untypical and rare. But the damage these speech codes cause goes far beyond the few times they're ever enforced. For what they do is make free speech the issue and as a result undermine any reasonable effort to educate students about the problem the codes were meant to address: that words and symbols are laden with values and have the power to shape social expectations and relations. Rather than punish a student for making a bigoted remark, universities should teach how that bigoted remark can cause pain or feelings of isolation in those to whom it was directed. Students can be taught how segregationists called black men "boy" as a way to degrade and humiliate. They can be reminded that before the feminists invented the prefix "Ms.," women were identified only by their marital state—"Mrs." and "Miss"—which meant that women were labeled and judged according to their relationship to men, which has never been the case the other way around. They also can be taught about the assumptions we make when we call someone "fat," or when women are called "pushy" when the same behavior is called "decisive" in men, or when a white person uses the word "articulate" to describe a black. Done right, when the curriculum teaches students how their choice of language can hold down minorities, women, or others vulnerable in society, it can play a powerful role in reducing prejudice and promoting equality. According to a survey conducted in 2000, most Americans prefer a workplace free of sexist language and sexually explicit jokes, and they reject the notion that we've gone too far in restricting what is acceptable for people to say at work. That's because thirty years of Baby Boom feminism have educated America about the consequences of this language. At bottom, it's all about creating a society in which people respect one another because of and in spite of their differences. With the unfortunate exception of speech codes, that's exactly what universities in the Baby Boom era have been trying to do.

About a century ago the academic world was similarly roiled by a conflict between traditionalists and modernists, but back then it was the traditionalists trying to fend off the infusion of Shakespeare, Dante, Milton, and Machiavelli into what was a curriculum dominated by the ancient classics. Shakespeare in particular was condemned for writing violent and sexually explicit plays. But the modernists argued that these great works can teach us about human nature, about the best of us and the worst of us, and they wondered why the traditionalists feared them so. We now think of Shakespeare and Milton as pillars of the canon, and no one looks back on this long-forgotten academic controversy. It won't be any different with the academic controversies of today.

In the long run, all of the criticisms and accusations leveled at higher education today will fade away, and it's the university created by Boomers that will be left standing. It will be a university characterized by courses that challenge assumptions and scholarship that speaks truth to the status quo. It will ask students to look at the diversity of their world and to figure out how it fits into their lives. It will support the research that keeps the powerful from setting the agenda at the expense of the powerless. It will explore those same questions of human nature that the academic reformers of a century ago raised, but in ways that older generations never imagined exploring. And it will combine the lessons of traditional pedagogy with the findings of new disciplines. Henry Kissinger once said that academic politics are so vicious because the stakes are so small. But in truth they're not small. For a William Buckley it might be all about the pedigree, the coat-and-tie, and the literary canon. But for Boomer educators it's all about educating a citizenry capable of thinking beyond their cultural context and own self-interest. No other institution in America is doing so much to accomplish these goals. What began a generation ago with Boomer students demanding change in the old academy has morphed into a dynamic university culture based on Boomer values that is helping us adapt to the ever-changing present and future. It is one of the Baby Boom's most significant and enduring legacies.

# Chapter Twelve
# Grass-roots Nation

Teach your children well,
Their fathers' hell did slowly go by,
And feed them on your dreams
The one they pick's the one you'll know by.
—*Crosby, Stills, Nash & Young, "Teach Your Children," 1970*

**I**t was a frustrating three years for Colorado's leading environmental groups. In 2001 they drafted what to most neutral observers was reasonable legislation that would require the state's largest utilities to generate more of their electricity from renewable sources, and the bill seemed to have widespread popular support. But three years in a row the bill came up for a vote, and three years in a row the special interests knocked it down. In 2004 it was especially frustrating because the bill had the strong enthusiastic backing of leading labor, business, and agricultural groups, but it was still killed, this time three days before the legislative session ended. But these environmental groups didn't back down—convinced that their public support was real and decisive, they had a Plan B to circumvent the special interests and bring it directly to the people.

Rick Gilliam is one of those behind-the-scenes Baby Boomers who has long worked in the environmental policy trenches, and when the bill died in 2004 he was ready with an alternative. An energy policy expert at the Western Resource Advocates, a nonprofit conservation group founded in 1989, he had been preparing a ballot initiative for the November 2004 election that paralleled the standards proposed in the legislation. Western Resource Advocates is typical of the many grass-roots environmental organizations that came of age in the Baby Boom era—a feisty group of policy experts empowered by our new environmental consensus and dedicated to protecting natural resources and promoting greener practices. Over the years they've quietly succeeded in developing and passing energy and environmental standards in various Southwestern states, all aimed at improving air and water quality. So they knew what they were doing.

The day the legislature killed the renewable energy bill, Rick handed his ballot language to a coalition of politically savvy environmental groups, Coloradans for Clean Energy, and the sprint to November began. To get it on the ballot, the initiative needed about 68,000 signatures, but just to be safe the coalition wanted 100,000. So they mobilized 1,000 activists, and within ten weeks they gathered 115,000 names. But that was the easy part. Led by the rural electrical co-ops, the initiative's opponents began running an aggressive television ad campaign against it, eventually outspending the environmentalists by a three to one margin. With a message about higher costs for consumers, the utilities began to chip away at support for the initiative. But the environmental groups believed they had the majority on their side and took their case directly to the people. Activists from all over the state organized local meetings and town hall events and sessions with community and business leaders. They generated a letter-writing campaign, drafted letters to the editor, and eventually received endorsements from fifteen Colorado newspapers. They also raised money, albeit in small amounts, but enough to begin their own ad campaign. And they debated the opponents before city councils and on TV. On November 2, Amendment 37, as the initiative was known, passed with 53.4 percent of the vote. By 2015, Colorado utilities with forty thousand or more customers would have to generate at least 10 percent of their electricity from renewable sources, mainly wind and solar power. Despite all the special interest forces lined up against them, Rick Gilliam and his fellow green activists had written into law the environmental thinking of the Baby Boom era. And it would become, Rick says with pride, a model for other states to follow.

Rick Gilliam's story, though important on its own, is really emblematic of a much larger phenomenon in America over the past few decades, and that's the remarkable growth of professional civic activism and the rise of a nonprofit advocacy culture determined to preserve, protect, and defend the predominant values of the Baby Boom generation. Today our country is alive with organizations dedicated to expanding rights and freedoms to as many citizens as possible, and barely a day passes without reports of civic Davids challenging corporate or institutional or well-funded Goliaths to live up to the norms and values of Baby Boom America. What these nonprofits do, effectively, is institutionalize the social gains of recent years and fight any attempts to roll them back.

The rise of this nonprofit culture has not gone unnoticed among conservative opponents of Baby Boom liberalism. Frustrated that these advocacy groups effectively enfranchise Boomer values and serve as a political proxy for the majority of Americans who hold them, some conservatives have tried to "defund the left" by pressuring corporations and foundations to stop funding these groups and by trying to restrict the advocacy activities of any group that receives federal money, even if the group uses the money to feed AIDS patients or help girls overcome their fear of math or researches racial disparities in health care. They also issue reports labeling any number of mainstream consumer, environmental, civil rights, and women's groups "left-wing" or "radical left" or even "anti-Christian." And they've even tried revoking the nonprofit tax status of some groups, saying, as one conservative activist did with seeming disregard for the First Amendment, that "if you take taxpayer dollars, you ought not to get involved in controversial issues." We have to assume these conservative opponents will never get their way, nor should they if their goal is to stifle democracy, free speech, and pluralism. But they are on to something important: We now live in a grass-roots nation, and the bulk of the activism sustains and advances the values of Baby Boom America.

Anyone who has ever read Alexis de Tocqueville's classic study of America in the 1830s knows that civic associations have always been a mainstay of American life. Ethnic, neighborhood, occupational, and reform-minded groups flourished throughout the twentieth century, and venerable organizations such as the NAACP and B'nai B'rith's Anti-Defamation League have long stood as stalwart defenders of American ideals and their minority group constituents. But in the Sixties something seemed to change. Baby Boomers began to lose confidence in the political process—particularly in political parties and established institutions. They saw elected officials accommodate segregationists and vote for a war because their party leaders told them to do so. They saw how the forces of change came not from inside Washington or city hall but from outside the electoral framework—from civil rights groups, anti-war groups, women's groups, and student groups. And they saw how the empowerment of blacks and women and gays came not from congressional representation but from the power of advocacy groups to make their voices heard.

So Boomers started organizing around all the issues that interested them. Convinced that the political system was tilted toward the special interests, they revitalized the American civic tradition and began to create organizations in the public interest—organizations to fight government secrecy, monitor the courts, expose the polluters, root out discrimination, promote opportunities for women, advocate for women's health, protect religious minorities, uncover corporate malfeasance, and advance equality for gays. It was a variation on the old Chinese proverb, let a thousand organizations bloom, and so they did. Nor did Boomers just create the new. They also invigorated the stodgy conservation groups of old and turned them from bird-watching and park preservation clubs to forceful advocates of environmental protection. They expanded the focus of major civil rights and civil liberties groups, and when these organizations reached capacity they spawned a new generation of advocates and organizations to ensure equality for the most vulnerable among us. These Boomers flocked to Washington and the state capitals and to countless community organizations, earning far less than what the private sector paid but content to spend their lives working for their ideals.

So from the late Sixties onward a curious phenomenon began to develop in American public life: Membership in the traditional political clubs declined, but more and more Americans were forming groups and coalitions to solve both local and national problems. Boomers were setting up alternative political institutions that empowered citizens in ways their elected representatives never did. Citizen organizing, writes the political scientist Karen Paget, has since the Sixties become "a well-established feature of the American political landscape."

As of the early 1990s, according to Paget, about two million citizen organizations were operating in the United States, most of them liberal or "social change" groups, and they were actively engaging almost fifteen million citizens in community-based and national networks. Among them are the major groups—the Sierra Club and American Civil Liberties Union, for example—but also many that fly under the radar as loose confederations of like-minded citizens that never register as nonprofits with the Internal Revenue Service (IRS), the more so now with the Internet as an electronic town square for citizen action. Another scholar looking at IRS figures estimates that thirty thousand environmental and animal rights groups and about two hundred thousand social action groups have registered with the IRS but don't meet the revenue threshold requirement to file an annual IRS report, which means they're rarely included in the national tally of nonprofits. As for the formal nonprofit groups that do file their annual forms—including the big ones that receive membership dues by the hundreds of thousands—they too have shown remarkable growth in the Baby Boom years. In the ten years from 1989 to 1998, for example, the number of animal rights and environmental nonprofits reporting to the IRS more than doubled, from 3,504 to 7,497. These numbers track with the rapid growth of all nonprofits since the Sixties. From the late 1970s to the early 1990s, according to Michael O'Neill, author of *Nonprofit Nation,* the IRS was approving between thirty-five thousand and forty-five thousand applications for nonprofit status each year, compared with only about five thousand per year throughout the 1950s and early 1960s. And it was the Baby Boom generation that staffed these organizations and spurred their growth. Boomers simply animated the nonprofit sector and made advocacy an acceptable choice as an alternative career.

These numbers also track with the Baby Boom's overall approach to getting things done, which is to distrust the political process and the powers that be and to initiate change from the grass roots up. This is a legacy from the Sixties, that it took outside pressure from students and women and anti-war and civil rights activists to effect legislative and normative change. Recent surveys show that Americans overall but Boomers in particular see the political system favoring special interests at the expense of everyone else. But these same surveys, not surprisingly, also find that Boomers refuse to accept the crumbs of such a political system and instead are more likely than others to speak out and have their voices heard. A Simmons Market Research Bureau study found Boomers far more likely than other age groups to address public meetings, involve themselves in local civic issues, write letters to the editor, and raise money for causes. A 2002 survey of civic activity conducted by the Center for Information and

Research on Civic Learning and Engagement reached similar conclusions—that Boomers are more likely than other adult cohorts to contact the news media to voice their opinions, sign or write a petition about a political or social issue, and go door-to-door for a candidate or cause, and Boomers more so than other cohorts have participated in a protest march or demonstration and refused to buy a product because of the company's labor practices or overall conduct. For Boomers, advocacy groups are the perfect fit for this generational sensibility—these groups tend to be nimble, distrustful of authority, never complacent, and responsive to their members because without them these groups never would stay in business. This is democracy in action, Baby Boom style.

That these groups stand on the outside looking in should in no way be interpreted to mean that they lack effectiveness. Quite the contrary—which is probably why conservative activists target them so. What they do is blend legislative advocacy, legal action, issue research, investigative reporting, grass-roots organizing, and public relations into a program that generates press attention and political interest and thus cuts through the media clutter to raise awareness of issues that might otherwise be lost. According to the political scientist Jeffrey Berry, who has done ground-breaking research on Washington-based nonprofits, citizen advocacy groups are "greatly *overrepresented* in terms of participation in the legislative process and in the press coverage they received." Based on a review of advocacy work in 1991, Berry found that these predominantly liberal citizen groups, while less than 7 percent of the interest group population in Washington, accounted for 32 percent of all congressional testimony that year and 46 percent of all references to interest groups in network news coverage. And while business lobbies dwarf the resources available to these groups, "when they went head-to-head against business in policy conflicts," Berry found, "citizen groups won their fair share of the time."

The question, of course, is why they're so effective even when they're overpowered by the might and resources of larger and better-funded lobbying groups. And that gets back to the fact that the issues and causes they embody are based on the values and norms that Boomers have nurtured since the Sixties and now predominate in our culture today. For what these groups represent is a firewall against any retreat from the social progress our nation has made over the last generation. All the overheated talk show rhetoric notwithstanding, Americans are content with the greater freedom, equality, and tolerance we now have. Most people simply don't want to go backwards, and they look to these groups to make sure that doesn't happen. So when a politician tries to chip away at environmental protections or civil rights laws, we depend on these groups to speak out, object, and prevent or at least mitigate the rollbacks. Or when current laws fail to protect women and minorities at work, we expect these groups to push for new and better solutions. Or when social conservatives try to impose their religious morality on everyone else, we turn to these groups to protect our contemporary values. That is why millions of Americans join these groups and write them membership checks to sustain their mission. Americans simply depend on them to define the limits of how far politicians can go before violating the norms of our culture. We cannot underestimate how much our culture stands on the shoulders of what Boomers initiated in the Sixties. Even the sociologist Robert Putnam, no friend of Boomer civic culture, admits in his book *Bowling Alone* that "it is virtually impossible to overstate the impact of these social movements on the lives of most American communities and most American citizens. In our most private moments, as in our most public ones, our behavior and our values bear the imprint of these movements." It is through these advocacy groups that the Baby Boom generation stands vigilant.

It's hard not to be impressed with the breadth and depth of advocacy that takes place daily in America. Open the newspaper and there's one story, then another, then another about this organization exposing discriminatory practices or that organization planting trees to counteract pollution from automobiles. Just think of what any number of organizations do to promote equality for women. One day it might be a group of nonprofits suing Wal-Mart for discriminating against its female employees, for making it harder for women to work their way up and for giving a wink and a nod to male managers who tell women applying for promotions to "doll up" and "blow the cobwebs off" their make-up. Another day it might be a nonprofit announcing it's created an online network for women in technology and business. Yet another day it might be a group issuing a report on gender bias in vocational and technical education—how career education classes channel girls into traditionally female jobs and away from such trades as plumbing and pipe fitting. Still another day it might be a different group reporting on changes in the family and the fact that men are spending more time than ever with the kids and the housework. Or it might be a group raising serious questions about how many hysterectomies doctors perform on women.

Or think of all the groups fighting ethnic discrimination and promoting a more tolerant America. There are groups that send out black and white testers with almost identical resumes to see whether companies favor white applicants over blacks—and there are other groups that do the same testing with rental housing and mortgage loans. Other groups write reports on voting problems in minority neighborhoods, or the underrepresentation of Latinos in the financial services industry, or how certain automobile companies routinely charge African-Americans higher interest rates than whites, or how schools track black first-graders into low-level classes, or how the largely Latino population of day workers—landscapers and construction workers especially—are forced to work long hours without breaks or are told to operate heavy machinery without safety precautions or are cheated out of pay because employers charge them for transportation to the job site. And there are groups that are suing companies over employment discrimination—as in the case against Abercrombie & Fitch, which told managers to recruit employees at predominantly white fraternities and sororities and favored whites and especially blonds for its sales floor jobs, with one corporate official allegedly telling a California store that it had too many Asian sales clerks, most of whom were subsequently fired, and other stores steering minorities to apply for stockroom, cleaning, or overnight positions (Abercrombie settled the case in November 2004, agreeing to implement more diverse hiring practices, add more minorities to marketing materials that almost exclusively featured whites, and pay forty million dollars in damages).

Switch now to environmental and animal advocacy, and the same pattern appears. From local to global concerns, these groups lobby and educate and agitate to protect our resources and the natural world. So one group uses satellite imagery to show how urban areas have lost a fifth of their tree cover over the last decade—and then points out the serious consequences for clean air and energy costs. Another group petitions the state of Oregon to replace its eleven thousand state vehicles with more fuel-efficient ones—with the goal of reducing greenhouse gas emissions by seventy thousand tons over the next decade. Other groups purchase shares in banking, chemical, automotive, and forestry companies so they can introduce shareholder resolutions urging greater concern for the environment. Then there's the coalition of environmental groups that's been working with McDonald's to phase out the growth-stimulating antibiotics that its poultry and meat suppliers use. Or there are the countless groups that push for reduced pesticide use, stronger food safety rules, faster toxic cleanup, and greater fuel efficiency. And there are all the local groups that hold town meetings on zoning issues, raise a ruckus over polluted streams, spend weekends cleaning up nearby riverbeds, improve community recycling practices, and throw roadblocks in front of developers who try to build near fragile ecosystems.

The list can go on and on—from groups that protect civil liberties to those that protect press freedom to those that file Freedom of Information requests to uncover government malfeasance to those that investigate the too often cozy relationship between regulators and the industries they supposedly regulate. Were it not for the American Civil Liberties Union, the Denver police might still be keeping secret files on nearly thirty-five hundred citizens, including Quakers and Catholic nuns who protest government policy. Were it not for the National Security Archives and its dogged researchers, the real story about the Iran-Contra scandal might never have come to light. Were it not for a slew of public health and public interest groups, the tobacco industry might still have free rein to market Joe Camel to teens. Were it not for the group Project Vote, one million minority citizens might not have registered to vote in 2004, which would have left them without a voice in that critical election. Were it not for groups like Common Cause and the Center for Responsive Politics, we might know a lot less about the revolving door between politicians and their lobbyist friends—and have fewer conflict-of-interest laws in place.

And the people behind these many groups, the Rick Gilliams of America—these are the unsung heroes of this generation. They're people like Sandy Newman, born in 1952, a brilliant lawyer who could have earned millions over his career but instead dedicated his life to making the American Dream a real possibility for all of our people. So what he did was create an organization that reached across partisan lines with the goal of giving kids a chance to lead a life of opportunity rather than crime. His organization, Fight Crime: Invest in Kids, brings together twenty-five hundred sheriffs, police chiefs, district attorneys, and crime victims to fight not for tougher criminal penalties but for better after-school programs so that latchkey kids have a good place to go and not get into trouble. This is a group that speaks to what Lincoln called our "better angels"—they coalesce not to express anger at crime but to express an inclusive vision that sees the equal worth of all Americans.

Or they're people like the late Anita Borg, a successful computer scientist who refused to accept the stereotype that only men enjoyed technology and gave much of her life to encouraging women in the field. "Well-behaved women rarely make history," was the line on a T-shirt she enjoyed wearing, and she lived it in her work. In 1987 she created an online community for women engineers, and within a decade it grew to twenty-five hundred members from forty countries. A decade later she founded the Institute for Women and Technology, a group dedicated to helping women enter the technology industry, which she ran until her untimely death from brain cancer in 2003, at the age of fifty-four. And in her last few months of life she received hundreds of letters and cards from women thanking her for opening doors that a generation ago would have been locked shut with no way in. "What I heard from you was that I could be both a technologist and a woman," one wrote with heartfelt gratitude.

And there are so many others are like Gilliam, Newman, and Borg, millions of unheralded Boomers who in big and small ways have dedicated their lives to advocating for a better and more just America. There are attorneys who have given up lucrative practices to join nonprofits as litigators. There are scientists who work at environmental groups rather than chemical companies because they want to bequeath a world less toxic than the one they inherited. There are professors who create think tanks to address racial disparities in law and society. There are executives who leave their corner offices to work for the homeless or for people with AIDS. There are writers and journalists and homemakers and teachers and veterans and Boomers of every background who have spent all or part of their lives in big and in small ways working to preserve and advance the social progress of the last generation. All of these individuals and all of these organizations, they each have their own stories to tell, compelling stories about winning childcare benefits for workers or exposing racial discrimination in the insurance industry or promoting environmentally sound construction practices or teaching children not to hate or pushing athletic opportunities for girls or any of the untold other causes that make each of our lives and all of society incrementally better day by day. Yes, there are stories, millions of them to share. But like points on a painting these individual stories matter less than the larger story they tell, that of a generation whose collective efforts have made America a more vibrant, tolerant, just, and equal country. Even amid the grimmest of days, let us celebrate how much of a better nation we've become over the last generation. What could be a better way to end this portrait of the Baby Boom legacy?

# Coda
# Unfinished Business

Will you still need me,
Will you still feed me,
When I'm sixty-four?
   —*The Beatles, "When I'm Sixty-Four," 1967*

Only the beginning.
Only just the start.
   —*Chicago, "Beginnings," 1969*

**I**t was only a few decades ago that Boomers, filled with youthful determination and an unstinting belief in American ideals, challenged the
hypocrisies and shortcomings of American life and set in motion the seismic social changes that would rejuvenate our country and transform how
we live. Back in the Sixties there were plenty of naysayers who mocked
Boomer idealism and advised them with paternalistic solicitude not to tilt
at too many windmills. Pursue your private dreams and don't worry
about changing the world, these elders counseled. But Boomers refused
to listen and the result is a better America, a more tolerant, equal, and inclusive America.

Now Boomers are facing their twilight years. In only a decade or two
they will begin to pass the torch of leadership to a new generation. With
work and family obligations winding down, they will once again feel rich
with opportunity and time. And once again they will be advised to spend
their days in private pursuits. This time it won't be elders telling them
what to do, but rather the siren song of marketing that will tempt them to
live out their years accumulating new toys, adventures, and badges of
youth, with alluring images of fun, fun, fun till the Reaper takes their T-
bird away. And of course the media will duly report it all, writing wry
stories about graying and feeble Boomers desperately trying to surround
themselves with the illusions and trappings of youth.

But as with much of the conventional wisdom about Boomers, such stories will tell only a part of what is likely to happen. For in spite of what the critics have said over the years, Boomers have never bought such a pinched and narrow interpretation of the American Dream, that it's all about me, that the pursuit of happiness is mine and only mine. Yes, Boomers have tried to succeed, to enjoy life, to stay youthful and have fun. But aren't these universal hopes and aspirations—ones we find throughout history and literature? Does it make all who share them narcissistic? In the rush to indict Boomers, what's too often forgotten is how—from the Sixties onward—they have engaged society and sought to make this a better world. In their schools and families and offices and communities, in the very settings and institutions that make up our lives, they've insisted on righting wrongs, including others, and believing with unwavering innocence that ideals are meant not to be ignored but to be realized. It is this determined idealism that has changed America. And there is no evidence to suggest that Boomers won't be as determined and idealistic in their remaining years.

So let us close with a final inquiry: What is this generation's unfinished business? What should Boomers do for their final act on the public stage? What did they start in the Sixties that they should try to complete now?

Perhaps there is no greater task facing Boomers than to bequeath a far cleaner environment than what they inherited just a few decades ago. As the original green generation, Boomers made a solemn pledge at the first Earth Day in 1970 to improve the environment and infuse a green ethic into national policy and our daily lives—and over the years they have done their best to fulfill that pledge. But more must be done. Recently, Boomers emerged as the early adopters of the new hybrid cars, which cost more than conventional cars but are nearly twice as fuel-efficient. It's only one indicator, but it suggests that Boomers are increasingly willing to spend a little more for a better environment, which hopefully will translate to a growing market for green products. Boomers also were early adopters of social investing—putting their savings into mutual funds that invest in environmentally progressive companies. These funds are burgeoning and there's every indication that Boomers will continue to put their money where their trees are. As for the millions of soon-to-be-retired Boomers looking to make a difference with their newfound freedom, don't be surprised if many return to their youthful days at the grass roots and volunteer their time, energy, and expertise to the countless environmental and community-based organizations that their generation helped to establish over the years. And as voters, expect Boomers to insist not just on green rhetoric but on green policies—and to give environmental protection a greater sense of electoral urgency. A generation that showed outrage at unjust wars and racial discrimination can now transfer that outrage to toxic waste and climate change—because in the long run they can give no greater gift to their children and grandchildren than a cleaner and more sustainable earth.

Second, as the first American generation to celebrate rather than deny our nation's diversity, Boomers can use their twilight years to make some important statements that affirm our new national norm of racial tolerance and inclusion. The segregated neighborhoods that Boomers inherited from their parents may have hardened over time, but the new communities that Boomers built—mostly in the West and Southwest—are among the most integrated in the country. Boomers can continue to model this new America by seeking out and indeed promoting racially integrated retirement communities. In fact for white Boomers there should be no excuse not to do so since the rationale behind white flight—bad schools and crime—has no relevance in retirement areas. Boomers also can promote integration at the most intimate level by giving full and unequivocal support to the interracial and interfaith relationships that their children and grandchildren are increasingly entering. Boomers are already the most racially and religiously tolerant generation of parents in American history, and welcoming these most personal of family relationships would surely move Boomers even closer to fulfilling their longstanding goal of eliminating prejudice, celebrating diversity, and treating people as people with the same hopes and dreams and abilities as anyone else regardless of who they are or where they're from. At the political level, Boomers already have shown little tolerance for intolerant politicians, and they must demand that our leaders offer more than lip service and Kumbaya images of diversity. There is no question our nation has made great strides since the days when President Nixon quite cynically appealed to Greatest Generation whites by sowing resentment toward blacks—what he and his advisors called the

Southern Strategy. Now any politician or party that makes overt or even covert appeals to racial bigotry suffers in the press and at the polls. But it's not enough for the absence of hostility to define our race relations today. Boomers should remain fully committed to the diversity culture they created, the culture that teaches the very basic lesson that all who are different have equal worth.

Third, Boomers must continue as an unflagging voice for women's rights, and in their graying years they have an opportunity to tackle one of the most stubborn and odious gender problems of all: our society's hidden contempt for older women and the subtle discrimination that arises from it. This is a contempt driven partly by outmoded images of beauty and partly by the lingering notion that women don't have much of value to offer once they've raised their children. It's a contempt that in many ways can be summed up by two films starring the actress Sally Field, who in the 1988 movie *Punchline* played Tom Hanks's love interest but only six years later played his mother in the box-office hit *Forrest Gump*. In the popular imagination, older men appear dignified, handsome, and wise, whereas older women come off as unattractive and overly meddlesome, a nuisance because they have nothing better to do with their time now that their children have left the roost. Occasionally there's a story in the news asking where all the older women are in television and film, especially older women who come off as distinguished, attractive, interesting, and sensuous. And from time to time there's a woman over forty cast in such a role—most notably Rene Russo, Sela Ward, Laura Linney, and Diane Keaton in recent years. But addressing an ingrained cultural bias requires more than just a few leading roles. What Boomers must do is raise the issue as relentlessly as they hoisted the women's rights banner three decades before, and demand not only more discussion of the problem but also more media attention, magazine covers, and roles on TV that don't fall back on the stereotypes of old.

Of course any change in how we view older women must be accompanied by an unbending resolve to sustain and support the gender role transformation that Boomers began in the Sixties. Boomers must continue to reinforce and encourage their daughters as they advance in the workplace, and they must reinforce and encourage their sons as they take on more responsibility at home. Certainly one way to do this is for Boomer executives to accelerate the recent progress toward more family-friendly workplaces and more liberal family leave policies. But the challenge remains as much psychological as programmatic. And so Boomers and their progeny must continue to challenge the subtly demeaning attitudes that linger from the old days and continue to hamper full equality. For example, some among us still label mothers who work without needing the income as have-it-all yuppies concerned more about themselves than their kids. But don't we all, men and women, share a universal desire for satisfying work? Why is it that women and not men are singled out for such criticism? There are also a number of underlying assumptions that disparage men who contribute to housework and childcare—that they're less than manly, that they're doing it not because they want to but because it's an obligation and a favor to their partners and wives, that they'd rather be doing something more important instead. But why must we persist in seeing such work as natural and enjoyable for women but not for men? Why must we assume it's central to the identity of women but can't be equally central to men? Talking about these issues has been a staple of Baby Boom culture, and there's no reason to think it won't remain that way. Boomers should continue to gather family and friends around the proverbial kitchen table and raise these issues till their final days.

Fourth, as a generation that spoke truth to power, Boomers now must make power speak the truth. If there ever was a threat to American democracy in recent years, it's come from the alienation of large numbers of citizens who simply don't believe their leaders are leveling with them and speaking honestly. Boomers saw it with Vietnam and Watergate and with so many other big and small lies that have metastasized into a spreading and thickening cultural cynicism. Anyone looking to explain declining social trust in America should begin here. Perhaps even more troubling today is how political leaders shamelessly try to manipulate public opinion by using the power of public relations to create images and impressions that are designed to contradict the reality behind them. So they label a proposal Clear Skies when in fact it would do the opposite. Or they cut the ribbon at a senior citizens home even though their budget slashes funding for senior citizens' housing. Boomers have always challenged authority, but now they should take that one step further and demand straight talk and candor as the price for their support and vote. Today we live in the most media-saturated country in human history, yet our nation continues to rank near the bottom of all industrialized countries in teaching its citizens how to understand and decode the imagery of mass media. So one way to force politicians to speak the truth is to teach media literacy in our colleges and schools. Teach them to pull the curtain away from the wizard and expose his machinations and illusions. We have national education goals and standards for every form of literacy but one: media literacy. As the first mass media generation, Boomers grew up amid the power of images. Now they can help reclaim the power from these images—and from those who manipulate them—by insisting that we all become literate in the language of media.

Finally, it's time for Baby Boomers to come to their own defense. Boomers must defend their generational legacy more forcefully and vigorously—not only because it's right, but because Baby Boom detractors have used their criticism of Boomers as a pretext to attack many of the social gains and accomplishments Boomers set in motion a generation ago. So Boomers must reassert control of their generational narrative and end the revisionism that has reduced their reputation to the level of carpetbaggers and Herbert Hoover. Reviving the Boomer legacy, speaking with pride about bettering America, will remind us of how remarkably far we've come in just a few short years. That we have not become a perfect society does not mean we are not a far better society. That we have not eradicated poverty does not invalidate our many other social gains. That discrimination still remains does not mean we haven't achieved breathtaking and unprecedented progress toward a more tolerant and inclusive society. That some can't handle personal freedom does not negate the flourishing individuality, expressiveness, and culture of choice that has enriched and enlivened our nation. It is always easier to criticize, far harder to defend. Boomers must show that it is just as patriotic to challenge corrupt and entrenched power as it is to salute the flag; that the bonds of society are strengthened, not weakened, by diversity and individual expression; that economic growth without environmental safeguards will ultimately undermine our economy; that the insistence on equal rights is not a zero sum game but rather in the interest of all. It's neither self-serving nor self-congratulatory to say that things have changed and to take proper credit for changing them. Other generations receive their due for their accomplishments. Isn't it time we stop begrudging the Baby Boom?

Maybe all we need is a little reminding. Survey after survey shows that most Americans embrace the advances of the Baby Boom years and shudder at those who want to roll back the greater freedom and equality we now have at home and at work and in the daily rhythms of our lives. But in the long run it probably matters little what the critics say about Baby Boomers. These critics may win a few battles along the way, but there is no turning back from the Boomer consensus that predominates today, and in fact the more these critics push, the more Boomers and their progeny will push them back and expose them for what they are, a force at the margins that's angry at how the world has passed them by. Whether the critics like it or not, we have become a nation written in the image of the Baby Boom.

As for me, I will enter my twilight years doing what I've always loved: seeding the public dialogue, joining the debate over issues and ideas, and continuing to teach younger generations that *what* they think is far less important than *how* they think. My deepest faith is in a principle, that knowledge, reason, and education are the best antidotes to ignorance, prejudice, and fear, and I remain inspired by the wisdom of our founders, that the essence of democracy is not merely the consent of the governed but the informed consent of the governed. Call me an idealist. Call me a Baby Boomer.

# Notes and Sources

## 1: The Greater Generation

ON BLACK AMERICAN LIFE IN THE GREATEST GENERATION ERA

The Elks leader who said, "We're not racists, believe me," is quoted in "Rogue Elk," *Newsweek,* December 13, 1971. On polls of Greatest Generation whites saying that blacks smell bad, laugh a lot, and are less intelligent than whites, typical are the Harris polls done for *Newsweek* in 1963 and 1966, with 71 percent of whites in 1963 saying blacks "smell different" and about 55 percent saying the same in 1966 (that year *Newsweek* broke it down according to lower- and upper-income whites, so this number is extrapolated). The same polls also found 36 percent of whites in 1963 and 28 percent in 1966 would refuse to try on the same clothes as blacks; among Southern whites, the numbers were 57 percent in 1963 and 54 percent in 1966. On the 1971 Harris poll question that asked whether "self-respecting men would want to marry a girl they knew had been fooling around with people of a different race," 60 percent said no. *Newsweek*'s observation that white antipathy and revulsion toward blacks grew with the suggestion of greater physical contact comes from "Prejudice: Widespread and Deep," October 21, 1963.

ON THE CULTURE OF CONFORMITY IN THE GREATEST GENERATION ERA

Historian Geoffrey Perrett's statement that "a bearded stranger" would excite suspicion can be found in his 1979 book, *Dream of Greatness: The American People, 1945–1963,* page 299. The 1954 surveys of attitudes toward atheists teaching college and speaking out against religion are from the National Opinion Research Center (NORC). Will Herberg's observations about American religion are from his 1955 book, *Protestant—Catholic—Jew* (specific citations are from pages 2 and 59 of the 1960 edition). William H. Whyte's comments on personality tests at the office are from his 1956 book, *The Organization Man,* pages 196–197.

## ON GAYS AND LESBIANS IN THE GREATEST GENERATION ERA

Two outstanding sources are John D'Emilio's and Estelle B. Freedman's 1988 book, *Intimate Matters: A History of Sexuality in America,* pages 292–295; and a 1997 article in the *Florida State University Law Review* by William N. Eskridge, Jr., "Privacy Jurisprudence and the Apartheid of the Closet, 1946–1961." On the Greatest Generation clinging to their attitudes, two NORC survey questions from 1987 found that 64.4 percent of Americans born before 1929 opposed homosexuals teaching college, and 62.6 percent supported removing gay-themed books from the library, and it wasn't until the early 1990s that a majority of this cohort—albeit a slim majority—began to reject these views.

## ON WOMEN IN THE GREATEST GENERATION ERA

The Harvard Law story is told in Judith Richards Hope's 2003 book, *Pinstripes & Pearls: The Women of the Harvard Law School Class of '64 Who Forged an Old-Girl Network and Paved the Way for Future Generations,* pages 104–105. The male psychiatrists were interviewed in the December 24, 1956, issue of *Life.* Stephanie Coontz's quote comes from her 1992 book, *The Way We Never Were: American Families and the Nostalgia Trap,* page 32; she cites a study of hospitalized "schizophrenic" women in the San Francisco Bay Area during the 1950s. On women wishing they had been born as men, see Everett C. Ladd, "Everyday Life: How Are We Doing?" *The Public Perspective,* April–May 1999.

## ON THE NEW BABY BOOM NORMS AND THE GREATEST GENERATION'S RESISTANCE

On the woman denied partnership who was advised by her supervisor to "walk more femininely, talk more femininely, dress more femininely, wear makeup, have her hair styled, and wear jewelry," see *Price Waterhouse v. Hopkins,* decided by the United States Supreme Court in 1989. The "broad cultural shift" quote comes from Ronald Inglehart's 1990 book, *Culture Shift in Advanced Industrial Society,* pages 423–424. In his 1981 book *New Rules: Searching for Self-Fulfillment in a World Turned Upside Down,* Daniel Yankelovich describes how people may wax nostalgic about the old family life but don't want a return to old norms, with only 21 percent expressing a desire to go back to the way it was (page 104). The "silence of the good people" quote comes from Martin Luther King, Jr., in his 1964 book, *Why We Can't Wait,* page 50. The "silent revolution" idea comes from two sources: Quoted here is Paul C. Light in his 1988 book, *Baby Boomers,* pages 111–115; also see Ronald Inglehart's 1977 book, *The Silent Revolution: Changing Values and Political Styles Among Western Publics.* That civil rights laws could have passed in the generally resistant Greatest Generation era is an example of what the anthropologist Margaret Mead wrote in her 1970 book, *Culture and Commitment,* page 86: "The innovating idea may come from others, but the initiative for successful action must come from those whose privileges, now regarded as obsolete, are about to be abolished." Mead's point is that a groundswell for change leaves those in power with little choice, largely because their status quo is obsolete. Daniel Yankelovich's quote about the "universally held prescriptions" of the Greatest Generation era is from his previously cited book, *New Rules,* page 88. The Greatest Generation's continuing resistance to Baby Boom norms, lasting well into the Nineties, can be seen in findings from NORC's General Social Survey, which is available on NORC's Web site; to compare Greatest Generation and Baby Boom attitudes on the many issues discussed here, I analyzed NORC's survey questions using various age cohorts (those born in 1900–1928, 1900–1942, 1943–1964, 1965–1980, 1943–1980); most of the Greatest Generation results are based on the 1900–1928 cohort, though in some cases they come from the 1900–1942 cohort; most of the Baby Boom results are based on the 1943–1964 cohort. Martin Luther King, Jr.'s call for justice over order comes from his famous 1963 essay, "Letter from the Birmingham Jail," which he reprinted in *Why We Can't Wait.*

## ON BOOMER MORALITY, CIVIC LIFE, AND PATRIOTISM

William Bennett's comment condemning Boomer liberalism for "universal moral disarmament" is cited in Alan Wolfe's 1998 book, *One Nation, After All,* page 299. American aimlessness at the end of the Fifties is discussed in John W. Jeffries, "The 'Quest for National Purpose' of 1960," *American Quarterly,* Fall 1978, pages 451–470. The 1959 New Haven study was conducted by the sociologist Robert A. Dahl; he describes the anemic civic life of Greatest Generation America on pages 275–281 of his 1961 book, *Who Governs?* For the concerns raised by *Life* magazine in 1960, see especially the May and June issues of that year, which featured a series of essays on national purpose and cultural drift; the *Life* essays evoked a widespread response, and the magazine continued discussing these concerns throughout the year. Robert Putnam called the Greatest Generation the "long civic generation" in his 2000 book, *Bowling Alone,* though he originally outlined his idea about declining social capital in the January 1995 issue of the *Journal of Democracy.* The information on nonprofits is culled from Michael O'Neill's 2002 book, *Nonprofit Nation: A New Look at the Third America,* and from Independent Sector, an organization that represents and studies nonprofit organizations. The observation about the "reinvention" of civic life was made by Margaret Talbot in her June 25, 2000, *New York Times* review of Putnam's book. Edward Rothstein's comment on the lack of ethnic stereotyping after September 11 can be found in his February 14, 2004, *New York Times* column, "Is Fear Itself the Enemy? Or Perhaps the Lack of It?"

ON THE GENERATION-WIDE EMBRACE OF THE NEW BOOMER VALUES
Daniel Yankelovich has written extensively on how the "cultural revolution" spread from the campuses of the Sixties to the rest of America; see his 1998 speech, "The Shifting Direction of America's Cultural Values," available on the Internet, and also his various books from the Seventies and Eighties, *The Changing Values on Campus* (1972), *The New Morality: A Profile of American Youth in the Seventies* (1974), and *New Rules: Searching for Self-Fulfillment in a World Turned Upside Down* (1981). For the convergence of attitudes between the college graduates and the less schooled, see Paul DiMaggio, John Evans, and Bethany Bryson, "Have Americans' Social Attitudes Become More Polarized?" *American Journal of Sociology,* November 1996, pages 690–755.

## 2: The New Silent Majority

ON HOW THE LIBERAL CONSENSUS IS UNAFFECTED BY CONSERVATIVE POLITICAL VICTORIES
For an interesting analysis of the 2004 vote, see Scott Turow, "A Dominant GOP? How So?" *The Washington Post,* December 26, 2004; see also two of

my own post-election articles, "Scrooge's Nightmare," *Salon.com,* posted November 25, 2004, and "Why the Democrats Don't Have to Worry About the Voters Who Are Obsessed with Old-Fashioned Morality," *HistoryNewsNetwork.org,* posted November 12, 2004. For the Everett Carll Ladd quote on the relative unimportance of politics, see his 1999 book, *The Ladd Report,* page 71. For Tom Smith's analysis of the Reagan Eighties, see two articles he published in 1985, "Atop a Liberal Plateau? A Summary of Trends Since World War II," *Research in Urban Policy,* vol. 1, pages 245–257; and "Trends in Attitudes on Sexual and Reproductive Issues," *GSS Social Change Report,* No. 23, March 1985. See also Tom W. Smith, "Liberal and Conservative Trends in the United States Since World War II," *GSS Social Change Report,* No. 29, March 1989; and the previously cited article by Paul DiMaggio, John Evans, and Bethany Bryson, "Have Americans' Social Attitudes Become More Polarized?"

ON THE WIDESPREAD ACCEPTANCE OF THE NEW BOOMER CONSENSUS
The statement that "the emblematic values of the 1960s are being embraced by more and more Americans" comes from Paul H. Ray, "The Emerging Culture," *American Demographics,* February 1997. Arthur Marwick's quote that the Sixties movements have "permeated and transformed" America is from his 1998 book, *The Sixties.* Among the scholars who have analyzed and documented this new liberal and egalitarian consensus are Tom W. Smith of the National Opinion Research Center (NORC), James A. Davis, Daniel Yankelovich, Ronald Inglehart, Paul DiMaggio, John Evans, and Bethany Bryson. See especially Inglehart's *The Silent Revolution: Changing Values and Political Styles Among Western Publics* (1977), *Culture Shift in Advanced Industrial Society* (1990), and *Rising Tide: Gender Equality and Cultural Change Around the World* (2003, co-authored by Pippa Norris). For the question asking Catholics about ordaining female priests, see NORC's 1986 General Social Survey; according to my cohort analysis of the data available on the NORC Web site, 62 percent of those born before 1943 opposed women as priests, whereas 66 percent of those born from 1943 on favored it, which translates to 55 percent of all Catholics surveyed open to the change; subsequent surveys, such as a CBS/*New York Times* poll conducted in 2002,

show a clear trend in the more liberal direction, with two-thirds of all Catholics opposed to the prohibition on female priests.

## ON PUBLIC OPINION WHEN PRE-BOOMERS ARE FACTORED OUT

When the NORC surveys are analyzed to factor out various cohorts, they show clearly how Americans born before 1929 (the Greatest Generation cohort) and, to a somewhat lesser extent, Americans born before 1943, skew the overall public results in a more socially conservative direction. On a 2000 question about a close relative marrying a black, 61.6 percent of Greatest Generation Americans and 55.3 percent of all Americans born before 1943 oppose or strongly oppose it, whereas only 23.7 percent of Americans born from 1943 onwards oppose or strongly oppose it. On a 1994 question asking whether gender role reversal hurts a family, Greatest Generation Americans are almost three times more likely to say yes than Americans born from 1943 onwards; similarly, when asked during the 1990s if it was better for the man to work and the woman to tend the home, more than 70 percent of Greatest Generation Americans and about 60 percent of all Americans born before 1943 say yes, while more than 70 percent of Americans born from 1943 onwards say no. On whether sex before marriage is "not wrong at all," there is a 30 to 35 percent difference between the more socially conservative Greatest Generation Americans and the more liberal Americans born from 1943 onwards, and this margin has held steady for three decades. On a question asking whether people should always obey the law or follow their conscience if they find the law unjust, more than 60 percent of Americans born from 1943 onwards would follow their conscience, whereas nearly 60 percent of Greatest Generation Americans would obey the law; on whether young people should be taught to think for themselves or follow their elders, two-thirds of Americans born from 1943 onwards typically say think for themselves, while nearly two-thirds of Greatest Generation Americans say follow their elders.

## ON THE NEW BOOMER NORMS

On race, the *Washington Post* poll showing widespread "tolerance and even acceptance" of biracial couples is analyzed by Darryl Fears and Claudia

Deane in "Biracial Couples Report Tolerance," *The Washington Post,* July 5, 2001. The poll showing that 80 percent of Americans support "racially diverse" colleges was conducted in 2003 by the Associated Press. The Rev. Jesse Jackson's comments on racial progress are quoted in Michael Slackman, "Jackson's Neutrality Hinders Sharpton Campaign," *The New York Times,* October 29, 2003.

On women, the three scholars describing a "fundamental and profound shift in public expectations" are Leonie Huddy, Francis K. Neely, and Marilyn R. Lafay, who wrote "The Polls—Trends: Support for the Women's Movement," *Public Opinion Quarterly,* vol. 64, 2000, page 309.

On homosexuality, the survey showing widespread acceptance of gays among all age groups except pre-Boomers was conducted by the Center for Information and Research on Civic Learning and Engagement (CIRCLE) in 2002. For the *Fayetteville Observer*'s decision to publish same-sex civil union announcements, the newspaper's editor, Charles Broadwell, provided details and perspective in a telephone interview on January 5, 2004.

On accepting cohabitation before marriage, NORC surveys in the 1990s found wide disparities between those born before 1943 and those born afterwards, with Greatest Generation Americans—those born before 1929—most vehemently opposed. In 1994, for example, it was acceptable to barely 10 percent of Greatest Generation Americans and 19 percent of Americans born before 1943, whereas it bothered only three in ten Boomers and younger Americans. In 1998, the numbers for all cohorts grew slightly more liberal.

On Catholics becoming "more similar to religious liberals" on social, sexual, and gender issues, see Paul DiMaggio, John Evans, and Bethany Bryson, "Have Americans' Social Attitudes Become More Polarized?" *American Journal of Sociology,* November 1996, page 730. The finding that Catholics are more liberal than Protestants on reproductive attitudes and behaviors is from Tom Smith, "Trends in Attitudes on Sexual and Reproductive Issues," *GSS Social Change Report No. 23,* October 1985, published by the National Opinion Research Center at the University of Chicago, where Smith directs their major survey of American attitudes, the General Social Survey. For Hispanic attitudes toward birth control and family planning, see Mireya Navarro, "For Younger Latinos, a Shift to Smaller Families," *The New York Times,* December 5, 2004.

The abortion opponent who said her waiting period proposal was all about giving women a choice, not about restricting abortion, appeared on MSNBC's *Hardball* on May 27, 2003. On opponents of gay marriage claiming they're not intolerant, one is Ohio governor Bob Taft, who signed a law prohibiting same-sex unions but then claimed "this is not a law of intolerance." Also, Catholic bishops in Massachusetts sent a four-page flier to Catholic households saying their opposition to same-sex marriage was not based on bigotry but was simply about upholding tradition. The same-sex marriage opponent who bitterly said that "we're not even allowed to discuss it without being called bigoted and hateful" is cited in Evelyn Nieves, "Family Values Groups Gear Up for Battle over Gay Marriage," *The Washington Post,* August 17, 2003.

## ON THE LACK OF A GENERATION GAP BETWEEN BOOMERS AND THOSE BORN AFTERWARDS

The comparison of Boomer and Generation X attitudes is based on my cohort analysis of the NORC surveys. The Boomer cohort is for the birth years 1943 to 1964; the Generation X cohort covers the birth years 1965 to 1980. For the 1995 *American Demographics* article describing children of Boomers as the "first generation" to accept non-traditional norms as mainstream and noting how they see their parents as "cool," see Susan Mitchell, "The Next Baby Boom," October 1995. The NORC study describing no generation gap between Boomers and their kids is "Changes in the Generation Gap, 1972–1998," published in 2000; the AARP study, released in 2002, is "Tracing Baby Boom Attitudes Then and Now: A Comparative Look at the Attitudes of Baby Boomers in the 1970s and in 2002." The survey finding that 94 percent of Boomer kids share their parents' values is cited in Don O'Briant, "Millennials: The Next Generation," *The Atlanta Journal-Constitution,* August 11, 2003.

## ON THE NEW SILENT MAJORITY

For media reporting of the old silent majority and the subtle pressure to slant news away from Sixties youth and toward a mythic middle America, see the rather fascinating analysis in Godfrey Hodgson's 1976 history of post–World War II America, *America in Our Time,* pages 371–383. Typical of press reports showing children of Boomers in conflict with Boomer values are: "With Current War, Professors Protest, as Students Debate," *The New York Times,* April 5, 2003; "Product of '60s, Now the Mother of a Marine," *The Washington Post,* April 9, 2003; "Trust in the Military Heightens Among Baby Boomers' Children," *The New York Times,* May 27, 2003. For Paul Light's quote on how Boomers will remain complacent and even disengaged "in the absence of some strong catalyst," see his previously cited book, *Baby Boomers,* page 113.

On Republican conservatives using Baby Boom language to cloak their true intentions and win elections, see Frank Luntz's "Straight Talk" memo on the environment, which is available on the Internet. Luntz's comments on women are quoted in Deborah Tannen, "Let Them Eat Words," *The American Prospect,* September 2003. The *New York Post* editorial writer who said that conservatism must be "blunted to be presentable to the boomer-heavy electorate" is Robert A. George, who wrote "Conservatism Go Boom? The Right Must Defend Itself from Baby Boomer Creep" for *NationalReview.com,* April 7, 2000. The conservative columnist who called the 2000 Republican Convention "a parody of inclusiveness" is David Brooks, who is quoted in Al Kamen, "Dues and Don'ts," *The Washington Post,* July 19, 2004. Kamen's article is also the source for the 2004 Republican Convention Web site delegate profiles. The defunct magazine *Brill's Content* calculated the percentage of reaction shots featuring blacks during Colin Powell's 2000 Republican Convention speech. The line about "histrionic displays of diversity at GOP events" is from Dinesh D'Souza in his 2002 book, *Letters to a Young Conservative,* page 215.

## 3: The Revenge of the Luddites

### ON BOOMERS CHOSEN MAN OF THE YEAR

In a cover story for its January 7, 1967, issue, *Time* magazine named the twenty-five-and-under generation its 1966 Man of the Year.

## ON CRITICISM OF THE BABY BOOMERS

The quotes criticizing Boomers come from a random selection of print sources dating back to 1990 and drawn from the Lexis–Nexis database of newspapers and magazines; the sources for the quotes come from various publications, including *The New York Times, Denver Post, USA Today, St. Louis Post-Dispatch, Newsweek,* and *Vanity Fair,* among others. The comments on John Walker Lindh are from Andrew Sullivan, "Parallel Lives," *London Times,* December 16, 2001, and Sean Hannity's 2002 book, *Let Freedom Ring,* page 23. For the *Washington Post* book critic, see Ellen Ruppel Shell, "The Heavy Set," *The Washington Post Book World,* February 23, 2003, a review of a book that blames Boomers for obesity in America.

## ON THE GLORIFICATION OF THE GREATEST GENERATION

For examples of Greatest Generation hagiography, see Tom Brokaw, *The Greatest Generation,* and also his December 7, 1998, *Newsweek* article, "Living in the Shadow of Giants." Katherine S. Newman, in her 1993 book *Declining Fortunes: The Withering of the American Dream,* makes the reference to Horatio Alger, page 56. The quote on Boomers never proving "their mettle" the way the Greatest Generation did comes from Professor Gil Blackburn of Gardner-Webb University, quoted in Tom Mashberg, "Bush Bears Boomer Cross—Must Guide Conflicted Generation," *Boston Herald,* January 21, 2001. For the quotes on Bill Clinton epitomizing the Baby Boom's "alleged sins," see Joe Klein's 2002 book, *The Natural: The Misunderstood Presidency of Bill Clinton,* pages 9 and 165.

## ON YUPPIES AND BABY BOOM HYPOCRISY

For *Newsweek's* 1984 cover story, see "The Year of the Yuppie," December 31, 1984. Christopher Hitchens's *Vanity Fair* article, "The Baby Boomer Wasteland," was published in January 1996. The Daniel Okrent quote comes from his article, "Twilight of the Boomers," *Time,* June 12, 2000. The poll asking whether "the baby boom generation has made a special contribution to society" was conducted in August 1992 by *Time*-CNN; 57 percent of Boomers and 54 percent of Generation X said yes, but only 42 percent of pre-Boomers agreed.

## ON BOOMER LIBERALS UNDERMINING BOOMER SUCCESSES

The J. Walker Smith and Ann Clurman quote that Boomers make every fight into "a clash of moral principles" comes from their 1997 book, *Rocking the Ages,* page 49. Neil Howe and William Strauss make the same point in their 1990 book, *Generations: The History of America's Future, 1584–2069,* saying that Boomers possess "unyielding opinions about all issues."

## ON GENERATION X CRITICISM OF THE BABY BOOM

Ken Dychtwald's quote about Generation X seeing only Boomers on TV comes from Beth Ann Krier, "Behind the Bulge," *Los Angeles Times,* June 17, 1990. Writing that "every social and political issue orbits around" the Baby Boom's needs is Stephen Lynch, "Taking Stock of Gen X: It's Fallen Sharply," *The Washington Post,* April 25, 2001. The Douglas Coupland quotes come from his 1991 novel, *Generation X,* pages 20 and 135. On Boomers as "the most greedy, materialistic, and selfish" Americans, see Marjorie Hall, "Busting Baby Boomers," *The Atlanta Journal-Constitution,* August 30, 1999.

## ON THE CONSERVATIVE ASSAULT ON BOOMERS

George F. Will's observation that conservative political gains cannot overcome the Sixties sensibility is from his foreword for a book of essays on the Sixties, *Reassessing the Sixties,* edited by Stephen Macedo, page 3. Dinesh D'Souza's quotes on the Fifties and the liberal "Kumbayah mentality" can be found in his 2002 book, *Letters to a Young Conservative,* pages 180 and 205. D'Souza's desire to "destroy" liberal culture "at the root level" is on page 25 of this book. Sean Hannity's declaration of war against Boomer liberals, "Not just debate them, but defeat them," is on page 11 of his previously cited book, *Let Freedom Ring.*

For Lewis Feuer's critique of the Boomer Sixties, see his 1969 book, *The Conflict of Generations: The Character and Significance of Student Movements,* particularly chapter 8. For those who have expanded Feuer's critique, see various articles from the late 1970s and early 1980s by S. Robert Lichter and Stanley Rothman, as well as their 1982 book, *Roots of Radical-*

*ism;* also see two chapters in the previously cited *Reassessing the Sixties,* Harvey Mansfield, "The Legacy of the Sixties," and Jeremy Rabkin, "Feminism: Where the Spirit of the Sixties Lives On."

The George Will quotes are taken from columns he's written since the early Eighties, most available on the Lexis-Nexis database of newspapers. Ann Coulter's comment about Boomers in "their Berkeley dorm rooms" comes from her 2003 book, *Treason: Liberal Treachery from the Cold War to the War on Terrorism.* D'Souza's regret that the Greatest Generation "produced the spoiled children of the 1960s" is from his previously cited book, *Letters to a Young Conservative,* page 181. Bill O'Reilly's comment that white Boomers befriended blacks because it was considered "cool" is from his 2000 book, *The O'Reilly Factor,* page 158. The book of essays by conservative authors, *Beyond the Boom,* edited by Terry Teachout, was published in 1990. The *Economist* article calling George W. Bush the "anti-1960s candidate" was published September 19, 1998.

For David Brooks's critique of Boomers, see his 2000 book, *Bobos in Paradise;* see also his *Newsweek* article, "Why Bobos Rule," April 3, 2000, and his *Newsweek.com* live chat from March 29, 2000.

For Irving Kristol's declaration of a "real cold war" against "the liberal ethos," see "My Cold War," *The National Interest,* Spring 1993, pages 141–144. For Robert Bork's statement that the culture war is all about "opposition to the counterculture, the culture that became today's liberalism," see his 1996 book, *Slouching Toward Gomorrah,* page 35.

For Sandra Day O'Connor's notion that law develops from "an emerging social consensus," see her 2003 book, *The Majesty of the Law,* page 166. Margaret Mead's observation about the anger and alienation of the old are from her previously cited book, *Culture and Commitment,* pages 80, 84, and 91. Ann Coulter's comment about "elitist liberals" is from her previously cited book, *Treason: Liberal Treachery from the Cold War to the War on Terrorism,* page 283. Peggy Noonan made her statement about "the majority versus the elites in journalism and academia" on MSNBC's *Hardball,* February 27, 2004. The quote that describes working mothers as "a minority preference among women" is from Rich Lowry, *National Review* editor, cited by Bernard Goldberg in his 2001 book *Bias,* page 178. The comment that Boomers "perverted" human experience is from Roger Kimball, "Requiem for the Critical Temper," an essay in the previously cited book, *Beyond the Boom,* page 107. Paul Weyrich's letter, dated February 16, 1999, is available on the Internet.

The success of critics portraying Boomers as arrogant, ambitious, self–centered, selfish, materialistic, and less patriotic than others can be seen in two 1992 surveys, one conducted in August by *Time*-CNN and the other conducted in October by *The Washington Post.*

# 4: The Baby Boom DNA

## ON BOOMER IRREVERENCE

For the *Whole Earth Catalog*'s piece on *Consumer Reports,* see the Fall 1970 issue, page 54.

## ON BOOMER LIBERALISM

The Robert Pirsig quote comes from his 1974 book, *Zen and the Art of Motorcycle Maintenance,* page 267 (of the 1982 Bantam edition).

## ON QUESTIONING AUTHORITY

For *Mad* magazine's popularity, see Maria Reidelbach's 1991 book, *Completely Mad,* page 188, and Todd Gitlin's 1987 book, *The Sixties: Years of Hope, Days of Rage,* page 35. R. Crumb is quoted in Reidelbach, page 36. For the *Ramparts* magazine commentary on Vietnam, see the December 1967 essay, "The Redress of Their Grievances."

## ON A NATION OF IDEALS

Godfrey Hodgson discusses the "Mississippi metaphor" in his aforementioned 1976 history of post–World War II America, *America in Our Time,* pages 297–299. For research on young Boomers and their respect for American laws and ideals, see Robert D. Hess and Judith V. Torney, *The Development of Political Attitudes in Children,* 1967, pages 50–52. For a discussion of what Boomers were taught about America in school, see Frances Fitzgerald's 1979 book, *America Revised: History Schoolbooks in the Twentieth Century,* pages 177–178; according to the textbooks Boomers were assigned, Fitzgerald writes, "the United States was perfect and yet making progress all the time."

ON "DO NOT FOLD, SPINDLE, OR MUTILATE"

*The Port Huron Statement,* the 1962 manifesto of the liberal Students for a Democratic Society, is available online. Robert Pirsig wrote about technology in his aforementioned 1974 book, *Zen and the Art of Motorcycle Maintenance,* pages 260–262 (of the 1982 Bantam edition). The Boomer perception of the workplace is drawn partly from *The Port Huron Statement,* which specifically decries the notion that better personnel management and improved gadgetry can solve human problems. The Norman Mailer quote about the "cold majesty" of corporations is from his 1968 classic, *The Armies of the Night,* page 213. The Theodore Roszak quote characterizing the rationality of American society is from his 1969 book, *The Making of a Counter Culture,* page 21. Rachel Carson's quotes about deadly materials and DDT are from her 1962 book, *Silent Spring,* pages 174 and 179 of the fortieth anniversary edition published in 2002. The *New York Times* report about the Vietnamese woman burned by napalm is from September 6, 1965, as cited in Howard Zinn's 1973 book, *Postwar America: 1945–1971,* page 85. For the *Whole Earth Catalog* comment on large and remote institutions and the need to find one's own inspiration, see the purpose statement on the inside cover of the Fall 1970 issue. For Alvin Toffler's effusive description of the "personal computer," see his 1970 *Future Shock,* pages 433–435 (of the 1971 Bantam edition). For an in-depth discussion of new attitudes toward work and the workplace, see the 1991 book by Paul Leinberger and Bruce Tucker, *The New Individualists: The Generation After the Organization Man,* page 188.


ON "NEVER TRUST ANYONE OVER THIRTY"

For an article describing the Honda Element ad campaign and the Boomer rush to buy the car, see Daren Fonda, "Baby You Can Drive My Car," *Time,* June 30, 2003. The story behind the "Never trust anyone over thirty" quote is told by Jon Margolis in his 1999 book, *The Last Innocent Year,* pages 354–355. Margaret Mead's insightful discussion of youth, elders, generations, and change is from her aforementioned 1970 book, *Culture and Commitment,* pages 74–79. The leading educator who in 1962 called premarital sex "offensive and vulgar behavior" was Sarah Gibson Blanding, president of Vassar College from 1946 to 1964. On the different meaning of money to Boomers and Greatest Generation Americans, see Daniel Yankelovich in his 1981 book *New Rules,* pages 40–42, where he describes how the Greatest Generation bought cars to signify social status whereas Boomers bought them to express "freedom and independence and convenience." For a discussion of American culture in the Victorian era, see Gilman Ostrander's 1970 book, *American Civilization in the First Machine Age,* pages 70–76, and the 1976 book of essays, *Victorian America,* edited by Daniel Walker Howe, particularly Howe's essay, "Victorian Culture in America," pages 3–28.

## 5: Farewell, Donna Reed

ON THE CHANGING ROLES OF MEN

For the University of Minnesota study and Food Network numbers, see Pilar Guzman, "Hey, Man, What's for Dinner?" *The New York Times,* August 28, 2002. The researcher who hears about work–family balance from both men and women is Marcia Kropf, vice president of research and information services for Catalyst, a nonprofit that works to advance women in business, interviewed by the author September 19, 2003. For the study of men in dual-earner couples who have reduced work hours and job-related travel, see Margaret B. Neal and Leslie B. Hammer, "Dual-Earner Couples in the Sandwiched Generation: How They Manage Their Work and Family Demands," final project report for research funded by the Alfred P. Sloan Foundation, 2000. On the increasing number of men who choose jobs based on family needs, see "Two Careers, One Marriage: Making It Work in the Workplace," a 1998 study by Catalyst based on a survey by Yankelovich Partners; see also a 2000 Harris Interactive poll on the issue, and a 1991 survey conducted by DuPont that was reported in "Trouble at the Top," *U.S. News & World Report,* June 17, 1991. The 1998 Catalyst study also shows the number of working spouses who see their careers as equal. On working wives who make more money than their husbands, see Michelle Conlin, "Look Who's Bringing Home the Bacon," *Business Week,* January 27, 2003.

The scholar who describes "mounting evidence" of shifts in family roles and the amount of time fathers spend with their kids is Suzanne M. Bianchi, "Maternal Employment and Time with Children: Dramatic Change or Surprising Continuity?" *Demography,* vol. 37, issue 4, November 2000, pages 401–414. On housework, see Beth Anne Shelton and John Daphne, "The Division of Household Labor," *American Review of Sociology,* vol. 22, 1996, pages 299–323; Michelle Conlin, "Look Who's Barefoot in the Kitchen," *Business Week,* September 17, 2001. Also, the Institute of Social Research at the University of Michigan has been tracking housework; see its March 12, 2002, news release, "U.S. Husbands Are Doing More Housework While Wives Are Doing Less." The "intensive parenting" concept is from Anastasia H. Prokos, "Changing Fatherhood in the 21st Century: Incentives and Disincentives for Involved Parenting," Working Paper No. 45, May 2002, Center for Working Families, University of California, Berkeley. For the Census Bureau study on fathers taking care of children, see Lynne M. Casper, *My Daddy Takes Care of Me! Fathers as Care Providers,* Current Population Reports, Census Bureau, September 1997. For the quote on changing family roles and father involvement with their kids, see the aforementioned article from *Business Week,* "Look Who's Barefoot in the Kitchen." For statistics on fathers in the delivery room, see Maureen Downey, "A Father's Place," *The Atlanta Journal-Constitution,* May 30, 1995. The *Newsweek* quote on fathers doing more is from Kathleen Deveny, "We're Not in the Mood," June 3, 2003.

The "sensitive and caring" versus "rugged and masculine" survey was conducted by Roper in 1989. The survey showing how many thought the Fifties was the best decade for men was conducted by the communications firm Euro RSCG Worldwide in June 2003 and can be found in their publication, "The Future of Men: U.S.A."

For the number of families sharing housework versus those in which women do most, see Cheryl Russell's 1993 book, *The Master Trend: How the Baby Boom Generation Is Remaking America,* page 110. For the survey question that asked if women should take care of running their homes and leave running the country up to men, see the National Opinion Research Center (NORC), which has asked this question repeatedly over the years; the mid-life numbers are from surveys taken when each cohort was in its forties and fifties. The childcare comparison between fathers from the Northeast and South can be found in the aforementioned 1997 Census Bureau publication, *My Daddy Takes Care of Me! Fathers as Care Providers.*

On the way egalitarian couples are more likely to share housework, see Lucia Gilbert's 1988 book, *Sharing It All: The Rewards and Struggles of Two-Career Families,* pages 90–91; see also the aforementioned article by Anastasia H. Prokos, "Changing Fatherhood in the 21st Century: Incentives and Disincentives for Involved Parenting," Working Paper No. 45, May 2002, Center for Working Families, University of California, Berkeley. On men with working wives tending to be more supportive of equal rights and shared responsibilities than men whose wives stay at home, see Tom W. Smith, "Working Wives and Women's Rights: The Connection Between the Employment Status of Wives and the Feminist Attitudes of Husbands," *Sex Roles,* vol. 12, nos. 5/6, 1985, pages 501–508.

**ON WOMEN**

For many of the facts and numbers on female educational attainments and employment gains, I am grateful to Jan Combopiano, a researcher for Catalyst, a nonprofit that works to advance women in business.

The study of Radcliffe freshmen in the early 1960s is cited in Annie Gottlieb's 1987 book, *Do You Believe in Magic?: The Second Coming of the Sixties Generation,* page 319. For the government study of the high-school class of 1972, see *The National Longitudinal Study of the High School Class of 1972,* conducted by the National Center for Educational Statistics, U.S. Department of Education. The guest editor of *Mademoiselle* is quoted in Alex Witchel, "After 'The Bell Jar,' Life Went On," *The New York Times,* June 22, 2003. For demeaning attitudes in the legal profession, see *The Unfinished Agenda: Women and the Legal Profession,* a 2001 report prepared for the ABA Commission on Women in the Profession; see also the studies conducted in the early 1980s by various state bars, among them New York and California. On the way Boomer daughters identified not with their moms but with their dads or with role models outside the home, see the 1991 book by Paul Leinberger and Bruce Tucker, *The New Individualists: The Generation After the Organization Man,* page 134. Polls that show how Americans, as late as 1970, opposed efforts to change women's status in society can be found in the Roper Center archives online.

Employment numbers, specifically the proportion of women in certain jobs, are from the Census Bureau. The statistics on women college graduates with science degrees are from Natalie Angier and Kenneth Chang, "Gray Matter and the Sexes: Still a Scientific Gray Area," *The New York Times,* January 24, 2005. The numbers on college physics teachers are from Natalie Angier, "Women Shatter Science Ceiling," *International Herald Tribune,* May 8, 2003. On comparing female managers in the U.S. and overseas, see "How Women Fare," *The New York Times,* July 25, 2003. On the number of women earning more than the median income for men, see research conducted on this subject by the Employment Policy Foundation.

The Catalyst Award information and quotes are from my September 19, 2003, interview with Marcia Kropf, vice president of research and information services; she also supplied various publications describing the corporate initiatives honored since 1987, when the awards were first given out.

For the 1995 Yankelovich survey of Boomer women conducted for *Fortune* magazine, see the 1997 book by J. Walker Smith and Ann Clurman, *Rocking the Ages,* pages 216–217. For the Home Depot Do-It-Herself program, see Marci Alboher Nusbaum, "Breaking into More Male Strongholds," *The New York Times,* November 13, 2003.

## ON WOMEN AND SPORTS

For the Sally Jenkins quote in *The Washington Post,* see her May 22, 2003, article, "This Has Some Guys Really Teed Off." On the number of women who watched the Super Bowl, and the comparison to the number that watched the Academy Awards, see Keith Reed, "Making Sure Ads Play to Women, Too," *The Boston Globe,* January 28, 2004.

## ON WOMEN, HOME, AND CHILDREN

The Census Bureau is the source for the number of women who return to work after their children are born. On whether women would continue working even if they could afford not to, see the aforementioned 1998 publication by Catalyst, "Two Careers, One Marriage: Making It Work in the Workplace," which found that 67 percent would stay in the work world; see also "Women: The New Providers," a 1995 Harris survey for the Families and Work Institute and The Whirlpool Foundation, which found that half would continue working even if they didn't need the money. The 1995 Harris survey is also the source for the majority of women (56 percent) who said they didn't want to give up any of their responsibilities as nurturer and provider. On working women spending as much time with their kids as stay-at-home moms, see John F. Sandberg and Sandra L. Hofferth, "Changes in Children's Time with Parents, U.S. 1981–1997," presented at the Annual Meeting of the International Association of Time Use Research, University of Essex, Colchester, England, October 6–8, 1999. One scholar, Suzanne M. Bianchi, argues that despite all the working moms today, mothers may be "spending significantly more time per child than during the 'family-oriented' 1960s," largely because there are fewer children per family nowadays; see her aforementioned article, "Maternal Employment and Time with Children: Dramatic Change or Surprising Continuity?" *Demography,* vol. 37, issue 4, November 2000, page 404.

### ON COHABITATION AND FEMALE SEXUALITY

The poll showing that eight in ten say women can be happy even if they never marry was conducted by the advertising firm DDB Needham Worldwide in 2000. On the percentage of women who were in at least one cohabiting relationship, see Larry Bumpass and Hsien-Hen Lu, "Trends in Cohabitation and Implications for Children's Family Contexts in the United States," *Population Studies,* vol. 54, March 2000, page 32. The financial planner who said grandma is cohabiting was quoted in Rebecca Gardyn, "Unmarried Bliss," *American Demographics,* December 2000. Andrew Hacker's finding on women initiating divorce is from his 2003 book, *Mismatch: The Growing Gulf Between Women and Men,* page 28.

For Daniel Yankelovich's finding that respect for female sexuality spread quickly throughout the Baby Boom generation, see his 1974 book, *The New Morality: A Profile of American Youth in the Seventies,* page 96. The AARP finding that older women are dating younger men—and the comment attributing it to the Baby Boom generation—is from AARP's 2003 survey of unmarried women, ages 40–69; the survey found that one-third of those who date go out with younger men.

ON FAMILY LIFE

For the demographer Cheryl Russell's comments on the families of old, see her aforementioned 1993 book, *The Master Trend: How the Baby Boom Generation Is Remaking America,* pages 119–120. See also the 1992 book by Stephanie Coontz, *The Way We Never Were: American Families and the Nostalgia Trap.* The 1974 poll that found "serious problems" between parents and teens was the Mood of American Youth survey, conducted by the National Association of Secondary School Principals and the Horatio Alger Association of Distinguished Americans; the other 1974 survey finding, on teen discomfort with their parents, is from Gallup. The 1971 survey showing that college students were far more likely to identify with fellow students than with their family—by a margin of 21 percent—is from Daniel Yankelovich's 1972 book, *The Changing Values on Campus,* page 87.

The Gallup poll showing more than nine in ten kids trust their parents today was conducted in 1997. The quote comparing thirty years ago with today is from the *State of Our Nation's Youth* study for 1997–1998, published by the Horatio Alger Association of Distinguished Americans. The information on today's parents as role models comes from the 2003–2004 edition of *The State of Our Nation's Youth.* For the 80 percent who have little or no difficulty with their parents today, see the 1997–1998 edition of *The State of Our Nation's Youth;* contrast that with an earlier version of this report, the 1974 *Mood of America* survey, which found "serious problems" between young people and their parents in 1974. The author who said there have never been better relations between parents and teens in "the history of polling" is William Strauss; he was quoted in Anna Bahney, "High School Heroes: Mom and Dad," *The New York Times,* May 16, 2004. The quote on Boomer parents as "accessible and understanding" is from the 1997–1998 edition of *The State of Our Nation's Youth.* On the greater openness between kids and parents, see Susan Mitchell, "The Next Baby Boom," *American Demographics,* October 1995. For the Ellen Goodman quote, see her November 22, 2000, column in the *Pittsburgh Post-Gazette,* "What Do We Tell the Kids?"

For the 1964 "underclass" quote by the NAACP official, see "The Negro's Search for a Better Job," *Newsweek,* June 8, 1964, page 79. For the number of children born to cohabiting parents, see the aforementioned article by Rebecca Gardyn, "Unmarried Bliss," *American Demographics,* December 2000. For the percentage of cohabiting households with children, see the Census Bureau's June 2001 report, "America's Families and Living Arrangements."

The mother writing in *Newsweek* about her five-year-old girl hockey player is Mary Charest Iorio, "My Three-Foot-Nine-Inch Symbol of Freedom," June 3, 2002, page 14.

# 6: All-American Diversity

FOR THE SPRING 2003 SNAPSHOT OF DIVERSITY

Of the thirty-two wedding and celebration announcements in the May 11, 2003, *New York Times,* seventeen were identifiably interracial, interfaith, interethnic, lesbian, or gay. The numbers on multiethnic TV ensemble series are from "Blacks, Whites Watching More of the Same TV Shows," *Jet,* May 19, 2003. On the Tony Awards, there were ten phone and sixty-eight e-mail complaints, according to Frank Rich, "Gay Kiss: Business as Usual," *The New York Times,* June 22, 2003.

ON RACIAL ATTITUDES IN THE GREATEST GENERATION YEARS

For a black soldier's experience during World War II, including the indignity of being seated behind German POWs, see Nurith C. Aizenman, "Black Soldiers Battled Fascism and Racism: Veterans Remember Bitterness of Bias-Tainted Homecomings," *The Washington Post,* May 26, 2004. The history text calling black children "pickaninnies" and slavery "benevolent" and "beneficial" is Ulrich B. Phillips's *American Negro Slavery,* which was originally published in 1918 and remained the authority on slavery throughout the Fifties, serving as the principal resource for school textbooks. For Wynton Marsalis's recollections, see Lucia Mouat, "Taking the Measure of Race Relations in U.S. Democracy," *The Christian Science Monitor,* March 13, 1995. The prominent Georgia senator is Richard Russell, who tried to amend the civil rights bill by saying that all states should have an equal proportion of blacks; see Jon Margolis in his book about 1964, *The Last Innocent Year,* page 165. The 1948 survey on working with different ethnic groups can be found in the January/February 1994 issue of *The Public Perspective,* published by the Roper Center. The finding that two-thirds of the Greatest Generation would oppose a close relative marrying a black is drawn from an average of responses to a General Social Survey question asked in 1990, 1996, 1998, and 2000. The 1971 Daniel Yankelovich poll showing how Boomers saw the indignities of the Greatest Generation years is from his 1972 book, *The Changing Values on Campus,* page 69.

## ON THE POSITIVE IMPACT OF DIVERSITY

For the impact of a racially diverse campus, see Patricia Gurin, "Expert Report of Patricia Gurin," submitted for the 2003 Supreme Court cases on racial diversity in college admissions, *Gratz, et al. v. Bollinger, et al.* and *Grutter, et al. v. Bollinger, et al.* Gurin has written various other reports documenting her findings. For other research on diversity's impact, see the brief for these Supreme Court cases submitted by the American Educational Research Association, the Association of American Colleges and Universities, and the American Association for Higher Education; Mitchell J. Chang, "The Impact of an Undergraduate Diversity Course Requirement on Students' Level of Racial Prejudice," paper presented at the Association for the Study of Higher Education conference, November 1999; and Susan M. Johnson and Xia Li Lollar, "Diversity Policy in Higher Education: The Impact of College Students' Exposure to Diversity on Cultural Awareness and Political Participation," *Journal of Education Policy,* vol. 17, no. 3, 2002, pages 305–320. For the impact on attitudes toward gays, see Rodger Streitmatter, "How Youth Media Can Help Combat Homophobia Among American Teenagers," a report funded by the GLAAD Center for the Study of Media & Society, November 2002.

## ON THE CROSSING OF RACIAL AND ETHNIC BOUNDARIES

For the findings and quotes from the director of the General Social Survey, Tom W. Smith, see his 2001 report to the American Jewish Committee, *Intergroup Relations in a Diverse America: Data from the 2000 General Social Survey,* especially pages 35 and 40. The finding on whether "mixed-blood children" and interracial marriage "violate God's law" is from a 1971 Harris poll. The findings on interracial dating among youth and the lack of parental opposition to it are from a Kaiser Family Foundation 2001 survey on the issue; Sarah Dutton, "School Colors: The Class of 2000 Weighs In on Race," *Public Perspective,* May/June 2001; and a 2001 Zogby poll question on parental reaction to interracial dating. For the 1990s statistics on marriage outside of ethnic groups, see Reynolds Farley, "Increasing Interracial Marriage: Trends Revealed by the Census and Census Bureau Surveys," preliminary draft, October 1996; for the numbers on Polish-American and Italian-American outmarriage, see Peter D. Salins, *Assimilation American Style* (1997), page 160; for Jewish intermarriage trends, see the *National Jewish Population Survey* issued by the United Jewish Communities in September 2003. The quote that almost every white extended family has "at least one member who has married across what two generations ago would have been thought an unbridgeable gap" is from the demographer Paul Spickard, cited in the testimony of the Harvard sociologist Mary C. Waters before the House Committee on Government Reform and Oversight's Subcommittee on Government Management, Information, and Technology, May 22, 1997. For the Gregory Rodriguez quote, see his article in the January/February 2003 *Atlantic Monthly,* "Mongrel America."

The cohabitation rates for blacks are from Rebecca Gardyn, "Love Is Colorblind . . . or Is It?" *American Demographics,* June 2000; the quote from the Institute for Social Research scholar, David R. Harris, is also from the Gardyn article. For the finding that one-fifth of Americans have a close family member of a different race, see J. R. Goldstein, "Kinship Networks That Cross Racial Lines: The Exception or the Rule?" *Demography,* vol. 36, no. 3, August 1999, pages 399–407. The numbers from the Population Research Center in Portland, Oregon, are from the Rodriguez article cited above, "Mongrel America." Demographer William H. Frey is quoted in Roberto Suro, "Mixed Doubles," *American Demographics,* November 1999.

For the "post-ethnic America" discussion, see Joel Kotkin and Thomas Tseng, "Happy to Mix It All Up," *The Washington Post,* June 8, 2003. Leon Wynter's quote, about today's youth not knowing "an America in which non-whites didn't occupy a disproportionately large space in . . . popular culture," is from his 2002 book, *American Skin: Pop Culture, Big Business, and the End of White America,* page 181.

## ON THE CROSSING OF GAY AND STRAIGHT BOUNDARIES

The marketing firm that developed the "metrosexual" idea is Euro RSCG Worldwide. The quote about the line between gay and mainstream fiction blurring is from Bruce Bawer, "Closing Time," *The New York Times,* January 13, 2003.

## ON THE CONSERVATIVE RESISTANCE TO DIVERSITY

For the Sean Hannity quotes, see his aforementioned 2002 book, *Let Freedom Ring,* pages 49–50 and 160.

## ON THE WIDESPREAD ACCEPTANCE OF DIVERSITY IN AMERICA

The 1995 survey question asking whether demographic changes and fewer non-Hispanic whites would make people uneasy about America's future was conducted by Scripps Howard and Ohio University and can be found in *The Public Perspective,* August/September 1995, page 11. The 2002 survey questions about ethnic traditions and differences are from NORC's General Social Survey. The 1998 survey on higher education and diversity was conducted by the Association of American Colleges and Universities. The 2000 survey question on whether the ethnic changes are good or bad for America is from NORC's General Social Survey.

## ON DIVERSITY IN OUR EDUCATIONAL INSTITUTIONS

The finding that two-thirds of colleges and universities require students to take at least one course dealing with diversity is from a 1998 survey by the Ford Foundation Campus Diversity Initiative. The 1998 survey of students who said they would take diversity courses even if they weren't required was conducted at Penn State, where more than a thousand students were surveyed; see Betsy Palmer, "The Impact of Diversity Courses: Research from Pennsylvania State University," *Diversity Digest,* www.diversityweb.org. Evidence showing the impact of diversity on social interactions can be found in Patricia Gurin, "Expert Report of Patricia Gurin," submitted for the 2003 Supreme Court cases on racial diversity in college admissions, *Gratz, et al. v. Bollinger, et al.* and *Grutter, et al. v. Bollinger, et al.;* also see the brief for these Supreme Court cases submitted by the American Educational Research Association, the Association of American Colleges and Universities, and the American Association for Higher Education; and Mitchell J. Chang, "The Impact of an Undergraduate Diversity Course Requirement on Students' Level of Racial Prejudice," paper presented at the Association for the Study of Higher Education conference, November 1999. For Jay Mathews's finding that parents seek out diversity in schools, see his May 20, 2003, *WashingtonPost.com* article, "What to Look for in a Good School."

### ON DIVERSITY IN THE MILITARY

For integration in the army, see Charles C. Moskos and John Sibley Butler in their 1996 book, *All That We Can Be: Black Leadership and Racial Integration the Army Way;* their quote is from page 71. Also see my co-authored 1999 book on race relations in America, *By the Color of Our Skin: The Illusion of Integration and the Reality of Race,* pages 228–233. For intermarriage among those who have served in the military, see Reynolds Farley, "Increasing Interracial Marriage: Trends Revealed by the Census and Census Bureau Surveys," preliminary draft, October 1996. For the high rates of residential integration near military bases, see Reynolds Farley and William H. Frey, "Changes in the Segregation of Whites from Blacks During the 1980s: Small Steps Toward a More Integrated Society," *American Sociological Review,* vol. 59, February 1994, pages 23–45.

### ON THE DECLINING APPEAL OF XENOPHOBIA IN POLITICS

For the failure of xenophobia in the 2002 Iowa State Assembly race, see Todd Dvorak, "GOP Pulls Support for Iowa Hopeful," *Associated Press,* October 29, 2002.

### ON THE GROWING ACCEPTANCE OF LESBIANS AND GAYS

The Little Rock incident, in which a school forced a gay student to listen to Biblical admonitions against homosexuality, was reported in the National Briefing column of *The New York Times,* July 18, 2003. The 1973 survey of college students on the morality of homosexuality is from Daniel Yankelovich's 1974 book, *The New Morality: A Profile of American Youth in the Seventies,* page 67. The number of schools with gay-straight clubs is from the Gay, Lesbian, Straight Education Network, at www.

glsen.org; the number is based on clubs that register with the Network, so there may be more. The 1999 Gallup poll on schools teaching "acceptance of people with different sexual orientations" was conducted in May of that year for Phi Delta Kappa, an association of educators. The 2001 poll of high-school sophomores, juniors, and seniors, which found that two-thirds supported legalizing gay marriage, was conducted by Hamilton College in August of that year. The quote from the chairman of MTV Networks is from Bill Carter and Stuart Elliott, "MTV to Start First Network Aimed at Gays," *The New York Times,* May 26, 2004. Maureen Dowd's comment that the Madonna and Britney Spears kiss "seemed more stale than shocking" is from her January 8, 2004, *New York Times* column, "Tizzy over Lezzies." The quote that "gay and lesbian issues are now so openly discussed in the mainstream media that it's almost as if gay literature were no longer niche publishing" is from Martin Arnold, "Gay Stores Feel the Pinch of Customers' Liberation," *The New York Times,* June 20, 2002. The number of newspapers that publish same-sex union announcements is monitored by the gay rights organization GLAAD. The *Newsweek* poll on Catholic acceptance of homosexuality is from Jon Meacham, "Sex and the Church: A Case for Change," *Newsweek,* May 6, 2002. On the link between diversity, innovation, and prosperity, see the 2002 book by the economist Richard Florida, *The Rise of the Creative Class;* the quotes here are from a column he wrote for *USA Today,* "Gay-Tolerant Societies Prosper Economically," May 1, 2003.

## ON RACE RELATIONS, BABY BOOMERS, AND THE GREATEST GENERATION

The finding that whites with felony convictions land jobs more easily than blacks with clean records is from research conducted by University of Wisconsin graduate student Devah Pager, whose doctoral thesis on the subject, "The Mark of a Criminal Record: The Consequences of Incarceration for the Employment Opportunities of Black and White Job Seekers," won the American Sociological Association's 2003 award for best dissertation; see also her article in the March 2003 *American Journal of Sociology,* "The Mark of a Criminal Record," pages 937–975; see also Brooke Kroeger, "When a Dissertation Makes a Difference," *The New*

York Times, March 20, 2004. For the study that found employers more likely to interview job applicants with white-sounding names than those with black-sounding names, see Marianne Bertrand and Sendhil Mullainathan, "Are Emily and Brendan More Employable than Lakisha and Jamal? A Field Experiment on Labor Market Discrimination," November 2002; the paper is available at http://gsb.uchicago.edu/pdf/bertrand.pdf, and is to be published in *The American Economic Review*. On the missed opportunity to integrate the suburbs after World War II, see the aforementioned article by Reynolds Farley and William H. Frey, "Changes in the Segregation of Whites from Blacks During the 1980s: Small Steps Toward a More Integrated Society," *American Sociological Review*, vol. 59, February 1994, pages 23–45; the specific quotes are from page 25. William Levitt is quoted in David Halberstam's 1993 book, *The Fifties*, page 141. The various survey questions showing the resistance of Greatest Generation whites to racial integration are from the National Opinion Research Center (NORC); for the 2000 survey question in which two-thirds of those born before 1943 felt that blacks shouldn't push themselves where they weren't wanted, it's worthwhile noting that two-thirds of those born from 1943 onwards rejected that view. For the Brookings Institution report on "low and declining segregation levels" in the newer metropolitan areas of the South and West, see Edward L. Glaeser and Jacob L. Vigdor, "Racial Segregation in the 2000 Census: Promising News," Center on Urban and Metropolitan Policy, The Brookings Institution, April 2001. The Farley and Frey quote is from their aforementioned 1994 article in the *American Sociological Review*, "Changes in the Segregation of Whites from Blacks During the 1980s: Small Steps Toward a More Integrated Society." The William H. Frey quote on Boomers having their greatest impact in the newer metropolitan areas is from an untitled article he wrote in *The Milken Institute Review*, Third Quarter 2001, pages 4–7.

## 7: Do Your Own Thing

### ON WEDDINGS AND FUNERALS

For the rise in civil marriages, see Cathy Lynn Grossman and In-Sung Yoo, "Civil Marriage on Rise Across USA," *USA Today*, October 7, 2003; most interesting is how this trend reaches into every region of the country, even the Bible Belt, with civil marriages accounting for 47 percent of marriages in South Carolina and 43 percent in Alabama. The information and quotes on funerals come from two sources: Lisa Takeuchi Cullen, "What a Way to Go," *Time,* July 7, 2003, and Peter T. Kilborn, "Funerals with a Custom Fit Lighten Up a Solemn Rite," *The New York Times,* February 11, 2004. For ethical wills, see Wendy Cole, "Leaving Your Values Behind," *Time* magazine, July 7, 2003.

## ON THE CONTRAST BETWEEN BABY BOOM AND GREATEST GENERATION PERSPECTIVES

The 1943 poll in which almost half of adults called premarital sex "wicked" was conducted by Roper; see Tom W. Smith, "Attitudes Towards Sexual Permissiveness: Trends, Correlates, and Behavioral Connections," *NORC Social Change Report 35,* June 1992. The 1971 Yankelovich survey showing how college students were rejecting Greatest Generation values and conformity is from Daniel Yankelovich, *The Changing Values on Campus* (1972), pages 28–29 and 35–36. The poll question on whether young people should be taught to think for themselves or follow what their elders think is from NORC's 1980 General Social Survey; the generational difference is from my cohort analysis of the data available on the NORC Web site. The 1972 Nixon administration commission on drugs, the National Commission on Marihuana and Drug Abuse, was known as the Shafer Commission, named after the chair, the former Republican governor of Pennsylvania, Raymond P. Shafer; the report they issued was called *Marihuana: A Signal of Misunderstanding.*

## ON THE MANY CHOICES IN THE BABY BOOM ERA

For Daniel Yankelovich's discussion of America's new "pluralism of lifestyles," see his 1981 book, *New Rules.* For Virginia Postrel's discussion of our "aesthetic abundance," see her 2003 book, *The Substance of Style: How the Rise of Aesthetic Value Is Remaking Commerce, Culture, and Consciousness.* On the growth of magazine choices, see the *National Directory of Magazines 2003,* published by Oxbridge Communication. See also *The Magazine Handbook 2002/03,* published by the Magazine Publishers of

America; and Robin Pogrebin, "Turn, Turn, Turn: Gleanings from that Magazine Jungle out There," *The New York Times,* April 26, 1998. The quote on Boomers fueling "the constant trial of new things" is from J. Walker Smith and Ann Clurman, *Rocking the Ages* (1997), page 225. For the way Boomers have transformed travel, see Mike Steere, "Adventure Travelers Move Up in Age," *The Baltimore Sun,* March 15, 1998; see also Eileen Ogintz, "Taking the Kids: Baby Boomers Spark Boom in Family Adventure," *Los Angeles Times,* July 11, 1993, and The National Tour Association's *Current Assessment Report for the Baby Boomer Market,* January 2002. For Cheryl Russell's observations on the increase in products carried by grocery stores, see her 1993 book, *The Master Trend,* page 58.

## ON BOOMER YOUTHFULNESS AND LIFESTYLE PRIORITIES

For the middle-aged Boomer "doing what I loved as a kid," see Christopher Noxon, "I Don't Want to Grow Up!" *The New York Times,* August 31, 2003. For Boomer concerns about the rat race, see Yankelovich's aforementioned 1981 book, *New Rules,* page 152. The survey on Boomer retirement plans was conducted by AARP, the lobby group for older Americans. The way Boomers are pursuing their interests outside the rat race is described in Kirstin Downey, "Setting Their Own Schedules: More Boomers Are Fitting Jobs Around Other Pursuits," *The Washington Post,* December 8, 2002.

## ON BOOMER SOCIAL LIBERALISM

The NORC numbers on teenage birth control, living together, and premarital sex come from my cohort analysis of General Social Survey data available on the NORC Web site. For Tom Smith's comment that openness has replaced puritanism, see his aforementioned 1992 NORC report, "Attitudes Toward Sexual Permissiveness." For the 2002 *Time* magazine poll on marijuana, see Joel Stein, "The New Politics of Pot," *Time* magazine, November 4, 2002. For the quote saying that the public has "a more nuanced view of morality" than that of the conservative moralists, see Froma Harrop, "Pundits Take Note: The Public Is Fed Up with This Circus," *Bergen Record,* August 24, 1998.

## ON BOOMERS AND RELIGION

The findings on Boomer religiosity and religious service attendance come from my cohort analysis of General Social Survey data available on the NORC Web site.

There's actually considerable controversy over how many Americans regularly attend church. Over the years, Gallup and others have claimed that 40 percent of Americans attend church weekly, give or take a few percentage points, and this number has been widely reported in the media. The finding is based on a poll question that asks Americans if they've been to church or synagogue in the last seven days. But critics say that people stretch the truth by giving pollsters what they think is the most socially acceptable answer—one that may not be accurate but allows respondents a chance to show their virtue. So someone who drops kids off for Sunday school or volunteers at a church function may say yes to the answer, even if it isn't wholly true, according to the critics. Two studies in particular, one based on time-use diaries and another using actual head counts in a sampling of communities, find that the real percentage of weekly churchgoers is much lower than the Gallup number, about 20–26 percent. The time-use diary study seems especially credible because it makes use of daily activity records kept by thousands of Americans in the mid 1960s, 1970s, and 1990s, and it avoids the social desirability bias found in polls because people were simply asked how they spent their time, not whether they went to church. This study, conducted by Stanley Presser of the University of Maryland and Linda Stinson of the U.S. Bureau of Labor Statistics, concludes that weekly church attendance fell from 42 percent in 1965 to 26 percent in 1994. Because of this debate, I decided to use the 2000 General Social Survey question as a reasonable compromise because it asks people to report their pattern of churchgoing behavior and gives them a number of choices (more than once a week, once a week, nearly every week, 2–3 times a month, once a month, several times a year, once a year, less than once a year, and never), some of which lapsed parishioners might find socially acceptable without feeling the need to mislead. Still, even this question could contain a churchgoing bias. For more on the debate, see C. Kirk Hadaway, Penny Long Marler, and Mark Chaves, "What the Polls Don't Show: A Closer Look at U.S. Church Attendance," *American Sociological Review,* December 1993, pages 741–752; C. Kirk Hadaway, Penny Long Marler, and Mark Chaves, "Overreporting Church Attendance in America: Evidence That Demands the Same Verdict," *American Sociological Review,* February 1998, pages 122–130; Richard Morin, "Bearing False Witness to the Pollster," *The Washington Post,* May 17, 1998; Andrew Walsh, "Church, Lies, and Polling Data," *Religion in the News,* Fall 1998.

For the declining number of Americans giving money and time to religious organizations, see the 2001 publication by the group Independent Sector, *The New Nonprofit Almanac in Brief: Facts and Figures on the Independent Sector 2001.*

For religious conservatives, see the comprehensive analysis written by General Social Survey director Tom W. Smith, "Are Conservative Churches Growing?" *GSS Social Change Report No. 32,* January 1991. There's actually a great deal of confusion over the terms "religious conservative," "fundamentalist," "evangelical," and "born-again Christian," with different scholars using different terms to describe similar cohorts. For example, the Barna Research Group, a Christian research organization, says that born-again Christians represent about 40 percent of the population and evangelicals 6 percent, numbers that have remained relatively stable for years, with evangelicals distinguished "by their commitment to biblical theology," whereas born-again Christians span the spectrum from liberal to conservative; others, such as Wade Clark Roof, in his book *A Generation of Seekers,* break it down between fundamentalist-leaning or religious conservative Americans and evangelical moderates, and he offers slightly different numbers for each. Still others use the term "evangelicals" to represent the larger group of born-again Christians, with fundamentalists being the Biblical conservatives. So for some, born-again Christians are the same as evangelicals, whereas for others, evangelicals are the same as fundamentalists or religious conservatives. I use the term "religious conservatives" here because it speaks to a worldview, not a religious belief, and according to most of the current research, their percentage of the population has shown little or no gain during the last couple of decades.

For the rapid growth of Americans who claim no religious identity, see Barry A. Kosmin, Egon Mayer, and Ariela Keysar, *American Religious Iden-*

*tification Survey 2001,* published by the Graduate Center of the City University of New York. The report challenges the popular perception that America has grown more religiously conservative in recent years. "In sharp contrast to that widely held perception, the present survey has detected a wide and possibly growing swath of secularism among Americans. The magnitude and role of this large secular segment of the American population is frequently ignored by scholars and politicians alike."

The quotes, statistics, and conclusions from Wade Clark Roof are drawn from his considerable body of work, among them: *Spiritual Marketplace: Baby Boomers and the Remaking of American Religion* (1999); *A Generation of Seekers: The Spiritual Journeys of the Baby Boom Generation* (1993); "Religious Kaleidoscope: American Religion in the 1990s," *Temenos,* vol. 32, 1996, pages 183–193; "Baby Boomers and the Return to the Churches," with Sr. Mary Johnson, in David A. Roozen and C. Kirk Hadaway, eds., *Church and Denominational Growth* (1993), pages 293–310; "The Baby Boom's Search for God," *American Demographics,* December 1992.

For the religious training Boomers received when young, see Roof, "Baby Boomers and the Return to the Churches," with Sr. Mary Johnson, in David A. Roozen and C. Kirk Hadaway, eds., *Church and Denominational Growth* (1993), page 296. For the number of Americans in the Greatest Generation era who believed the Bible was the literal word of God, and how that's declined since then, see Norval D. Glenn, "Social Trends in the United States: Evidence from Sample Surveys," *Public Opinion Quarterly,* vol. 51, supplement, 1987, pages 109–126.

The Roof quote about Boomers abandoning their churches and temples in numbers rarely seen before—"Young people have abandoned their churches and temples in the past, but rarely in such large numbers"—is from his December 1992 *American Demographics* article, "The Baby Boom's Search for God." In that article he specified the Boomer dropout rate to be 58 percent, meaning the percentage of Boomers who have dropped out of church or synagogue at one time or another, but he revised it upwards to more than 60 percent in his 1993 book, *A Generation of Seekers: The Spiritual Journeys of the Baby Boom,* pages 54–55 and 154–155.

On Boomers seeking spirituality if not religion in the Sixties, see Andrew Greeley, "There's a New-Time Religion on Campus," *The New York Times Magazine,* June 1, 1969. The Paul Goodman quote that it's "religion that constitutes the strength of this generation" was found in Peter Clecak's 1983 book, *America's Quest for the Ideal Self: Dissent and Fulfillment in the '60s and '70s,* page 116. For the Tom Wolfe quote, see his famous Me Decade essay, "The Me Decade and the Third Great Awakening," which was originally published in the August 23, 1976, issue of *New York* magazine. For Annie Gottlieb's quote that Boomers were turning away from "the rote religion of our childhood," see her 1987 book, *Do You Believe in Magic?: The Second Coming of the Sixties Generation,* page 195.

For Roof's quote on the decline of religious conformity, see his 1996 article, "Religious Kaleidoscope: American Religion in the 1990s," *Temenos,* vol. 32.

For the Bill O'Reilly quotes, see his 2000 book, *The O'Reilly Factor,* pages 165 and 163, respectively.

For Boomers returning to religious institutions, see Roof, "Baby Boomers and the Return to the Churches," with Sr. Mary Johnson, in David A. Roozen and C. Kirk Hadaway, eds., *Church and Denominational Growth* (1993), page 298; and his 1993 book, *A Generation of Seekers: The Spiritual Journeys of the Baby Boom Generation,* pages 54–60 and 154–181. On "retraditionalizing," see Roof's 1999 book, *Spiritual Marketplace: Baby Boomers and the Remaking of American Religion,* pages 171–172. For the number of Americans switching denominations, and for the "mixing and matching" quote, see Richard Cimino and Don Lattin, "Choosing My Religion," *American Demographics,* April 1999; see also Roof's 1996 article, "Religious Kaleidoscope: American Religion in the 1990s," *Temenos,* vol. 32.

The number of Americans who find truth in one religion versus those who find basic truths in many religions is from a question in NORC's 1998 General Social Survey. For the number who believe in a higher consciousness or sense of the divine rather than a Biblical God, see Andrew Walsh, "Church, Lies, and Polling Data," *Religion in the News,* Fall 1998, where he cites the work of Christian researcher George Barna. The number of Americans who say morality is a personal matter is from a question in NORC's 1998 General Social Survey. On Hollywood and God, see Tim Appelo, "God: Still Ready for His Close-Up," *The New York Times*, May 11, 2003.

For Roof on the surge in alternative religious groups, see Sandi Dolbee, "Spiritual Growth," *The San Diego Union-Tribune*, September 22, 2000. The 2003 Episcopal Church report is entitled *Restoring the Ties That Bind*. The quote from the self-proclaimed Christian thinker is from the Web site www.ginkworld.net; see also John Leland, "Hip New Churches Pray to a Different Drummer," *The New York Times*, February 18, 2004. For the study of Americans in their twenties, see Jeffrey Jensen Arnett and Lene Arnett Jensen, "A Congregation of One: Individualized Religious Beliefs Among Emerging Adults," *Journal of Adolescent Research*, September 2002, pages 451–467.

For the 20 percent of Americans sympathetic to New Age ideas, see Robert C. Fuller's 2001 book, *Spiritual, But Not Religious: Understanding Unchurched America*, page 99. For the twenty million who attend yoga studios, see Suzanne Smalley, "Tantric Tunes," *Newsweek*, May 12, 2003. For the amount spent on New Age books, see the aforementioned article by Richard Cimino and Don Lattin, "Choosing My Religion," *American Demographics*, April 1999. The advertisement welcoming "people with pierced body parts" is from a church in Walkersville, Maryland.

On the number of Catholics attending Mass weekly, see James D. Davidson, "American Catholics and American Catholicism: An Inventory of Facts, Trends, and Influences," written for a July 2003 forum on the future of the Catholic Church, *The Church in America—The Way Forward in the 21st Century*, sponsored by the Boisi Center for Religion and American Public Life. The percentage of Catholics calling themselves traditional and liberal is from a question in NORC's 2000 General Social Survey; the numbers for Boomers and everyone younger come from my cohort analysis of the data available on the NORC Web site.

On Catholics and church teachings, the numbers come from a May 2002 CBS/*New York Times* poll. On the most devout and committed Catholics rejecting church authority on moral issues, see William V. D'Antonio, James D. Davidson, Dean Hoge, and Katherine Meyer, *Ameri-*

*can Catholics: Gender, Generation, and Commitment* (2001). For the number of Catholics that marry outside the church, see the aforementioned publication by James D. Davidson, "American Catholics and American Catholicism: An Inventory of Facts, Trends, and Influences," written for a July 2003 forum on the future of the Catholic Church, *The Church in America—The Way Forward in the 21st Century.* For Catholics who marry outside the church but still call themselves "good Catholics," see James D. Davidson, "Generations Have Different Views of the Church," published as part of a Special Report for the *National Catholic Reporter Online.* For the percentage of Catholics separated or divorced, see the aforementioned publication, *American Religious Identification Survey 2001,* published by the Graduate Center of the City University of New York. The quote that "we're going to have nobody taking Communion" if the Catholic Church enforces its moral rules was made by the Reverend Thomas J. Reese, former editor of the Jesuit publication *America;* the source is Alan Cooperman, "Bishops in Political Crossfire over Issue of Communion," *The Washington Post,* June 25, 2004. On Catholic support for more democracy in the church, as well as the overwhelming lay belief that you can't be a "good Catholic" without being concerned for the poor, see Roof, "Baby Boomers and the Return to the Churches," with Sr. Mary Johnson, in David A. Roozen and C. Kirk Hadaway, eds., *Church and Denominational Growth* (1993), page 306. On Catholic support for church democracy, as well as the increasing lay reliance on individual conscience rather than church teachings, see the aforementioned book by D'Antonio, Davidson, Hoge, and Meyer, *American Catholics: Gender, Generation, and Commitment* (2001).

The Roof quote that Boomers may well be remembered "as a spiritually creative generation" that has "reclaimed something fundamental to the American religious experience" is from his 1993 book, *A Generation of Seekers: The Spiritual Journeys of the Baby Boom Generation,* page 243. For another book that reaches similar conclusions, with particular focus on how the countercultural impulse of the Sixties has transformed mainstream religion, see Mark Oppenheimer, *Knocking on Heaven's Door: American Religion in the Age of Counterculture* (2003).

## 8: Meet the New Boss

FOR OSBORNE AND DORAN

Much of the material here is based on various conversations and interviews I had with CEO Jeff Stegman. I am also grateful to Jeff for sending me company newsletters, internal memos, and what they call their "cultural training notebook," a binder given to all Osborne and Doran employees that details the company's philosophy.

ON THE WORK CULTURE IN THE FIFTIES AND THE BOOMER
RESPONSE TO IT

The 1971 findings from Daniel Yankelovich are from his book *The Changing Values on Campus* (1972), page 35. The David Halberstam quote is from his 1993 book, *The Fifties,* page 124. For the 1974 Yankelovich findings and quotes, see his book *The New Morality: A Profile of American Youth in the Seventies* (1974), pages 21, 29, 37, and 47. For the University of Michigan finding that American workers in the 1970s were embarrassed by what they made and wouldn't buy it for themselves, see Daniel Yankelovich's 1981 book, *New Rules: Searching for Self-Fulfillment in a World Turned Upside Down,* pages 43–44. The finding that Americans were unhappy with their jobs and with the "hierarchy gap" at work is from a 1977 survey conducted by Opinion Research Corporation. Yankelovich's 1974 observation that Boomer college students respected the right of business to make a profit but wanted more corporate responsibility is from his aforementioned book, *The New Morality,* page 63.

ON BOOMER WORKPLACE ATTITUDES AND REFORMS

The *Business Week* cover story, "Baby Boomers Push for Power: And They're Getting It—In Business, in Politics, and in the Marketplace," was published July 2, 1984, along with an editorial commenting on the article, "Baby Boomers Banging on the Door." Landon Jones is quoted in Lynn Rosellini, "You've Come a Long Way, Baby Boomers; When a Generation Turns Forty," *U.S. News & World Report,* March 10, 1986. For Robert Krulwich's quote, see his December 14, 1986, *New York Times* book review, "Don't Tell a Baby Boomer What to Do." J. Walker Smith's quote on "meaningful work" is from Irene Sege, "The Aging of Aquarius," *The Boston Globe,* May 12, 1998. For the two books that discuss how Baby Boomers have influenced the economy, see D. Quinn Mills, *Not Like Our Parents: How the Baby Boom Generation Is Changing America* (1987), and Paul Leinberger and Bruce Tucker, *The New Individualists: The Generation After the Organization Man* (1991). For the culture of our new economy, see the quintessential Nineties magazine on the high-tech industry, *Fast Company,* which offered four "New Rules of Business": Work Is Personal, Knowledge Is Power, Computing Is Social, and Break the Rules. For the new workforce priorities, *Information Week* conducted a survey of twenty thousand information technology and knowledge workers from 2000 to 2002.

## ON WORKER PARTICIPATION AND THE MOVE AWAY FROM ORGANIZATIONAL HIERARCHIES

For the academic article describing how managers would typically refuse to listen to workers because it "conflicts with traditional management-worker relations," see Curt Tausky and Anthony F. Chelte, "Workers' Participation," *Work and Occupations,* November 1988, pages 363–373. The book *The New American Workplace,* published in 1994, is by Eileen Appelbaum and Rosemary Batt; see especially pages 60–66. The Bristol-Myers Squibb example is drawn from Robert B. Tucker, "Seven Strategies for Generating Ideas," *The Futurist,* March/April 2003. The NORC numbers are from the 2002 General Social Survey. The banking executive critical of hierarchy is quoted in Joseph L. McCarthy, "Participatory Style: Antidote for Hard Times?" *American Banker,* January 3, 1991. The software company employee quoted in Christopher Cook, "The East Bay's Coolest Companies," *Diablo Magazine,* July 1997 (available online), was describing the culture and "entrepreneurial spirit" at PeopleSoft, Inc. For a more extensive discussion of flattening hierarchies in the workplace, see Ron Zemke, Claire Raines, and Bob Filipczak, *Generations at Work: Managing the Clash of Veterans, Boomers, Xers, and Nexters in Your Workplace* (1999).

## ON CASUAL DRESS AND FLEXIBILITY AT WORK

For the survey showing that nine in ten companies allow casual dress regularly or occasionally, see the 1996 survey of 505 human resource managers conducted by the Society for Human Resource Management and Levi Strauss Co. The quote about people coming to work "when they want" but always getting their work done is from Julie Connelly, "Youthful Attitudes, Sobering Realities," *The New York Times,* October 28, 2003.

## ON ENTREPRENEURSHIP AND THE GROWTH OF SMALL BUSINESSES

For the *Wall Street Journal* piece on small businesses, see Dale D. Buss, "The Broad View—Issue of the Decade: The Work Force Defined Small Business in the '90s—Beginning with a Flood of Potential Entrepreneurs and Ending with a Labor Squeeze," May 24, 1999. The information on entrepreneurship programs at business schools is from Julie Flaherty, "Entrepreneurship Courses: It Pays to Pick the School," *The New York Times,* April 1, 2004. For eBay, *USA Today* reported in 2004 that "about 430,000 individuals and small businesses make their livings from eBay"; see Jon Swartz, "eBay Evolves to Serve Small Businesses," *USA Today,* February 22, 2004.

## ON CORPORATE SOCIAL RESPONSIBILITY

For the survey that found half of Americans formed an impression of a company based on its social behavior, see the 1999 worldwide study by Environics International Ltd., and for the finding that more than three-fourths of consumers would switch to a brand or retailer associated with a good cause, see the 1997 survey by Walker Research. The 2002 study on the number of Americans that reported boycotting a company because of concerns about its business practices was conducted by EPIC-MRA for the organization Women in International Trade Charitable Trust. For background on "sustainability reports," see Amy Cortese, "The New Accountability," *The New York Times,* March 24, 2002, and Scott Fields, "Sustainable Business Makes Dollars and Sense," *Environmental Health Perspectives,* March 2002. The Internet site Corporate Register.com, which monitors corporate sustainability reports, listed 501 reports from American companies as of December 2004. The 2002 survey of companies and sustainability reports was conducted by the accounting firm PricewaterhouseCoopers; it found that 32 percent of surveyed companies have published reports, 18 percent plan to in two years, and 23 percent plan to in three to five years. The McDonald's Social Responsibility Report is available online at the McDonald's Web site. For the growth of socially responsible mutual funds, see Mark Hulbert, "Good for Your Conscience, If Not Your Wallet," *The New York Times,* July 20, 2003, which includes a graphic showing the Lipper Inc. statistics. The facts, statistics, and examples from the Social Investment Forum are from its *2001 Report on Socially Responsible Investing Trends in the United States.* The Harris poll showing that two-thirds of Americans would choose a socially responsible fund were it included in their employee retirement plan was commissioned by The Calvert Group, a socially responsible investment fund.

### ON BOOMERS AS CONSUMERS

The Harley Earl quote on hastening obsolescence is from Paul Leinberger and Bruce Tucker, *The New Individualists: The Generation After the Organization Man* (1991), page 391. For "mass customization," see J. Walker Smith and Ann Clurman, *Rocking the Ages,* page 64. For more on Boomers as consumers, see Paul C. Light's 1988 book, *Baby Boomers,* pages 114–115 and 155–157.

## 9: The Greening of America

### ON AUSTIN GRILL

For verification and quotes, I spoke with the restaurant chain's chief operating officer, Chris Patterson, in August 2004.

### FOR THE SURVEYS SHOWING THE NEW ENVIRONMENTAL NORM

The RoperASW survey showing the number of Americans that consider the environment when making a purchase is cited in Amy Cortese, "They Care About the World (and They Shop, Too)," *The New York Times,* July 20, 2003. The 1999 Gallup poll on the number of Americans who avoided buying products that weren't recyclable and who boycotted a company for environmental reasons was conducted in April of that year; the findings are available at *Public Opinion Online,* a service of the Roper Center at the University of Connecticut. The 1994 Schick survey on recyclable packaging was conducted by Roper Starch Worldwide in January and February of that year. The 2000 Rice University survey of Texans was conducted by the school's department of sociology in December of that year, with a sample size of one thousand Texans. For the 2002 RoperASW survey of potential computer buyers, which had a sample size of two thousand consumers, see its *Green Gauge Report 2002*. The NORC General Social Survey results can be found on the NORC site online; I conducted all cohort analyses using the available General Social Survey data; all questions cited here were asked in 1993, 1994, and 2000, except for the question that asked whether natural environments with endangered species should be left alone regardless of the economic benefits, which NORC asked in 1996.

## ON THE GROWTH OF ENVIRONMENTAL GROUPS

The increase in membership groups is described in Robert Lerner and Althea K. Nagai, "Explorations in Nonprofits," *Foundation Watch,* July 2002. The Census Bureau findings and other estimates on the number of environmental groups are from Michael O'Neill, *Nonprofit Nation: A New Look at the Third America* (2002), pages 136 and 11. The current membership numbers for the major environmental groups are available on their Web sites; for the earlier numbers and for a discussion of what local chapters do, see George Pettinico, "Civic Participation and American Democracy: Civic Participation Alive and Well in Today's Environmental Groups," *The Public Perspective,* June/July 1996. The 2000 Gallup poll showing widespread agreement with the environmental movement's goals was conducted in April of that year; the 2002 Gallup poll showing the number of adults who say they actively participate in or sympathize with the environmental movement was conducted in March of that year; these findings are available at *Public Opinion Online,* a service of the Roper Center at the University of Connecticut. For the number of households that contribute money to environmental groups, see the 2001 publication by the group Independent Sector, *The New Nonprofit Almanac in Brief: Facts and Figures on the Independent Sector 2001.*

## FOR RECYCLING NUMBERS

The recycling numbers are drawn from a variety of government sources, including the Environmental Protection Agency (EPA) and the Census

Bureau's *Statistical Abstract of the United States.* See especially the EPA's *Municipal Solid Waste in the United States: 2001 Facts and Figures.* Although curbside recycling serves half the population nationwide, the regional breakdowns show that the South in particular but also the Midwest lag and therefore drag down the national percentage; recycling serves 82 percent of people in the Northeast, 26 percent in the South, 40 percent in the Midwest, and 69 percent in the West. The General Social Survey result is from 2000.

ON ORGANIC FOODS

The *New York Times* comment that organic farming was "a fringe movement in the 1960s" is from an October 21, 2002, editorial, "A New Organic Era." The Roper poll showing that half of Americans thought organic foods to be worth the extra money was conducted in August 1999. For the Department of Agriculture report, which includes an analysis of survey research and trends in the organic food industry, see Carolyn Dimitri and Catherine Greene, "Recent Growth Patterns in the U.S. Organic Foods Market," Economic Research Service, U.S. Department of Agriculture. See also Margaret Webb Pressler, "Growing, Naturally: Organic Foods Get into the Mainstream," *The Washington Post,* July 26, 2003.

ON PROGRESS AND THE ENVIRONMENT IN THE GREATEST
GENERATION YEARS

For the Jon Margolis quote on "filmstrips celebrating . . . DDT," see his 1999 book, *The Last Innocent Year,* page 189.

ON BOOMERS AND THE RISE OF ENVIRONMENTAL AWARENESS

For recollections of the first Earth Day, see Gaylord Nelson, "Earth Day '70: What It Meant," *EPA Journal,* April 1980 (it was Nelson, then a United States senator, who first proposed Earth Day); Jack Lewis, "The Spirit of the First Earth Day," *EPA Journal,* January/February 1990; and John C. Whitaker, "Earth Day Recollections: What It Was Like When the Movement Took Off," *EPA Journal,* July/August 1988. Whitaker was the former Nixon cabinet secretary quoted here. See also Philip Shabecoff's 1993 survey of the environmental movement in America, *A Fierce Green*

*Fire: The American Environmental Movement.* For an analysis of what shaped the environmental movement, including a discussion of the counterculture's role, see Adam Rome, "Give Earth a Chance: The Environmental Movement and the Sixties," *Journal of American History,* September 2003; this article is also the source for the number of hippies in the Sixties. For the 1971 Yankelovich finding that college students would devote a year or two to reducing pollution, see his 1972 book, *The Changing Values on Campus,* page 55.

ON TECHNOLOGY VERSUS THE ENVIRONMENT

The 1970 quote from Ecology Action East, saying that we must separate technology's creative power from its destructive power, is from the group's essay, "The Power to Destroy, the Power to Create," originally published in the January 1970 issue of *Rat* and reprinted in Ian G. Barbour, ed., *Western Man and Environmental Ethics: Attitudes Toward Nature and Technology* (1973), pages 244–245. The Leo Marx quote is from his classic 1964 book, *The Machine in the Garden: Technology and the Pastoral Ideal in America,* page 226.

ON THE BOOMER ENVIRONMENTAL IMPACT

For Everett Carll Ladd's quote on the environmental movement's ascendancy, see his 1999 book, *The Ladd Report,* page 27. The EPA list of environmental laws can be found on its Web site under "Introduction to Laws and Regulations"; see www.epa.gov. The number of workers making air pollution control equipment can be found in the Census Bureau's *Statistical Abstract of the United States;* the statistic cited here is from 1999. For the numbers on our energy and oil consumption since 1980, see the op-ed article by former president Jimmy Carter, "Misinformation and Scare Tactics," *The Washington Post,* May 17, 2001. For the green-building movement and the number of buildings being certified as green, see the Web site for the U.S. Green Building Council, www.usgbc.org. The land conservation ballot initiatives approved in 2004 are described in Will Rogers, "It's Easy Being Green," *The New York Times,* November 20, 2004; see also Paul W. Hansen, "Green in Gridlock," *The Washington Post,* March 15, 2005.

ON BUSINESS AND THE ENVIRONMENT

The survey that found 85 percent of Americans praising new technology was conducted by Virginia Commonwealth University in August and September of 2001. The question on whether almost everything we do in modern life harms the environment was asked in the 1993, 1994, and 2000 NORC General Social Surveys; I conducted the cohort analyses using the General Social Survey data available online. The General Social Survey question on whether business or government should decide how to protect the environment was asked in the 1993, 1994, and 2000 General Social Surveys. The question asking people who they trusted for accurate information about pollution is from the 2000 General Social Survey. On whether businesses will cut corners and damage the environment without strong government regulation, see the *Los Angeles Times* poll conducted in April 2001. For an analysis of BP's environmental record, see Darcy Frey, "How Green Is BP?" *The New York Times Magazine,* December 8, 2002; see also BP's 2003 Sustainability Report, available on the company's Web site. For William Clay Ford, Jr., see Danny Hakim, "He Does Get Some Respect, but the Critics Still Have His Number," *The New York Times,* May 7, 2004; Danny Hakim, "Cloaked in Green, But Pushing Trucks," *The New York Times,* April 19, 2003; Danny Hakim, "Talking Green vs. Making Green," *The New York Times,* March 28, 2002; Russell Long, "The Broken Promise of Bill Ford, Jr.," *Alternet.org,* June 23, 2003 (Long is executive director of the environmental group Bluewater Network, which ran the Pinocchio ad critical of Ford); the Ford quote comes from Danny Hakim, "A Family's 100-Year Car Trip," *The New York Times,* June 15, 2003. I am grateful to my former graduate student at American University, Cory Davies, for his research and insights into corporate environmental public relations, the result of which is an exceptional master's thesis, "Wag the Dog: How Environmental Public Relations Efforts Are Beginning to Drive Business Practices," April 2004.

# 10: Power Corrupts

ON THE OLD JOURNALISM

The Leonard Downie and Robert Kaiser quote is from their 2002 book, *The News About the News: American Journalism in Peril,* page 67. Russell

Baker's observations were captured in Timothy Crouse's classic 1973 book on the traveling press corps in the 1972 presidential campaign, *The Boys on the Bus,* page 195 (in the 1973 hardcover edition).

## ON BOOMER VIEWS OF POLITICS IN THE SEVENTIES

The Daniel Yankelovich findings and quotes are from two of his books from the early Seventies, *The Changing Values on Campus* (1972), page 50, and *The New Morality: A Profile of American Youth in the Seventies* (1974), page 45.

## ON OPENNESS IN GOVERNMENT

The Woburn, Massachusetts, couple's freedom of information effort is profiled in Micah Morrison, "How They Uncovered the Truth," *Parade,* January 25, 2004.

## ON BOOMER ALTERNATIVE JOURNALISM

For an excellent treatment of the underground journalism movement in the Sixties, and for examples of stories broken by the underground press, see Abe Peck, *Uncovering the Sixties: The Life and Times of the Underground Press* (1985).

## ON POLITICAL HUMOR

The various jokes cited here are drawn primarily from the late-night monologues of Jay Leno and David Letterman. For an excellent source of political humor, see the Political Humor Web site, http://politicalhumor. about.com/. For the Pew study on the influence of late-night comedy, see the Pew Research Center for the People and the Press, "Cable and Internet Loom Large in Fragmented Political Universe," January 11, 2004, specifically its table entitled "Learn Anything New?"; Pew has been tracking late-night comedy's rising political influence over the last few years.

## ON POLITICAL DEALIGNMENT

The early-1970s numbers on Boomers leaving political parties are from the aforementioned 1972 book by Daniel Yankelovich, *The Changing Values on Campus,* pages 59–60 and 129. The 2000 NORC General Social Survey numbers are from a question that asks whether people think of themselves as a strong Democrat, a not very strong Democrat, an Independent but close to Democrat, an Independent, an Independent but close to Republican, a not very strong Republican, or a strong Republican; NORC has asked this question a number of times over the years; the Boomer and younger cohort findings came from my analysis of the data available on the NORC Web site.

ON CONSERVATIVES

Dinesh D' Souza's "social guerillas" quote is from his 2002 book, *Letters to a Young Conservative,* page 26; his "anti-establishment" quote is from a February 14, 1988, *New York Times Magazine* story, "Reagan's Disappearing Bureaucrats," by Phillip Longman.

ON THE REVOLUTIONARY GENERATION

Historian Bernard Bailyn's quote is from his 2003 book, *To Begin the World Anew: The Genius and Ambiguities of the American Founders,* page 2.

# 11: Take Over the Administration Building

ON CRITICS OF HIGHER EDUCATION

The George Will headline is from a September 1990 syndicated column, which claims that we're seeing "political indoctrination supplanting education" on many campuses; Will often writes on this subject. Phyllis Schlafly is quoted in "Thought Control Replaces Academic Freedom," a column printed on her organization's Web site, www.eagleforum.org, March 26, 2003; "indoctrination" and "thought control" are words she frequently uses when describing higher education. For the Robert Bork quotes, see his 1996 book, *Slouching Toward Gomorrah: Modern Liberalism and American Decline,* pages 208 and 22, respectively. Bork's book is essentially a tirade against what he calls the Sixties generation and Sixties culture, replete with warnings of how the "malignant" Sixties has returned to "metastasize more devastatingly throughout our culture," especially in the universities where these radicals are "indoctrinating" the young (pages 52–53). For the Dinesh D'Souza quote, see his 2002 book, *Letters to a Young Conservative,* page 41; according to D'Souza, Boomer radicals have taken over the universities "to dominate their fetid little ponds, to impose their political values on a new generation of students"; D'Souza made waves with his first book in 1991, *Illiberal Education: The Politics of Race and Sex on Campus,* which attacked higher education and labeled it a den of politically correct thinking. For Robert Brustein's quote on English departments, see John K. Wilson, "Come Not to Bury Shakespeare; He Lives," *Chronicle of Higher Education,* February 14, 1997. The quote saying universities study rap artists in equal proportion to Shakespeare is from Seth Forman, "The New Rigidity," *The American Scholar,* Autumn 1997. The quote that "only literature professors now believe in socialist revolution and centrally planned economies" is from the July 2003 "Foundation Watch" newsletter published by the conservative group Capital Research Center. The Jeremy Rabkin quote criticizing women's studies is from his chapter, "Feminism: Where the Spirit of the Sixties Lives On," in *Reassessing the Sixties,* edited by Stephen Macedo, page 60. *The Closing of the American Mind* is the title of an influential 1987 book by Allan Bloom, a conservative critic of the modern university.

## ON DISSERTATIONS

For the information on theses and dissertations, I consulted the *Dissertation Abstracts* database of more than two million theses and dissertations, available online through my university. I obtained my final numbers in September 2004. Although most of the theses and dissertations listed come from American universities, the database also includes dissertations written elsewhere. Unfortunately, the database as structured enables researchers to find out exactly how many theses and dissertations were written in other countries, but not how many were written in the United States. To obtain my numbers, I therefore found out the total number of dissertations written on a certain topic or during a certain decade and then subtracted the number written in Canada and Great Britain, which had the most entries besides the United States, as well as some other countries depending on the topic. In a few cases there may be a small number of dissertations written in countries I didn't eliminate, so it's possible that my final numbers could be off by a marginal amount. But the thrust of the data is accurate and true.

**ON THE NUMBER OF COURSES FEATURING CERTAIN AUTHORS**

My primary source here is a 2000 report written by the National Association of Scholars, "Losing the Big Picture: The Fragmentation of the English Major Since 1964."

**ON THE NEED FOR CHANGE IN THE SIXTIES**

The 1992 U.S. Department of Education report, "Tourists in Our Own Land: Cultural Literacies and the College Curriculum," by Clifford Adelman, was based on findings from the National Longitudinal Study of the High-School Class of 1972; it specifically looked at the higher education experience of those who went to college and concluded that their colleges and universities gave them only limited exposure to cultures outside the Western world, with only a small number of elite schools offering opportunities to study non-Western cultures and American minority groups. For the 1967 William Buckley quote, see Jerome Karabel, "The Legacy of Legacies," *The New York Times,* September 13, 2004.

**ON CRITICISM OF MULTICULTURALISM**

For Sean Hannity's quote, see his 2002 book, *Let Freedom Ring,* page 151. Robert Bork's quote comes from his aforementioned 1996 book, *Slouching Toward Gomorrah: Modern Liberalism and American Decline,* page 89.

**ON FACULTY APPROACHES TO TEACHING**

The survey of English professors showing that they teach both diversity and tradition was conducted by the Modern Language Association in 1991. For the survey of undergraduate teachers nationwide showing that they are equally committed to Western civilization and diversity, see "The American College Teacher: National Norms for the 1998–1999 H.E.R.I. Faculty Survey," published by the University of California at Los Angeles Higher Education Research Center.

**ON THE CURRICULUM AT AMERICAN UNIVERSITY**

All the information cited here comes from the university's 2004–2005 catalog.

ON FACULTY PRIORITIES FOR THEIR INSTITUTIONS

For the finding that faculty consider the intellectual development of students their highest priority—and teaching students how to change society one of their lowest priorities—see the H.E.R.I. survey cited above.

ON DIVERSITY COURSES AND OTHER INNOVATIVE CURRICULUM

An excellent source for diversity courses and other innovative curriculum is the Association of American Colleges and Universities. Their publications include: "To Form a More Perfect Union: Campus Diversity Initiatives" (1999), "Globalizing Knowledge: Connecting International and Intercultural Studies" (1999), "Connecting Diversity and Democracy: The American Commitments Series" (1995), and their quarterly *Diversity Digest*. See also Debra Humphreys, "Diversity and the College Curriculum: How Colleges and Universities Are Preparing Students for a Changing World," a 1998 paper prepared for the Ford Foundation Campus Diversity Initiative.

ON SCHOLARSHIP

For the conservative view that academics today produce "many-footnoted obfuscation," see Walter Olson, "The Split-Level Generation," in Terry Teachout, ed., *Beyond the Boom: New Voices on American Life, Culture, and Politics* (1990), page 35. For the dissertation topics, see the *Dissertation Abstracts* database cited above.

ON THE BENEFITS OF DIVERSITY

The study of Harvard and University of Michigan law students is cited in Jeffrey F. Milem, "Why Race Matters," *Academe,* September/October 2000. For a summary of other studies, including the report on women's studies courses, see the aforementioned 1998 paper by Debra Humphreys, "Diversity and the College Curriculum: How Colleges and Universities Are Preparing Students for a Changing World," prepared for the Ford Foundation Campus Diversity Initiative. Other studies are described in chapter 6 of this book and cited in the notes and sources for that chapter under the heading "On Diversity in Our Educational Institutions." See also William G. Bowen and Derek Bok, *The Shape of the River: Long-term*

*Consequences of Considering Race in College and University Admissions* (1998), which offers considerable evidence on the benefits of diversity. For more on faculty views of diversity in the classroom, see a nationwide survey of faculty sponsored by the American Council on Education and the American Association of University Professors, as reported in Peter Schmidt, "Faculty Members Prize Campus Diversity, Study Finds," *Chronicle of Higher Education,* May 26, 2000.

### ON OFFENSIVE LANGUAGE

The 2000 survey showing that most Americans prefer a workplace free of sexist language and sexually explicit jokes, and that most reject the notion that we've gone too far in restricting speech, was sponsored by Shell Oil Company and conducted by Peter D. Hart Research Associates, with a sizable sample of 1,453 adults; 58 percent agreed with the statement that people shouldn't use sexist language or tell sexually explicit jokes at work, whereas only 35 percent said we've gone too far in restricting what is acceptable for people to say at work.

### ON THE MODERNIST VERSUS TRADITIONALIST DEBATE OF A CENTURY AGO

See W. B. Carnochan, *The Battleground of the Curriculum: Liberal Education and American Experience* (1993), and Lawrence W. Levine, *The Opening of the American Mind: Canons, Culture, and History* (1996).

## 12: Grass-roots Nation

### ON COLORADO'S AMENDMENT 37

Much of my information comes from a December 13, 2004, interview with Rick Gilliam of the Western Resource Advocates based in Boulder, Colorado; I am grateful for his insights and time. See also Kirk Johnson, "Coloradans Vote to Embrace Alternative Sources of Energy," *The New York Times,* November 24, 2004.

### ON "DEFUNDING THE LEFT"

The idea of "defunding the left" was hatched in 1981 by the ultra-conservative Heritage Foundation, a think tank that gained prominence in the Eighties in part because it provided intellectual ballast for Ronald Reagan's agenda and in part because of generous support by right-wing industrialists who had been funding far-right causes for years. For a typical example of how the "defund the left" campaign works, see the Capital Research Center's 2001 publication, "Patterns of Corporate Philanthropy: A Mandate for Reform," which rates nonprofits on an ideological scale ranging from "radical left" to "market right," calls groups such as the National Alliance of Business and Catalyst, an organization that promotes working women, "liberal," argues that corporate America is funding radicals, liberals, and environmentalists "hostile" to our economic system, and urges corporations to stop funding them. See also the Capital Research Center's *Foundation Watch* newsletter; in its December 2002 issue, for example, the center urges corporations and foundations to stop funding women's organizations such as the National Organization for Women (NOW) and the League of Women Voters (LWF), saying that NOW "revels in attacking Christianity and traditional values" and accusing LWF of indoctrinating its members, concluding that these groups "have no popular following, but represent ideological advocates whose views alienate the constituency they claim to represent." For a sampling of conservative writings related to "defunding the left," see a piece by the far-right activist Grover G. Norquist, "Defunding the Left," *The American Spectator,* September 1995; Jarol B. Manheim, "Biz-War: Origins, Structure, and Strategy of Foundation–NGO Network Warfare on Corporations in the United States," which was presented at the American Enterprise Institute on June 11, 2003; and Marshall Wittman and Charles P. Griffin, "Lobbyists Bring Scare Tactics to Your Hometown," a September 21, 1995, commentary published on the Heritage Foundation Web site that attacks the National Council of Senior Citizens, an organization that accepts taxpayer money for its senior assistance programs, for speaking out on issues of importance to seniors. Anyone interested in a chronology of efforts to "defund the left" should use that phrase in a newspaper database search for articles dating back to the early 1980s—a search that will uncover various attempts to choke off funding for nonprofits. For a review and discussion of the conservative attack on public interest advocacy groups, see Karen M. Paget, "The Big Chill: Foundations and Political Passion," *The Ameri-*

*can Prospect,* May/June 1999. For the quotation from the conservative activist who said that nonprofits getting any federal money should not "get involved in controversial issues," see Hank Hoffman, "Massive Attack," *In These Times,* September 3, 2001.

## ON CITIZEN ORGANIZING AND THE GROWTH OF NONPROFITS

The late public opinion researcher Everett Carll Ladd wrote frequently about the fact that traditional political activity was being replaced by the more informal civic activism and organizing discussed in this chapter; see, for example, his aforementioned 1999 book, *The Ladd Report,* especially pages 98–105, as well as his essay in the June/July 1996 *Public Perspective,* "Civic Participation and American Democracy: The Data Just Don't Show Erosion of America's 'Social Capital.'" See also the 1995 book by Sidney Verba, Kay Schlozman, and Henry Brady, *Voice and Equality: Civic Voluntarism in American Politics,* which uses data from a survey of fifteen thousand citizens to examine changes in political participation over the last few decades. Karen Paget's comment that citizen organizing has become "a well-established feature of the American political landscape" and her estimate on the number of citizen organizations are both from her June 1990 article in *The American Prospect,* "Citizen Organizing: Many Movements, No Majority." For the number of environmental, animal rights, and social action groups registered with the Internal Revenue Service (IRS), see Michael O'Neill's 2002 book, *Nonprofit Nation: A New Look at the Third America,* page 11. For the number of animal rights and environmental nonprofits reporting to the IRS, see Elizabeth T. Boris and Jeff Krehely, "Civic Participation and Advocacy," in Lester M. Salamon, ed., *The State of Nonprofit America* (2002), page 315. For the rising number of new nonprofits since the 1950s and 1960s, see the aforementioned book by Michael O'Neill, *Nonprofit Nation: A New Look at the Third America,* pages 15–18.

## ON THE BABY BOOM APPROACH TO POLITICAL ACTION

The Simmons survey of Baby Boom public and political activities was conducted in 1992 and was based on a sample of twenty thousand adults, from which the comparison between Boomers and other adults was made. The Center for Information and Research on Civic Learning and Engagement (CIRCLE) survey of 3,246 adults was conducted in April and May of 2002.

## ON THE EFFECTIVENESS OF ADVOCACY GROUPS

For Jeffrey Berry's conclusions, see his chapter, "Effective Advocacy for Nonprofits," in *Exploring Organizations and Advocacy,* published in 2001 by the Urban Institute, pages 1–5. The Robert Putnam quote is from his aforementioned 2000 book, *Bowling Alone,* page 152.

## ON THE UNSUNG HEROES OF THE BABY BOOM GENERATION

I am grateful to Sandy Newman for sharing his vision of Fight Crime: Invest in Kids during a telephone interview on October 3, 2004. Anita Borg's life and accomplishments were noted widely after her death in 2003; see Katie Hafner, "Anita Borg, 54, Trailblazer for Women in Computer Field," *The New York Times,* April 10, 2003; Carrie Kirby, "Anita Borg—Champion of Women in High Tech," *San Francisco Chronicle,* April 9, 2003; and Dawn Marie Bracely, "One Woman Who Made a Difference," *Buffalo News,* April 27, 2003.

# Acknowledgments

I breathed a lot more than ideas into this book. I breathed the support and love of family and friends who believed in my work and sustained me during those long and preoccupied hours of researching and writing. To them I owe this book. And I owe it to everyone who has humored me over the years in conversation after conversation about the state of our country, the legacy of the Sixties, and our continuing pursuit of a more free and equal America. You know who you are, and you'll probably see a little glimmer of yourself in these pages. That I might not mention you by name does not mean you haven't contributed in some small way to what I've written here.

Special thanks must go to my hearty graduate research assistants, who helped me dig up and find mounds upon mounds of material—and who patiently tracked down page after page of leads and citations I gave them. Julie Moyer, Rosaline Juan, and especially Aaron Johnson—you were a tremendous help, and the reams of research sitting on the floor of my study attest to your hard work. Anna Oman deserves particular mention here, not only because she so diligently checked and double-checked every fact in the book, but also because her comments on the first draft were perceptive and helpful. I also want to thank my former student Cory Davies, who rolled up his research sleeves for me at the last minute with some well-needed material on environmental issues, and whose M.A. thesis stimulated my thinking on the new environmental norm in our country. And I would be remiss not to express thanks to all of my students, past and present, whose work in class has fertilized and enriched my thinking.

I am especially grateful to a small group of friends who read the manuscript with care and gave thoughtful, detailed suggestions for making it better. To Wendy Swallow, Rick Shenkman, Brent Crane, and Lissa Muscatine—this is a stronger book because of you, and I deeply appreciate your insights, comments, interest, and time. I'm also indebted to David Sobel for the many conversations and e-mails that helped me shape this book at its earliest stages. And I owe thanks to my friend Frank Sesno, whose probing questions over dinner one night made me tighten my argument and write a better book.

I interviewed a number of people for this book, and they were all very generous with their ideas and time: Jeff Stegman, whose company and rather exemplary management philosophy I feature in chapter 8; Marcia Kropf, a vice president at the nonprofit group Catalyst, whose thoughts on women, family, and work provided valuable insight; Rick Gilliam, whose work on Colorado's renewable energy ballot initiative is detailed in chapter 12; Sandy Newman, truly an unsung hero, whose nonprofit work for at-risk kids I also highlight in chapter 12; Charles Broadwell, editor of *The Fayetteville Observer,* who walked me through his principled decision to run same-sex civil union announcements in his Bible Belt newspaper; and Chris Patterson, whose environmental initiatives at his Austin Grill restaurants are described in chapter 9. I also owe thanks to my friend Ellen Babby, who pulled together some of her colleagues at the American Council on Education to discuss trends in higher education. I'm grateful as well to Scott Ward for the background material he gave me on corporate social responsibility. My thanks also to Jan Combopiano, a researcher at Catalyst, who very graciously shared with me her data on women's educational and employment gains.

A book like this could not have been written without the support, encouragement, guidance, and wisdom of my editors at St. Martin's Press, Tom Dunne and Sean Desmond, whose belief in this book was evident from the day we first met, and whose gentle but smart recommendations have materially improved my work. I also could not ask for a better advocate than my agent, Gail Ross, who believed in this project since day one and has always provided candid and clearheaded advice and counsel.

But it is to my family that I owe the most. It must surely be trying to live with a writer, with his highs and lows and his hopes and frustrations and his long days and late nights; I can only imagine how many times I've driven you all to despair. So please forgive me. To my wife, Sabine, my best friend and soul mate, I could not have even imagined this book without your love, reassurance, patience, and support. You know me so well, you know my thinking, you know how to bring me out, and my ideas are that much richer just from talking them through with you. Sometimes I don't tell you how much it all means to me, so let me say it here: It means every-thing to me. To my kids, Ariella and Max, ages twelve and nine, you in-spire me and brighten even the toughest of days. How lucky I am to see the world through your eyes, because every time I do, I learn about life anew. I'm grateful to be your dad, and it is to you, the next great genera-tion, that I dedicate this book. Let me also thank my mom, Adele, whose stories about life in the Fifties textured my view of that decade, and who never once stopped believing in me, which is one of the reasons I am who I am and I do what I do. And to my late dad, Paul, I wish you could be here to read this, but thank you, wherever you are.

# Index

AARP, 106, 269
Abercrombie & Fitch, 238
abortion, 35, 39, 157, 258
advertising, 36, 47, 82, 129, 131–32
advocacy groups, 231–41, 245, 299–302
affirmative action, 11, 30–31, 40, 61
African-Americans. *See* blacks
American Civil Liberties Union, 234, 239
*American Demographics,* 29, 36
*The American Journal of Sociology,* 26, 34
American University (AU), 213, 218–22, 293, 297
Anheuser-Busch, 191
anti-Semitism, 22–23, 117
AOL, 171
Ariel Fund, 176
*The Atlantic Monthly,* 121
Austin Grill, 179, 289
authority, questioning, 66, 67–72, 87, 247–48
automobiles. *See* cars

Baby Boom generation. *See also specific areas of interest*
civic life, 20–22, 253–54
criticism of, xi, 17–19, 23–24, 44–64, 65, 124, 144, 145, 146–47, 178, 185, 243–44, 248–49, 252–59, 261–63
defending, 248–49
definition of, xi–xvi
drugs and, xi, xv, 69, 85, 142, 148, 278
egalitarianism of, 90, 93, 98, 101, 109, 116, 167
as Greater Generation, 13
Greatest Generation and, 1, 9–26, 74–76, 251–54
hypocrisy, 45, 48–51, 75–76, 77, 185, 261
liberalism of, 17–18, 24, 65–67, 147
morality, 17–19, 253–54
patriotism of, 22–23, 207, 248, 253–54
religion and, 139–40, 141, 147, 148–59, 280–85
Sixties roots of, 23–24, 50, 77–78

technology and, 77–82, 169, 170, 171, 264
unfinished business of, 243–49
youth culture fixation of, 82–87, 145–46, 264–65
Bailyn, Bernard, 207
Baker, Russell, 196
The Beatles, 35, 43
beauty ideal, 122–23
Belafonte, Harry, 3
Ben & Jerry's, 174
Bennett, William, 17, 19, 61, 124
Berkeley. *See* University of California at Berkeley
Berry, Jerry, 236
Betty Crocker, 123
Bianchi, Suzanne, 265–66, 269
bigotry. *See* discrimination; ethnicity; prejudice; race
Bill of Rights
"Academic," 217
U.S., 207, 208
Birmingham, Alabama, 12
birth control. *See* contraceptives
births, out of wedlock, 109–11
blacks. *See also* discrimination; ethnicity; prejudice; race
black history and, 212, 218, 219–21
black power and, 76
discrimination against, 1–5, 16–17, 72–73, 136–38, 238, 245–46, 251, 277
in Greatest Generation era, 1–5, 12, 16–17, 115, 251, 271–72
interracial marriage and, xi, 3–4, 16, 30, 116, 120–22, 129, 251, 256
out of wedlock births among, 109–10
police and, 12, 72, 136
slavery and, 115, 271
as soldiers/veterans, 2, 115
Blanding, Sarah Gibson, 264
The Body Shop, 174
Boeing, 191
Boise, Idaho, 6